Ethnopolitics in Cyberspace

Ethnopolitics in Cyberspace

The Internet, Minority Nationalism, and the Web of Identity

Robert A. Saunders

LEXINGTON BOOKS
A division of
ROWMAN & LITTLEFIELD PUBLISHERS, INC.
Lanham • Boulder • New York • Toronto • Plymouth, UK

Published by Lexington Books
A division of Rowman & Littlefield Publishers, Inc.
A wholly owned subsidiary of The Rowman & Littlefield Publishing Group, Inc.
4501 Forbes Boulevard, Suite 200, Lanham, Maryland 20706
http://www.lexingtonbooks.com

Estover Road, Plymouth PL6 7PY, United Kingdom

British Library Cataloguing in Publication Information Available

Library of Congress Cataloging-in-Publication Data
Saunders, Robert A., 1973–
  Ethnopolitics in cyberspace : the internet, minority nationalism, and the web of identity
/ Robert A. Saunders.
    p. cm.
  Includes bibliographical references and index.
  ISBN 978-0-7391-4194-6 (cloth : alk. paper)   ISBN 978-0-7391-4195-3 (pbk)
  1. Political anthropology. 2. Politics and culture. 3. Mass media and culture. 4. Mass
media and international relations. 5. Internet—Political aspects. 6. World Wide Web—
Political aspects. I. Title.
  GN492.S28 2011
  302.23'1089—dc22

                                    2010042989

For Kieran

For Stewart

Ubi bene ibi patria ('Where one is happy, there lies the homeland').

— Anonymous

Each person is the Son of his Nation, and at the same time, the Son of his Age.

— G. F. W. Hegel (1831)

There's no such thing as heroes, just a bunch of ones and zeros.

— Lyrics by Immaculate Machine

Contents

Acknowledgments

The driving force behind this book is an attempt to address the question "What is national identity?" While I do not expect to fully answer this question, nor do I anticipate a definitive answer in my lifetime, I believe the attempt to understand the issue is a worthy pursuit. My hope is that this work will shed at least a small beam of light on the issues surrounding national identity in the age of globalization.

I wish to thank all those who have inspired, shaped, and challenged my research on the national question over the past two decades. For her mentorship and careful dedication to detail, I thank Maria Todorova. I am particularly indebted to Alexander Golovko for introducing me to the complexities of what it means to be a man without a nation. I am indebted to the tutelage of Ted Czupryk, Wolf Schäfer, Gary Marker, Haig Der-Houssikian, George Eisenwein, and Alice Freifeld, who tutored me in the finer points of nationalism in all its various incarnations.

To Joel Vessels, Justin Wyble, Michal Řezníček, Martin Doskočil, Jonell Sanchez, and Georgi Tsekov, my good friends and occasional intellectual foils, I give thanks and salutations. I want to single out for adulation Valters Ščerbinskis and Vlad Strukov, both of whom went above and beyond in their assistance with this project. I also wish to thank Karim H. Karim and my editor, Joseph C. Parry, who provided me with a host of helpful comments and suggestions on the final version of the text. I could not have completed the research entailed herein without the invaluable help of my in-country and cyberspatial guides: Ruslans Osipovs, Dennis Babkov, Naeem Ahmed, Fatmir Fanda Ibraimi, and Paul Chiş.

Special thanks are due to the late, great Frank Pellegrini for his help in securing a course reduction to allow me to put the finishing touches on the manuscript. I would also like to thank my students at Farmingdale State College, Rutgers University, and elsewhere for their queries and comments on this work, each one of which pushed me to work harder and smarter. This undertaking was possible only through access to the vast array of electronic and print materials of the libraries of Rutgers, The State University of New Jersey and the State University of New York.

While pursuing my Ph.D. dissertation at Rutgers University, I was fortunate enough to work with Yale Ferguson, Rey Koslowski, and Richard Langhorne, all of whom shaped this endeavor and helped me to grow as a scholar. In particular, my dissertation advisor, Alexander J. Motyl, deserves my deep gratitude for his patience, guidance, and constant support. My most heartfelt thanks, however, go to my wife, Michelle. Throughout this project, she has been my inspiration, intellectual partner, and long-suffering copy-editor.

I would like to note that portions of Chapter 6 were supported in part by a grant from IREX (International Research & Exchanges Board) with funds provided by the U.S. State Department through the Title VIII Program. None of these organizations is responsible for the views expressed.

Portions of the work have previously appeared elsewhere, most notably in my thesis "Unweaving the Web of Identity: Assessing the Internet's Impact on Identity among National Minorities," Ph.D. dissertation, Rutgers, The State University of New Jersey (May 2005). A version of Chapter 4 appeared in "Virtual Irredentism? Redemption and Reification of the Albanian Nation in Cyberspace," *Albanian Journal of Politics* 1, no. 2 (December 2005). Chapter 5 is adapted from my chapter "New Media, New Russians, New Abroad: The Evolution of Minority Russian Identity in Cyberspace" in *The Post-Soviet Russian Media: Power, Change and Conflicting Messages*, edited by Birgit Beumers, Stephen Hutchings, and Natalya Rulyova (Routledge, 2009). Lastly, Chapter 7 was published under the title "The Ummah as Nation: A Reappraisal in the Wake of the 'Cartoons Affair,'" *Nations and Nationalism* 14, no. 2 (April 2008).

Introduction
Turning the Tables on Procrustes

The ancient Greeks spoke of a man named Procrustes who kept a house by the side of a well-traveled road. He would invite travelers into his home so that they might rest their tired bodies after a long day's journey. Procrustes would provide his guests with a fine meal and engaging conversation before showing them to their quarters for the night. He promised a special treat for his visitors: a bed with magical properties. Procrustes guaranteed that the bed would perfectly contour to the shape of its guest. What he did not volunteer was that once his unwitting caller lay down, he would bind them and then stretch their bodies on a rack until they met the very edge of the iron bed. Afterward, any body part which happened to extend beyond the bed's perimeter would be viciously cut off. Needless to say, none survived a night of Procrustean slumber. That is until Theseus paid a visit to the fiendish innkeeper. The Greek hero turned the tables on Procrustes and forced him to sleep on his own bed, bringing a bloody end to the villain.

Since Europe's early modern period, the state's relationship to the nation has been roughly analogous to that of Procrustes' bed to its unfortunate guests. While the two terms are frequently conflated, a nation is any named human population that shares a historical territory, common myths, and historical memories, and enjoys a mass, public culture. The nation exists as a psychological link between individuals and the collective based on the above-mentioned attributes. In contrast, a state is a political organization that exercises sovereignty over a defined territory. Nations have been pulled and stretched to cover the political space of emerging states from France to Hungary to Greece. In the process, indigenous minorities living within those states have been assimilated or eradicated. Those who refused to submit to this process came to be known as *national minorities*, typically confined to marginalized roles in the new polity.[1] Other peoples ended up on the "outside" of their nation's state-building project, effectively exiled to other states. Like those unfortunate extremities that did not fit on Procrustes' bed, these marooned nations were cut off from the rest of their nation, eventually becoming another state's national minorities.

The creation of nation-states—that is, legally recognized, ostensibly sovereign geographic entities dominated by a single ethnic group that enjoys political, economic, cultural, and social dominance—is an ongoing process.[2] However, we can begin to date the process with the abatement of the religious wars which wracked Europe during the mid-seventeenth century. In the wake of the Peace of Westphalia (1648), the system of nation-states steadily came to dominate Europe, and then quickly spread beyond the continent (principally through imperialism) displacing competitive systems in Asia and eventually Africa.[3] Various scholars of nationalism have identified striking similarities in the processes of crafting of national identity projects around the globe from Portugal to Japan. A national identity project is an "ongoing rhetorical achievement of a social network" aimed at distinguishing the ethnic "self" from the "other" through linguistic, spatial, and cultural bounding practices.[4] In order to win support for such projects, elites needed to craft grand narratives that would win over the masses. English-American philosopher Kenneth Boulding distinguishes between elites, "the small group of people who make the actual decisions which lead to war or peace, the making or breaking of treaties, the invasions or withdrawals, alliances, and enmities which make up the major events of international relations," and the masses, "ordinary people who are deeply affected by these decisions but who take little or no direct part in making them."[5] During earlier periods of history, these masses had tended to identify themselves in religious and/or communal terms. In order for these narratives to promote political loyalty, acute social change was requisite. The widening availability of mass media, an increase in the intellectual skills of intended audiences, and revolutionary changes in the distribution of information precipitated such developments.

As nationalism scholar Benedict Anderson has pointed out, the age of mass media and near universal literacy allowed the political, commercial, and cultural elites of these burgeoning nation-states to speak for the nation. This process gave rise to what Anderson calls *print capitalism*, an epiphenomenon that gave fixity to particular "national" languages, which then began to squeeze out their competitors to become the only true medium of communication for a given nation-state.

> Print language laid the bases for national consciousness in three distinct ways. First and foremost, they created unified fields of exchange and communication below Latin and above the spoken vernaculars. Speakers of the huge variety of Frenches, Englishes, or Spanishes, who might find it difficult or even impossible to understand one another in conversation, became capable of comprehending one another via print and paper. In the process they gradually became aware of the hundreds of thousands, even millions, of people in their particular language-field, and at the same time that only those hundreds of thousands, or millions, so belonged. These fellow-readers, to whom they were connected through print, formed, in their secular, particular, visible invisibility, the embryo of the nationally imagined community.[6]

According to Anderson, this community is inherently limited and sovereign; a member of a nation will never know or even see most of his co-nationals no matter how small the nation, yet they feel an interconnectedness, or as Anderson puts it, "a deep, horizontal comradeship."[7] Adhering to the territorialized principles of the Westphalian state system in which the exclusion of external actors from domestic authority structures are sacrosanct, international borders became a salient factor in determining the scale of such community-building. Furthermore, the nationalizing project typically was directed at all residents of the state. As such, minorities within the state and members of the nation outside the state were effectively marginalized by the development of ubiquitous mass media whether in the form of the newspapers, radio programming, motion pictures, or television broadcasts. Such media delivered powerful and ubiquitous messaging intended to promote the idea of national unity based on the ideals of the elites who spoke for the "nation." In conjunction with state control of education and the military, media emerged as one of the preeminent shapers of identity and lifeways during the late nineteenth century. Furthermore, the state's ability to police, regulate, and subtly influence media reinforced pervading notions of identity through the first half of the twentieth century.

The rapid evolution of technology after World War II, however, complicated state-based informational monopolies and challenged the cultural hegemony of national elites. Starting with satellite television in the 1970s, new information and communications technologies (ICTs) opened hitherto unimaginable venues for communication across international and intercultural borders. Fax machines, VHS cassettes, and the decreasing costs of telephony complemented this evolution. This deterritorialization/reterritorialization of media has been of particular value to those who had been denied access to the productive capacity of previous broadcast media platforms. Furthermore, new options have become available that to these constituencies that allow for consumption of mass media in their own languages/dialects and/or content that caters to their particular cultures. Stateless nations, subaltern ethnic groups, marooned nationalities, and diasporic communities have been directly impacted by this shift.

In particular, the Internet has radically altered the media environment for the creation and maintenance of national identity because of its global structure, anonymity, and functionality. Cyberspace allows for the multifold digital replication of all pre-existing media platforms (texts, newspapers, motion pictures, radio, and television). Furthermore, the Internet is a universally-oriented communication platform that delivers the functions of the post, telephone, and fax machine, while simultaneously offering innovative ways to interact, from instant messaging to blogging to telepresence. The deterritorialized nature of the platform allows communication and media consumption without regard for geographic location, assuming the user has access to the Web. The Internet also provides its users with near simultaneity, allowing its users not only to bridge space, but time as well. This effect is compounded by the capacity of cyberspace to function as timeless reservoir for storing data, sound, and images, effectively functioning as a time capsule for future generations. Furthermore, the medium allows for high levels of anonymity and, despite the best efforts of governments, the Web has proved difficult for states to regulate.

Such developments, though still very much in the nascent stage, are impacting local, national, and global politics. However, it is already clear that cyberspace is evolving into a decentralized nodal area that links the nation—however its members define it—across borders and oceans. I argue that sustained Internet activity has thus created a new ecumene that enables many of the communicative, cultural, and socio-economic exchanges which, in the previous 150 years, could only have existed within the structure of a nation-state. With widening Internet access in the developed and developing worlds, Internet-enabled elites now have the ability to construct nearly limitless media ecosystems in cyberspace. These environments can favor even the smallest ethnic or linguistic groups. In his recent essay on the Japanese anime sensation *Ghost in the Shell*, Austin Corbett argued that though our ubiquitous and accelerating dependence on technology, especially information and communication technology (ICT), we have become—as a species—cyborgs. He states: "If we are all cyborgs, then a modern cyborg politics becomes a pressing concern."[8] This study uses Corbett's assertion as a starting point and attempts to provide an incipient understanding of the cyborg politics of the world's emerging new media spaces *and* lingering ideological orientations which shape the digital body politic, as well as "real world" politics.

National elites among minority groups, what Victoria Bernal calls "Internet intellectuals,"[9] of many different types are utilizing computer-mediated communication to establish direct linkages with their co-nationals in the ethnic homeland and elsewhere the world. My research demonstrates that new media, and especially the Internet, allow marginalized national groups to transcend statist media monopolies embedded in the Westphalian state structure. National minorities are particularly well-served by the advent of the Internet and cyberspace. The secessionist movements of the Chechens, Kashmiris, and Basques have all migrated into cyberspace; operatives, fundraisers, and propagandists of such movements regularly use the Internet for advancing their respective causes. The Web has also become a bastion for the defense of cultural and linguistic diversity among small nations across the European continent and elsewhere. In Italy, representatives the Northern League are using the Internet to craft a Padanian nation replete with passports; young people in Scotland are using chatrooms such as Clishmaclaiver to gain fluency in the Scots language; and Internet-enabled Slovene schoolchildren in Italy regularly communicate with co-nationals in Ljubljana to prepare themselves for higher education in Slovenia. Nearly every regional and minority organization in Europe has annexed a bit of cyberspace to articulate their political goals, demand independence, lobby for greater rights, and/or replicate the benefits of mainstream media.[10]

National minorities are not the only beneficiaries of this transformation. Immigrant diasporas now also have the capacity to use the Internet to connect with their ethnic kin, often across borders, oceans, and even time.[11] The current era of media globalization and greater mobility enables sustained, dependable, and diverse connections between diasporas on multiple continents and their ethnic homelands in such a way that has never been possible in the past.[12] Social anthropologist Arjun Appadurai argues that mediascapes—the global distribution of media images and texts that appear on our computer screens, in newspapers, television, and radio—are creating "diasporic public spheres, phenomena that confound theories that depend on the continued salience of the nation-state as the key arbiter of important social changes."[13] Industrialized countries with large immigrant populations have witnessed an explosion of foreign-produced satellite TV consumption among their immigrant population over the past two decades. The advent of the Internet allows distant expatriates to maintain daily contact with their homeland though local news Web sites, email, Internet radio stations, and instant messaging. New Internet telephony and Webcasting services such as Skype are perhaps the most radical innovations, making communication between diasporas and their patrias instantaneous and free; such platforms also take the state's monopolistic control of the postal and telephone systems out of the equation. Even financial sovereignty has been impacted with the advent of electronic remittances.

By historical comparison, the last major wave of American immigration (1890-1910) was defined by communication practices between immigrants and their native countries that could take as long six months if not more, and correspondence was always in danger of being seized by government authorities. Furthermore, the information provided through newsletters and newspapers was meager at best and often lacked the right "local" component. Today, communication is cheap, instantaneous, and reliable. Likewise, the dynamics of the Internet allow information to be "pulled" rather than "pushed" to immigrants as they are able to decide what types of information they want and when. Thus, the socio-geographic conditions which encouraged the development of tight ethnic ghettos in previous centuries have somewhat lessened (though traditional *entrepôts* such as Marseille, London, New York, and Vancouver still attract new immigrants and sustain centuries-old ethnic communities).

Today, an immigrant can use a combination of e-commerce, instant messaging, satellite TV, "push-to-talk" wireless, Internet telephony, and Web-based news sources to create a conceptual micro-universe of the homeland, one which is vastly superior to any comparable replication of the "old country" available to earlier generations living abroad. In North America and Western Europe falling prices for high-speed Internet access, satellite television, and mobile telephony have made new media accessible to even to those with modest incomes. Furthermore, children born in diaspora can now use the Web for connecting to their peers in their ethnic homelands, as an educational resource, and for other identity-building purposes. Both those who leave the home country and those who "stay put" become part of a continuum of cultural experimentality based on flows of information and ideas.[14] As communications scholar Maya Ranganathan has shown with case studies on the Internet-enabled Kashmiri and Tamil diasporas, the combination of immigrant and minority identity has been especially impacted by mass mediation.[15] When oppressed minorities emigrate to information-rich Western environments, the use of ICT becomes a major tool for national liberation and a way to pierce the hegemonic information practices of their home countries. Likewise, indigenous populations are tapping into digital media as a cheap and effective way to create alternative narratives to dominant culture's control of media practices. Thus, the Internet—in conjunction with other deterritorialized ICT platforms—is enabling countless Theseuses among minority communities who are looking to turn the tables on the old Westphalian System.

The purpose of this study is twofold: to complement existing, often inchoate studies that suggest a seminal role for the Internet in national identity production and maintenance, and to contextualize cyberspatial national identity building projects within the larger field of nationalism studies.[16] I do this through a comprehensive examination of the relationship between the Internet and the stateless nations, national minorities, and dispersed immigrant communities that use it for purposes of community building, cultural exchange, and political action. While a number of empirical case studies and theory-based treatments of the topic exist in article format, there has yet to be a book-length analysis which attempts to tackle more than a single case study.[17] With this text, I hope to partially address this void through a thorough examination of a much-talked about, but often poorly studied, aspect of globalization—Internet use—and its impact on national identity.

By focusing on the historical relationships between states, nations, and the minorities trapped between these powerful identifiers of modernity, I hope to provide a better understanding of how the old rules of national identity production and state-building are changing. I argue that the governing norms of these processes are being re-written with the advent of the Internet, a deterritorialized global medium for communication, news, entertainment, and coordination. My analytical framework combines media theory with the constructivist school of nationalism. I employ methodologies for investigating the impact of globalization derived from anthropology and cultural studies. The historical and theoretical portion of the book is followed by four in-depth case studies of individual nationalities (Albanians outside of Albania, "near abroad" Russians, the Roma, and the transnational ummah) and their activities in cyberspace. Accompanying my case studies are briefer discussions of dozens of other online national movements and Internet-enabled diasporic communities that share characteristics with one of my four paragons, i.e., electronic irredentists (Albanians), post-imperial digerati (Russians), the cybernetic vanguard (Roma), and virtual prophets (ummahists).

My thesis is that the impact of Internet use by national minorities, subaltern nations, and diasporas is *not* neutral. When a sizeable percentage of the nation or diaspora has access to the Web, elites within the community are employing the communicative and publishing capacity of the Internet and cyberspace to affect political, social, and cultural cohesion and/or advancement of the nation through what Gayatri Spivak defines as "strategic essentialism," or a useful—if sometimes artificial—solidarity for purposes of social or political action.[18] Interestingly, Internet use is simultaneously leading to a globalization of identity among those who use it. Pre-existing organizational, demographic, economic, and political characteristics of a given group play a large role in determining which of the above-mentioned phenomena is more keenly realized. In short, there are some groups for which the Internet *increases* their sense of national identity while others find that cyberspace *weakens* ethnic unity and promotes globalism. A secondary aim of this book is to document the myriad ties and interactions which link national minorities and diasporas across borders, continents, oceans, and time through the medium of cyberspace. As I narrate these cross-border negotiations, I am careful to explain their impact on nation-states, intergovernmental organizations, domestic and transnational social movements, economic and labor markets, commercial networks, international security, and religious communities.

Although this text focuses on cyberspace and minorities, its ultimate value comes from expanding the understanding of globalization and identity in the post-Cold War universe. I focus on ethnic minorities, stateless nations, and diasporas because these communities tend to have a strong sense of identity which has been formulated and maintained outside of the Westphalian state system. I posit that as deterritorialized communication and mass media increase globally, there will be ever more groups that will use the Web to achieve the benefits won by the minorities discussed in this text. By using the Internet—which combines the functionality of newspapers, telephones, radios, and television on a single platform—national minorities and diasporans now have the capacity to challenge media monopolies of the states in which they live.

The end of the Cold War and the accelerating economic, cultural, social, and commercial interconnectedness that has characterized the globe since 1989—deemed by many authors as the "era of globalization"—has enabled the mass popularization of the Internet (at least in the advanced economies and urban areas of the developing world). My tertiary goal is to address the extent to which elites among national minorities are becoming shapers of national consciousness and what role cyberspace plays in this process. As nation-states face new and variegated challenges to their dominance as the central trope in identity production, I believe this to be an important question to address. As European historian Panikos Panayi states, "The leaders of peoples which do not conform to the dominant real and created values of individual nation states manufacture their own alternative sub-nationalism," but such action is only relevant when combined with organization and politicization.[19] It is therefore necessary to understand not only how new identities are created, but also who they manifest in the political space of the real world. My intention is to investigate the role of the Internet in identity projects among ethnic minorities and assess the impact of sustained Internet use on national identity.

Cyberspace: An Imaginary Space or a Space for Imaginaries?

Cyberspace is a concept that is often difficult to define due to the abstract nature of the psychogeographic environment which it describes.[20] William Gibson, who coined the term in his novel *Neuromancer*, defines cyberspace as "a consensual hallucination experienced daily by billions of legitimate operators, in every nation...the graphical representation of data abstracted from the banks of every computer in the human system."[21] Network researcher Michael Benedikt expands Gibson's groundbreaking concept by describing cyberspace as a new, parallel universe "created by the world's computers and communication lines" sustained by a "common mental geography, built, in turn, by consensus and revolution, canon and experiment" connected and ultimately bordered by "corridors [that] form wherever electricity runs with intelligence."[22] Ronald Deibert identifies cyberspace as "the artificial 'space' one enters on computer networks."[23] Technology studies professor Jim Falk states, "The result of browsing the Web is to experience movement over an information terrain, mapped not by geography solely or even particularly, but by a multidimensional set of categories and themes."[24] Others conceive of cyberspace as a new electronic frontier built only to be colonized by the rich, white, and powerful.[25] Globalization expert Saskia Sassen points out that the Internet's digital space is clearly divided between private and public realms, much like territorial space, and this leads to important distinctions in access, communication and content in cyberspace.[26] I define *cyberspace* as the conceptual universe created by and sustained through electronic interactions of humans over global computer networks and shaped by ever-changing geographies of digitized information.

As to its functionality, cyberspace represents an alternate universe with unlimited potential for the storage and preservation of symbols of national identity including anthems, folk songs, legends, contested versions of history, alternative forms of orthography and dialects, genealogies, art, photos, recipes, etc. According to anthropologist Diane Nelson, it is the ultimate public sphere.[27] Furthermore, the deterritorialized nature of the Web genuinely unleashes the power of imagination in terms of nation-building, which, as Menderes Candan argues, "does not crucially depend on physical proximity the community's members."[28] Chat rooms, instant messaging and email—all of which run over the Internet—are being utilized to reinvigorate dead, dying or moribund languages. The ability to post personal Web pages, Web logs (blogs), and links to other sites is enabling minorities to provide frank, incendiary and even exaggerated or outright false content regarding their situation within their state. The Internet provides such communities with mass-mediated imaginaries, that is, spaces of memory (*lieux de memoir*) psychically tethered to real world geography, but free of many—if not all—of its restrictions. Furthermore, it assists in the development of a Habemasian transnational public sphere where marginalized groups can "produce and debate narratives of history, culture, democracy, and identity."[29] Via the Internet, these groups are also informing the outside world (and more importantly, their co-nationals) of the conditions in which they live and how they are faring economically, politically and socially. Certain groups also use the Web to articulate their political goals, demand independence, and lobby for greater rights in their states of residence.

In terms of national identity production—a related, but distinct aspect of the politicization of the nation—I have found that the Internet is being used by elites among national minorities in an attempt to affect the following:

- *Activation*: while rare, some elites are attempting to form entirely new nations based on contrived differences from currently recognized national groups or encourage members of other nations to join theirs

- *Maintenance*: nearly ubiquitous among minority communities, influential Internet-enabled elites are using the Web to keep the nation alive and well without attempting to "re-tell" the story of the nation in a way that differs greatly from generally accepted norms both within and outside of the community

- *Re-Articulation*: though not as common as maintenance, certain elites within national minorities are using the communicative abilities and reservoir capacity of cyberspace to "imagine" the nation in new and innovative ways.

All this can be done with a great deal of anonymity (if desired). The private nature of Internet identity projects is especially welcome among the Roma who are discussed in Chapter 6, many of whom are reticent to make public their submerged identity, but are supportive of the nationalist cause or social justice for their in-group. On the Web, nationalist agitation can be conducted in an environment which is typically beyond the reach of hostile state authorities. As the chapter on Internet-enabled Albanian irredentists shows, the Web is a powerful tool for promoting discrete political goals even in the face of strong—even violent—statist forces bent on maintaining the status quo. Though, as I explore later, the state is not without its own tools to combat this phenomenon.

Paradoxically, the Internet is also a mechanism for fashioning oneself as a global citizen, effectively denationalizing its users. As we will see in the chapter on near abroad Russian netizens, the very structure of cyberspace as a corporatist, non-nationalist space can often massage identity in a way that weakens rather than promotes nationalism. The constant bombardment by messages of consumption and cosmopolitanism poorly serve the interests of both the homeland and the nation and instead promotes a globalized mélange.[30] Digital landscapes of global commerce, intellectual and ideological freedom, and personal mobility dominate the information superhighway, whereas geographically or nationally-bounded thought-realms are pushed into the less traversed, though not inaccessible, byways of cyberspace. However, as I demonstrate in the discussion of certain groups, the juxtaposition of global capitalism and nationalist rhetoric is also a viable option for many diasporic

Web users. The Internet is also emerging as a tool for linking previously uncon-
nected groups due its structural immunity to the challenges of physical geography, as
the chapter on the virtual ummahists will demonstrate.

This study limits its scope to minority groups which possess a triad of attributes
that would enable the community to participate in viable national identity projects.
The attributes are as follows:

- Direct access to the Internet among elites who can and do act as preceptors of
  information and ideology within the community
- Perception of inequality based on nationality/ethnicity/immigrant status within the
  state of residence which could lead to political activity on the Web
- An "external" audience with the capacity to implement political, economic, and/or
  social reforms to improve the conditions impacting the nationality in question
  (e.g., the state of residence, friendly foreign powers, transnational non-
  governmental organizations, etc.)

While possession of these attributes does not necessarily guarantee effective Web-
based national identity projects, they are the minimum requirements for achieving
the outcomes mentioned above. Roma academics in Transylvania, Russian entrepreneurs in Riga, Albanian journalists in Kosovo, and imams in Copenhagen all meet
the above requirements and will be discussed forthwith. That being said, it is prudent
to define my own concept of the nation before proceeding further.

It is my contention that the nation is built on perceived or, more accurately, *imagined* or fictive ties of primordial kinship between a group of people who aver that
they share a common history, language and set of values and customs, often deemed
culture.[31] Emotional attachment to a particular state or territory is a common—but
not necessary—component of nation.[32] Political scientist Montserrat Guibernau
points to the necessity of five dimensions (psychological, cultural, territorial,
political, and historical) for any nation to constitute itself.[33] One of the founders of
the interdisciplinary field of nationalism studies, Anthony Smith, similarly argues
that we must also incorporate the following into our definition of nation: 1) a named
human population; 2) a mass public culture; 3) common legal rights and duties for all
members; and 4) a common economy and territorial mobility for all members.[34] It is
also important to include philosopher Ernest Gellner's requirement of mutual
recognition, i.e., "two men [sic] are of the same nation if and only if they recognize
each other as belonging to the same nation."[35] The centrality of sentiment to the
nation is unequivocal in German political economist Max Weber's writings: "One
might well define the concept of nation in the following way: a nation is a community of sentiment which would adequately manifest itself in a state of its own: hence a
nation is a community which normally tends to produce a state of its own."[36] The
desire to be one community—despite barriers of language, faith, geography, and/or
international borders—is the keystone of the nation.

I see little value in employing the definitional split used by Czechoslovak-
American social scientist Karl Deutsch and others who distinguish between "nation"
(a people with a land to call their own) and "nationality" (a people aspiring to
political, economic and cultural autonomy),[37] especially in the context of Soviet-era
national identity projects and their continued resonance after 1991. The "national
republics" of the Ingush, Tuvans, Tatars, etc. exist within the structure of the Russian
Federation, while the Transnistrians, Abkhazians, South Ossetians, and others have

established statelets in other former Soviet Republics (Moldova for the first and Georgia for the latter two), thus making Deutsch's definition meaningless without clarification of what he means by statehood in the post-1991 context.[38] I define *nation* as a named group of people who imagine themselves to be part of a community based on common history, language, and a set of traditions/culture, and who strive towards common legal rights, political responsibilities and rewards and economic interaction for all members of the group. I thus place myself firmly within the constructivist school and am unwilling to link historical homogeneity or persistence in physical attributes to the concept of *nation*.

Case Studies, Methodology, and Structure

The text is composed of two parts: 1) a historical and theoretical overview of mass media's impact on the process of state-building and national identity projects, as well as current global trends that have impacted these processes as they relate to national minorities, stateless nations, and immigrant diasporas; and 2) an empirical portion that addresses the differing ways in which the Web is employed by minority communities. While the latter half of the book is constructed around four case studies, it also includes anecdotal information on dozens of other Internet-enabled national identity projects.

Part I, entitled "The Color and Shape of a Cyberspatial World," provides an introduction to the theories and historical events which gird the case studies found in the second half of the book. This section begins with a chapter that covers the historical relationship between the nation-state and mass media. The principal aim of "From Bibles to Bollywood: Mass Media, Identity, and the State" is to recount the rise of mass media as a tool for garnering loyalty to the state. I also explore the role of the media in shaping national identity and excluding competitive identity projects. The next chapter, "Media Unbound: The Internet, Cyberspace, and Nationalism on the Web," provides a brief history of the Internet to position subsequent analyses within the overall development of cyberspace. The first half of the chapter charts the history of the Web with a special focus on the politicization of cyberspace. The second half examines the unique attributes of the Internet and cyberspace with an eye towards national identity projects. The last chapter in this section, "New World (Dis)Orders: National Identity and Ethnic Politics in the Global Era," explores the realities of the fractured and anarchic world which were unveiled as the Cold War came to an end. In this chapter, I explore the sometimes complementary though usually competing theories which attempt explain post-1989 global milieu. I explore the emergence of new states after the collapse of communism and the increasing number of nation-state-like entities (Kosovo, Transnistria, etc.). This is followed by a discussion of globalization, immigration, and the perspectival constructs that Appadurai has labeled mediascapes, technoscapes, ethnoscapes, financescapes, and ideascapes.[39] I end the chapter with a brief overview of the types of national minorities that exist in the twenty-first century and make some observations on their particular characteristics, thus preparing the reader for the second half the book.

In "Part II: *Homo-Cybericus*—Genus and Species," I devote a chapter to each the four archetypes that I have identified among cyber-minorities. My research is

TABLE 1: *Cyber-Minority Case Studies*

Nationality	Estimated population	States of residence (as a minority)	Issues	Characteristics
Albanians outside of Albania	3-5 million	Kosovo (Serbia), Turkey, Macedonia, Greece, Italy, United States, Canada, other countries in Western Europe	Irredentism, nationalism, migration issues, cultural preservation	Solidarity: High Activism: Moderate
Russians outside of the Russian Federation	20-30 million	Ukraine, Kazakhstan, Belarus, Latvia, Uzbekistan, Kyrgyzstan, Estonia, other post-Soviet republics, United States, Germany	Economic issues, social networking, citizenship/language rights	Solidarity: Low Activism: Low
Roma (including Sinti and those who self-identify as "Gypsies")	5-10 million	Romania, Turkey, France, Bulgaria, Hungary, Greece, Russia, Italy, Serbia, Slovakia, other European countries	Human rights, cultural/linguistic preservation, social justice	Solidarity: Low Activism: Moderate
Western European Muslims	15-20 million	France, Germany, Great Britain, Spain, Austria, Netherlands, Sweden, Belgium, Switzerland, Denmark, Italy	Ethno-religious identity, social issues, Islamism, "Clash of Civilizations"	Solidarity: High Activism: High

based on small-*n*, interview-based studies among Netizens in the four selected populations: Albanians outside of Albania, Russians outside of Russia, Roma, and Western European and North American Muslims.[40] My research focuses on those whom Linda Leung, author of *Virtual Ethnicity: Race Resistance and the World Wide Web* (2005), identifies as techno-elites, i.e., members of ethnic minorities who are integrated into the "educational, media, cultural, and political institutions and networks in the West [and] who travel and migrate virtually as geographically."[41] Interviews with members of the North American, Macedonian, and Kosovar Albanian populations were conducted in person and online between May 2003 and December 2006. Interviews with Russian residents of Kazakhstan, Latvia, and Estonia were conducted in person and online between October 2002 and May 2005. In-person interviews of Transylvanian Roma were conducted in May-June 2006; online interviews with Roma in Germany, Great Britain, and the United States were conducted between September 2006 and May 2007. In-person interviews of Dutch Muslims were conducted in December 2004 and my interviews with British Muslims took place in April 2006; online interviews with Danish and North American Muslims took place between May 2005 and January 2006. In addition to face-to-face and online interviews, I also monitored English-, Albanian-, German-, and Russian-language YouTube postings, blogs, and personal web sites dedicated to issues important to the minorities in question.[42]

Through a synthesis of this original research with the extant literature on nation-building in cyberspace, I have attempted to provide an analysis of developing trends among "stationary" minorities that I hope will complement the work of Jennifer Brinkerhoff, Linda Leung, Arjun Appadurai, Victoria Bernal, and other scholars who have focused on new media-based nation-building among immigrant populations and reconfigurations of the concepts of citizenship and identity. In doing so, I also hope to provide a partial and tentative answer to the question posed to the attendees of the 2006 Ernest Gellner Nationalism Lecture at the London School of Economics and Political Science by Thomas Hylland Eriksen: "What kinds of creatures will form what kinds of communities in an electronic age of instantaneous, transnational communication?"[43]

"Electronic Irredentists" provides a case study of the Albanian Internet and irredentist politics, examining those ethnic entrepreneurs who seek to "redeem" their nations in cyberspace and achieve political advancement in real space—up to including territorial acquisition and state-building efforts. Research for this chapter was conducted among Albanian-Americans who emigrated from various Balkan states, including Macedonia, Serbia, and Kosovo. The subsequent chapter, "Post-Imperial Digerati," explores the impact of the Internet on identity formation and maintenance among those ethnic minorities who descend from or once-comprised the ruling elites of now defunct empires. This chapter includes a case study of the near abroad Russians based on field research conducted in Estonia, Latvia, Kazakhstan, and cyberspace. "The Cybernetic Vanguard" explores the challenges of small, weak, and stateless nations that seek to preserve their identity in the face of near certain acculturation in their states of residence. The geographic focus of this chapter is squarely on Europe, with the Roma (Gypsies) constituting the case study. My treatment of Romani cyberspace stems from research conducted among upwardly mobile Roma in Transylvania, as well as monitoring and participation in Romani chatrooms and Internet groups. The focus of this chapter is on those zealous coteries of ideologues who commit significant time and resources to breathing new life into their endangered ancestral tongues though cultural work in cyberspace. The last chapter in this section, "Virtual Prophets," discusses the self-appointed architects of pan-ethnic unity who hope to forge new, contrived "imagined communities" in cyberspace. This case study explores the impact of Web-enabled ummahists, who are rapidly crafting a "nation" out of the various ethnicities which constitute the transnational community of Muslims. My analysis explores the rapid identity shift which occurred among de-ethnicized Muslims living in the West after the publication of the infamous Danish cartoons depicting the Prophet Muhammad in 2005.

In the conclusion, I attempt to tie together the complex and often contradictory impacts that the Internet has had on minorities to reify and then defend my thesis that the impact of Internet use on minorities is *not* neutral. My ultimate finding is that the Web is a double-edged sword for national identity projects. On the one hand, cyberspace provides an alternate universe with unlimited potential for the storage and preservation of national totems. Furthermore, chat rooms, instant messaging, IP telephony, and email—all of which run over the Internet—are being utilized to reinvigorate dead, dying, or moribund languages as well as to create virtual propinquity and conceptual contiguity among dispersed and divided nations. This is a boon to challenged minorities and those immigrants wishing to maintain vibrant and daily contact with their co-nationals and ethnic homeland. However, I also consider the denationalizing aspects of the Internet. The frequent use of English for research and international communication, the deterritorialized nature of cyberspace, the atomizing effects of regular Web use, and the Western-derived, socially-liberal, multicultural, and consumption-centric esprit of the Internet all combine to create a seductive nexus of globalism, which tends to work against the promotion of narrowly-defined nationalisms.

Following the recapitulation of my findings, I critique the Web's ability to facilitate political action, something which is undeniable but certainly also underdeveloped and, at best, interstitial. I then move on to state-based responses to Web-based national identity projects among national minorities and immigrant populations. I look at the various efforts of totalitarian, authoritarian, and liberal-democratic governments to censor, contest, and co-opt such projects. The section includes some policy recommendations for IGOs, nation-states, and multinational corporations seeking to take advantage of and/or further the cyberspatial activities of minorities around the globe. I suggest ways to discourage virtual communities which might be prone to violence from pursuing such a route. I also offer new directions for research in the field. In the final pages, I return to my analysis of previously discussed theories and make some observations on how cyberspace enables or retards the eventualities prophesied by the likes of Samuel Huntington, Benjamin Barber, Gilles Kepel, and others.[44]

Notes

1. A national minority is any group that a) forms a numerical minority in a given state b) does not dominate politically c) differs from the majority population due to ethnic, linguistic or religious characteristics, and d) expresses feelings of intra-group solidarity in preserving their own culture, traditions, and language. It should be stated that in some states, ethnic or

national minorities, in fact, enjoy statistical superiority, but are denied political influence commensurate with their numbers, the indigenous peoples of Bolivia being a case in point.

2. This definition intentionally fails to include states which have been forged through the creation of multicultural and multiethnic societies, such as the United States, Canada, Switzerland, and contemporary South Africa. According to John Milton Yinger, it is now inconceivable that any actions, either in terms of migration or redefinition of boundaries, could produce the "ethnically homogenous populations" that would turn these countries into "nation-states"; John Milton Yinger, *Ethnicity: Source of Strength? Source of Conflict?* (Albany: State University of New York Press, 1994), 11.

3. Within a half century of the establishment of the American Republic, the system of sovereign states spread across the Western hemisphere. However, the fact that these societies were composed of mixed immigrant (European, African, and Asian) and indigenous popula-tions, the concept of nation-state as defined above did not and could not apply.

4. Kiran Pervez, "Narrating the 'Nation': A Relational Methodology Exploring the India-Pakistan Conflict." Paper presented at the annual meeting of the International Studies Association, Montreal, Quebec, Canada (20 March 2004).

5. Kenneth E. Boulding, "National Images and International Systems," *Journal of Con-flict Resolution* 3, no. 2 (June 1959): 120-131.

6. Benedict Anderson, *Imagined Communities: Reflections on the Origin and Spread of Nationalism* (London: Verso, 1991), 44.

7. Anderson, *Imagined Communities*, 7.

8. Austin Corbett, "Beyond the Ghost in the (Human) Shell," *Journal of Evolution and Technology* 20, no. 1 (March 2009): 43-50.

9. See Victoria Bernal, "Diaspora, Cyberspace and Political Imagination: The Eritrean Diaspora Online," *Global Networks* 6, no. 2 (April 2006): 161-179.

10. Representative examples include: the Bavarian Party (bayernpartei.org); the Two Sicilies independence movement (duesicilie.org); the Sami Parliament (sametinget.se); and North Frisian Radio (nfradio.de).

11. See, for instance, James Tyner and Olaf Kuhlke, "Pan-National Identities: Representa-tions of the Philippine Diaspora on the World Wide Web," *Asia Pacific Viewpoint* 41, no. 3 (December 2000): 231–252; Abril Trigo, "Cybernation (Or, La Patria Cibernetica)," *Journal of Latin American Cultural Studies* 12, no. 1 (March 2003): 95-117; Rachel C. Lee and Sau-ling Cynthia Wong (eds.), *AsianAmerica.Net: Ethnicity, Nationalism, and Cyberspace* (New York: Routledge, 2003); and Karim H. Karim (ed.), *The Media of Diaspora* (London: Routledge, 2003).

12. According to Peters, diaspora "implies a relation to identity based on 'real or imag-ined relationships among scattered fellows, whose sense of community is sustained by forms of communication and contact such as kinship, pilgrimage, trade, travel, and shared culture.' This shared culture includes language, ritual, and both print and electronic media"; see Nicola Mai, "The Albanian Diaspora-in-the-Making: Media, Migration and Social Exclusion." *Journal of Ethnic and Migration Studies* 31, no. 3 (May 2005): 543-561.

13. Arjun Appadurai, *Modernity at Large* (Minneapolis: University of Minnesota Press, 1996), 4.

14. Mai, "The Albanian Diaspora-in-the-Making," 544.

15. See Maya Ranganathan, "Nurturing the Nation on the Net: The Case of Tamil Ee-lam," *Nationalism and Ethnic Politics* 8, no. 2 (Summer 2002): 51-66 and "Potential of the Net to Construct and Convey Ethnic and National Identities: Comparison of the Use in the Sri Lankan Tamil and Kashmiri Situations." *Asian Ethnicity* 4, no. 2 (June 2003): 265-279.

16. See Ranganathan, "Potential of the Net to Construct and Convey Ethnic and National Identities;" Rohan Jayasekera, "Waiting for the Kingdom: Nations in Cyberspace are No Substitute for the Real Thing," *Index on Censorship* 29, no. 3 (May/June 2000): 140-145; Kilic Kanat, "Ethnic Media and Politics: The Case of the Use of the Internet by the Uyghur

Diaspora," *First Monday* 10, no. 7 (July 2005): 1-6; and Donna M. Kowal, "Digitizing and Globalizing Indigenous Voices: The Zapatista Movement," in Greg Elmer, *Critical Perspective in the Internet* (Lanham: Roman & Littlefield Publishers, Inc., 2002), 105-126.

17. See, for instance, Daniel Miller and Don Slater, *The Internet: An Ethnographic Approach* (Oxford: Berg, 2000) on the Web-enabled Trinidadian diaspora and Neil Blair Christensen, *Inuit in Cyberspace: Embedding Offline, Identities Online* (Copenhagen: Museum Tusculanum Press, 2003) on the Inuit.

18. See Gayatri C. Spivak, "Can the Subaltern Speak?" in Bill Ashcroft, Gareth Griffiths, and Helen Tiffin, *The Post-Colonial Studies Reader* (London and New York: Routledge, 1995).

19. Panikos Panayi, *An Ethnic History of Europe since 1945: Nations, States and Minorities* (Harlow: Longman, 2001), 138.

20. Robert M. Kitchin, *Cyberspace: The World in Wires* (Chichester, UK: John Wiley and Sons, 1998), 2.

21. William Gibson, *Neuromancer* (London: Gollancz, 1984), 67.

22. Michael Benedikt, *Cyberspace: First Steps* (Cambridge: The MIT Press, 1992), 1-2.

23. Ronald J. Deibert, *Parchment, Printing and Hypermedia: Communication in World Order Transformation* (New York: Columbia University Press, 1997), 114.

24. Jim Falk, "The Meaning of the Web," *Information Society* 14, no. 1 (November 1998): 285-293.

25. Ziauddin Sardar, "alt.civilizations.faq: Cyberspace as the Darker Side of the West," in Ziauddin Sardar and Jerome Ravetz, *Cyberfutures: Culture and Politics on the Information Superhighway* (New York: New York University Press, 1998), 14-41.

26. Saskia Sassen, "The Impact of the Internet on Sovereignty: Unfounded and Real Worries," in Christoph Engel and Kenneth H. Heller, *Understanding the Impact of Global Networks in Local Social, Political and Cultural Values* (Baden-Baden: Nomos Verlagsgesellschaft, 2000), 195-209.

27. Diane E. Nelson, "Maya Hackers and the Cyberspatialized Nation-State: Modernity, Ethnostalgia, and a Lizard Queen in Guatemala," *Cultural Anthropology* 11, no. 3 (August 1996): 287-308.

28. Menderes Candan and Uwe Hunger. "Nation Building Online: A Case Study of Kurdish Migrants in Germany," *German Policy Studies* 4, no. 4 (2008): 125-153.

29. Bernal, "Diaspora, Cyberspace and Political Imagination," 162.

30. Jan Nederveen Pieterse, *Globalization & Culture: A Global Mélange* (Lanham: Rowman & Littlefield, 2003).

31. See Anthony Smith, *National Identity* (Reno: University of Nevada Press, 1991) and Benedict Anderson, *Imagined Communities: Reflections on the Origin and Spread of Nationalism* (London: Verso, 1991).

32. Ernst Gellner, *Nations and Nationalism* (Ithaca, NY: Cornell University Press, 1983), 1.

33. Montserrat Guibernau, *Nationalisms: The Nation-State and Nationalism in the Twentieth Century* (Cambridge: Polity Press, 1996).

34. Smith, *Imagined Communities*, 14; Smith's definition (probably inadvertently) proscribed many nationalities of the USSR and other totalitarian states from achieving nationhood since the *propiska* (residence permit) tradition which prevents free movement limits "territorial mobility."

35. Gellner, *Nations and Nationalism*, 7.

36. Cited in John Hutchinson and Anthony Smith, *Nationalism* (Oxford: Oxford University Press, 1994).

37. Karl Deutsch, *Nationalism and Social Communication: An Inquiry into the Foundations of Nationality* (Cambridge: The Technology Press of the Massachusetts Institute of Technology, 1953), 3-4.

38. Although these political entities lack international recognition, they conform to the requirements of states in every other major way. They possess a defined territory, a permanent resident population, a government, an organized economy, a circulation system, and sovereignty. In some cases, these statelets more resemble states than a number of those entities recognized by the United Nations as part of the community of nations, e.g., Somalia, Sierra Leone, etc.

39. Appadurai, *Modernity at Large*.

40. The range per ethnic population of the interviews ranged from 20 to 200.

41. Linda Leung, *Virtual Ethnicity: Race, Resistance and the World Wide Web* (Farnham, UK: Ashgate, 2005), 167.

42. My thanks to Fatmir Fanda Ibraimi and Vlad Strukov for their help in this regard.

43. Thomas Hylland Eriksen, "Nationalism and the Internet," *Nations & Nationalism* 13, no. 1 (January 2007): 1-17.

44. See Samuel P. Huntington, "Clash of Civilizations," *Foreign Affairs* 72, no. 3 (Summer 1993): 22-49 and *The Clash of Civilizations and the Remaking of World Order* (New York: Simon and Schuster, 1997); Benjamin R. Barber, "Jihad vs. McWorld," *Atlantic Monthly* 269 (March 1992): 53-65 and *Jihad vs. McWorld: How Globalism and Tribalism Are Reshaping the World* (New York: Ballantine Books, 1996); and Gilles Kepel, *The Revenge of God: The Resurgence of Islam, Christianity, and Judaism in the Modern World* (University Park: Penn State University Press, 1994) and *The War for Muslim Minds: Islam and the West* (Cambridge, MA: Harvard University Press, 2004).

Part I
The Color and Shape of a Cyberspatial World

Chapter 1
From Bibles to Bollywood: Mass Media, Identity, and the State

After the fall of Rome in AD 476, Europe experienced a millennium in which even the most basic forms of mass media were limited in their availability. During the Dark Ages, the Catholic Church established and maintained a rapacious monopoly on the written word, with vetted liturgical works soon becoming almost the only acceptable content for publication. Even within this extremely limited field, the Church vigorously policed the boundaries of "acceptable" works. Furthermore, the very act of book-making became confined to the cloistered monasteries of the church itself. In cash-poor medieval Europe, few possessed the resources to fund the labor-intensive process of transcribing old texts, much less to create new ones. As a result, libraries became the bailiwicks of bishops and kings, and literacy dwindled among all but the highest aristocratic castes and the upper echelons of the clergy. Even something as simple as a letter was a rare sight, and typically required the use of a village scribe or a semi-educated priest to interpret the arcane scribbling upon it. Europe from AD 400 to 1400 was—for all intents and purposes—a culture of the spoken word.

Mass media were virtually unknown outside of a few narrowly circumscribed avenues of human existence, namely the priesthood and the aristocratic household. Such an environment—that is, one almost totally devoid of mass media—allowed the Church to achieve near dominance over the production of identity and collective consciousness. As media theorist James Curran argues, the role of the Church during the Middle Ages was to interpret and make sense of the world to the mass public.[1] In absence of mass media, the Church effectively dominated identity production.[2]

In pre-Renaissance Europe, peasants were simultaneously part of two communities. The first community was that of Christendom. This community was too large, diverse, and amorphous to provide medieval Europeans with any meaningful way of differentiating themselves from others (with the possible exception of Jews or Muslims living amongst them or invaders from abroad such as the Mongol/Tatar hordes).[3] The second community to which Europeans belonged was one based on residence. Typically, this space was constituted by the familiar space around a particular village or settlement that could be traversed on foot in less than a single day. However, in most cases these areas were often much smaller. Unlike the imagined community of Christendom, this societal formation was much tighter, and did not require an outside agent to maintain it (though the village priest or itinerant monk often served this purpose). The languages to which the peasantries were exposed reflected these two disparate communities: Latin was the language of the Church,[4] while a local dialect was employed in all other situations.[5] In both cases, group identity was comparatively weak since almost everyone an individual came in contact with was, in fact, part of the same community, i.e., Christian and local.[6]

During the fourteenth century, a series of plagues swept across the continent, rocking Europe to its very core. Between a third and one half of the population perished as a result of the epidemic. This keenly impacted the relationship between the rulers and the ruled. The reduction in manpower made the peasantry more valuable to landlords, who were forced to increase their remuneration for services rendered. Serfdom began to fade as wage labor became more common and the standard of living for the lowest of the low began to rise. As a result of these societal shifts, upward and outward mobility soon became comparatively common. By the beginning of the fifteenth century, the European world was no longer exclusively constituted by serfdom, fiefs, and rural living. Instead, the continent witnessed the nascent stages of a transformation based on industrialization, the establishment of nation-states, and urbanization. The shift from a spoken to a written culture that accompanied the expansion of mass media was both a trigger for and the result of this process.

The Renaissance (1450-1600) marked the beginning of centuries of massive socio-economic change. A number of factors coalesced to produce an environment conducive to such new developments. Certainly labor-saving advances and climatic factors played a role, but there were also important intellectual, socio-economic, and cultural forces as well, including: the tangential influence of the *Pax Mongolica* ('the Mongol peace'); the weakness of the Catholic Church in the wake of the Black Death; acquisition of Arabic texts as part of the Reconquista; a flood of Greek scholars into Western Europe fleeing the Ottoman conquest of Constantinople; and a precipitous increase in the wealth and power of certain merchant families in northern Italy. This "rebirth" of culture, knowledge, and learning quickly translated into a catalyst for the increased production of printed works of science, art, anatomy, mechanics, literature, and theology. Scholars operating outside—but not necessarily in opposition to—the Universal Church sought to expand the frontiers of the human experience and knowledge by locating and interrogating long dormant works of the "ancients" such as Cicero, Homer, and Plato.

Printing the Nation

While the Italian city-states of Florence, Milan, and Siena were principle sites of the assimilation of "lost" Greek and Arabic knowledge, perhaps the most important Renaissance development occurred north of the Alps. In the mid-fifteenth century, the goldsmith Johannes Gutenberg invented the moveable type printing press.[7] His first printed text in 1451 was a version of Aelius Donatus's schoolbook on Latin grammar entitled *Ars Minor*. However, his most famous work—which would ultimately bear his name—came four years later. With the *Biblia Sacra*, Gutenberg demonstrated the economic, social, and political power of the printing press. For a fraction of the price of a scribe's labor, Gutenberg produced a copy of the Christian holy book. In the space of a year, the German entrepreneur produced 180 copies of the text. In the same timeframe, a monk working away in a scriptorium would have been lucky to finish a single copy. Furthermore, all the versions were identical in their content, and thus did not suffer from the endemic mistakes and omissions which characterized their scriven counterparts. This event marked the beginning of the "Age of the Printed Book."

Twenty years after making his first book, Gutenberg's presses could be found in twelve European cities. The dawning of the Age of Discovery in the late 1400s soon infused the new medium of printed texts with extraordinary vigor. Advances in map-making, combined with the spread of printed works on geography, yielded huge benefits for explorers. In the wake of Christopher Columbus' *Epistola* (1493), a report to King Ferdinand II of Aragón and Queen Isabella of Castile, the allure of the printing press became almost irresistible to monarchs and merchants alike. In fact, both groups saw the press as a mechanism for diminishing the Church's influence over their affairs. Literacy among the wealthy soon became a prerequisite to occupational success and/or political advancement. No longer was the ability to read and write the exclusive seigniory of the clergy and nobles, the sons (and sometimes daughters) of the merchant class were now joining the literati.

With the advent of the printing press, increasing literacy, and the subsequent popularization of printed materials (theological, fictional, pornographic, etc.), there emerged a new impetus towards "national languages." These new, standardized tongues grew out of established dialects, usually those spoken in the largest cities of Europe. Not coincidentally, these localities were precisely where the sovereign resided. Karl Deutsch describes the localities that determined the national languages, and ultimately national identities, as nodal areas.[8] These central locations came to dominate the communication ecumene, and ultimately define the nation during the classic age of nation-building.[9] As a result, London, Paris, Berlin, Madrid, Stockholm, and Lisbon all came to function as nuclear areas of culture, learning, and language. These and other cities came to dominate the communication ecumene of the future nation-states of Europe. A precipitously improved economic milieu and its resulting impact on demography, combined with the expansion of literacy beyond the realm of a small religious elite laid the groundwork for greater distribution of literary works in these new vernaculars.

As written works experience an increase in linguistic intelligibility and physical availability, as well as a comparative decrease in their cost, Europe's various national vernaculars flowered. As a result, Europeans began to conceive of themselves as part of fledgling communities which were less expansive than Christendom yet larger than those constituted by village life; these new communities would eventually become the various "nations" of Europe.[10] Such a transformation was neither spontaneous, nor accidental; it occurred under the direction of emergent elites who actively sought to harness the power of these new socio-culturo-political constructs. One might argue that such an undertaking was the greatest marketing effort in history.

Without the creation of these "national" audiences who could understand the idiom of message transmission, media products such as François Rabelais's novels *Gargantua and Pantagruel* and Niccolò Machiavelli's political treatise *The Prince*—both first published in 1532—would probably have been confined to laughable small readerships. Author of *The Gutenberg Galaxy*, Marshall McLuhan states, "Scribal culture could have neither authors nor publics such as were created by typography."[11] Not only new works benefited from this phenomenon; older works, such as *The Divine Comedy* (1308-1321), *The Decameron* (1350-1353), and *The Canterbury Tales* (1369-1372), now flourished within their rapidly expanding national audiences. Latin—a language which had once united a small coterie of elites across the European continent—now competed against more than a dozen languages empowered by kings and nobles, who saw their newly-minted written forms of English, French, and Spanish as equal in stature to the moribund tongue of the Romans (and the Church). While these texts certainly benefited from the creation of these new national vernaculars, they also served to solidify them. Collectively, these publications came to function as a primer for the new national languages of Europe, as aspirant elites sought to mimic the diction, vocabulary, and syntax of the Renaissance authors.

Perhaps the most famous of the early vernacular texts to gain wide distribution was the Bible. Martin Luther's doctrinal battle with the Papacy led to a hitherto unknown interest in personal interpretation of the Holy Scripture. Luther's posting of the *Ninety-Five Theses on the Power of Indulgences* in 1517 set off a chain of events that prompted an entire generation of literate Europeans to investigate the vagaries of their religion. They did so by reading mass-produced printed works including the Bible, and then acting upon the knowledge they obtained. Such distribution would have been impossible without the use of Gutenberg's printing press over fifty years earlier. Interestingly, the printing press was both a catalyst for and a tool of Luther's heresy. The Dominican friar Johann Tetzel's selling of mass-printed indulgences prompted Luther to pen his ninety-five theses, which in turn were printed en masse in the local German dialect of Wittenberg.[12]

Political scientist scholar Ronald J. Deibert draws a clear connection between the popularization of Martin Luther's writings and other works produced for mass consumption in the fifteenth and sixteenth centuries and social, political and economic change. "Distributional changes undercut some social forces while they advance[d] the interests of others."[13] The Catholic Church's monopoly on ideas was dashed by the printing press. During his lifetime, Luther's works surpassed those of Catholic disputants by a factor of five to one in terms of publication.[14] German princes and nobles quickly realized the potential of mass-produced works in the vernacular and began to make deft use of the printing press to serve their own ends. Canadian communications theorist Harold Adam Innis states, "With printing, paper facilitated an effective development of the vernaculars and gave expression to their vitality in the growth of nationalism."[15] As Luther's heresy was transformed into a genuine movement, a fecund nexus of religiosity, the pursuit of political power, and ideological conflict was created, with the printed word at its center.

Empowered by didactic power of the printing press, new views of space and territory evolved. This transformation was amplified by the cartographic revolution and a steady centralization of bureaucracy, enabled by increasing literacy rates among the bourgeois/burgher classes.[16] Such a milieu allowed European monarchs to increase their own power. Faith proved to be the greatest motivating force. A series of religious wars ravaged France from 1562 to 1598, subsiding only after the signing of the Edict of Nantes. The bloodshed between French Catholics and their Huguenot brethren served as a vicious prologue for the Thirty Years War (1618-

1648) in central Europe, which pitted increasingly powerful monarchies against one another, ostensibly in the name of Christianity. In 1648, a series of treaties collectively known as the Peace of Westphalia brought an end to the carnage, but not before a third of Germany's population had perished. The treaty officially recognized the existence of the Swiss Confederation and the Dutch Republic, as well as other sovereign territories on the European continent.

Theorists of international relations tend to use this event to mark the beginning of the modern system of nation-states. This was in great part due to the application of *cuis regio, eius religio* ('as goes the king, so goes the religion'). Thus, monarchs—not priests and bishops—came to be masters of identity production in Early Modern Europe. Rather than loose corporate identity based on Christendom, England, Spain, France, and other burgeoning states began to promote collective identity projects forged in the geopolitical territory to which their rulers laid claim.[17] From the mid-1600s onward, the rise of the nation-state steadily translated into the reification of sovereignty based on territorial rather than spiritual borders. Consequently, the diplomatic system that evolved in the post-Westphalian era reinforced the notion that the body politic of the ruler and the ruled were one. Thus, neither God nor the village served as the final arbiter of identity; they had been both been trumped by the nation. Incipient forms of mass media were integral to this process. Plays, posters, novels, and other forms of information transmission instructed the Englishman on how to be English, the Frenchman on how to be French, etc.

Europe's sacralization of the state system in the eighteenth and nineteenth centuries created an environment where governing elites were now able to collect, correlate, and distribute information about the souls living within increasingly well-delineated boundaries. Such taxonomic power soon led to the process of national homogenization within the nation-state. In the words of anthropologist David W. Anthony, states adopted "policies that forced Welsh...to speak English, and the Breton to speak French [which] were rooted in politicians' need for an ancient and 'pure' national heritage for each new state."[18] Steady displacement of the rural population promoted urbanization, which in turn became tied to industrialization. These socio-economic disruptions forced individuals to compete in new environments which differed greatly from the medieval village. German sociologist Ferdinand Tönnies describes this transformation as a shift from *Gemeinschaft* (community) to *Gesellschaft* (society).[19] In this process, organic forms of community—based on blood, locality, kinship, and neighborhood—were exchanged for mechanical, transitory, and superficial links based on individualism, self-interest, and monetary gain. This societal shift abetted the various national projects of Europe's states by diminishing the value placed on rooted, local difference and genuine, verifiable connections of kith and kin. Small, organic ecumenes linked to the village were abandoned in favor of large, artificial ecumenes associated with the machinery of the burgeoning nation-state.

At the heart of this change was mass media, which promoted new "imagined communities" based on the nation. Increasing literacy rates prompted a shift in the distribution of power which began alter society at several levels. Marshall McLuhan, who once called nationalism the "child of print technology," underscores the relationship stating,

Another feature of the penetrative powers of print technology, in addition to uniformity and repeatability, is the complimentary of individualism and nationalism.... Not only does print vividly discover national boundaries, but the print market was itself defined by such boundaries, at least for early printers and
publishers. Perhaps also the ability to see one's mother tongue in uniform and re-
peatable technological dress creates in the individual reader a feeling of unity and
power that he shares with all other readers of that tongue.[20]

The world order transformation described by the media theory school[21] involved the
codification of law, the distribution of maps, and the advent of careful record keeping—all of which formed the basis of the modern state, which is dependent on an
efficient system of taxation.

While citizens had to bear this new burden, they could expect two tangible
benefits: security and the potential for better economic conditions in the future. As
the nation-state began the long and rather complicated process of "drawing in"
those over whom it now claimed sovereignty, the need to reduce other loyalties
became an integral part of the process of state-building. Historian Panikos Panayi
describes the nation-state as "a method of political organization which has developed in the age of industrialization and in which the life-blood consists of an artificial culture which has been introduced by those who dominate political power, who
usually control the economy."[22] This mechanical, artificial culture was reified
through the press, works of popular fiction, and other media outlets. Certain minority traditions were adopted by the national culture, but regional and ethnic minorities
were generally subsumed within the now dominant national identity.

Ernest Gellner pioneered the notion that nationalism and industrialization were
inextricably linked in his magnum opus, *Nations and Nationalism* (1983). Just as
industrialization inevitably arrived in different locales at different times, so did the
contagion of nationalism. However, Gellner notes that nationalism tended to be the
most explosive when it was combined with "early industrialism (dislocation, mobility [and] acute inequality not hallowed by time and custom)."[23] In such realms of
confrontation and competition, nationalism often turned bloody. It is here that we
can begin to date the identification and "othering" of national minorities as a requisite part of the nation-building process which so-defined the modern era. My use of
the concept of the "Other" is drawn from the writings of postcolonial theorist Edward Said who stated:

> The development and maintenance of every culture require the existence of anoth-
> er, different and competing *alter ego*. The construction of identity . . . involves the
> construction of opposites and "others" whose actuality is always subject to the con-
> tinuous interpretation and reinterpretation of their differences from "us."[24]

Just as Christendom had defined itself against the pagan, the Jew, and the Moor in
an earlier era, nascent European nations now began to identify themselves against
their neighbors in other states, as well as in contrast to internal "strangers" in their
midst. The notion of "us" soon became differentiated from the notion of "them"
through the delineation of linguistic, cultural, and geopolitical spaces to which the
dominant group belonged, and, more importantly, the *foreigner* (external other) or
minority (internal other) did not. It is helpful in this context to divide nationalism
into two separate but equally important categories: external nationalism (contrasting

the national self versus the external other) and internal nationalism (drawing division between the dominant nation and internal others, i.e., ethnic and/or religious minorities). The former became wedded to the national project before industrialization, the latter emerged as an important factor in its wake (or alternatively, in its absence). Media technologies played a key role in the process of shaping both forms of nationalism. France provides a compelling example of both phenomena.

The French Revolution (1789-99) marked a new stage in the development of mass media. The proliferation of inexpensive and easily reproducible leaflets about political developments, and the emergence of semi-professional class of persons who wrote about events spawned the modern concepts of "news" and the "press." While both newspapers and reporters were becoming a staple of life in Britain and the American republic by the end of the eighteenth century, it was in France that the politicization of mass media reached its zenith. According to French historian Lynn Hunt,

> Yet, the large numbers of newspapers…did not make the politics of the Revolution revolutionary; the multiplication of politics outside the halls of government only made France seem more like England or the new United States. What made the French different, what made them seem to themselves and to observers alike "this new race," was their profound conviction that they were establishing a new human community in a present that had no precedent or parallel.[25]

The revolution itself was intricately linked to the emergence the "fourth estate," i.e., reporters. The term, coined by the Irish wit and anti-revolutionary Edmund Burke, embodies journalists' roles as both advocates for issues and their capacity to shape the perceptions of the masses. In France prior to the outbreak of violence, political discourse had generally been confined to the salons. However, the heady days of July 1789 brought political arguments onto the streets, with pamphlets and newspapers acting as the lightening rod of this process. After being freed from the shackles of censorship associated with the *ancien régime*, the press suddenly mushroomed and began reporting "daily events with the breathless immediacy that marked a turn to toward a new, more modern sense of journalistic time."[26]

As regicide deprived France of its uniting figure, the revolutionary regime put every available form of mass media to work to craft a community of allegiance and identity based on common ideals (liberty, equality, and fraternity) and membership in the nation. This symbolic framework was underwritten by government-subsidized posters, papers, bulletins, and other propaganda.[27] Paul Starr refers to this of the written word as France's "revolution in print."[28] The gathering chorus of enemies on France's borders made playing the national card both a natural and effective way to engender support for an increasingly terroristic regime. No longer did French fight, kill, and die for "king and country." After 1789, the denizens of the French Republic marched to the battlefield in the name of imagined community of the French nation.[29]

Just as France's revolutionary transformation entailed its embrace of external nationalism, its post-Napoleonic industrialization process facilitated the homogenization of its peoples of France into a new breed: the French. As it entered the modern period, France included a panoply of linguistic and cultural groups, from Celtic-speaking Bretons to pre-Indo-European Basques to Germanic Alsatians, most of whom lived at the country's periphery. Even at its core, a north-south linguistic divide cut the country into two parts: the northern lands where the Langue d'Oïl was spoken and southern zone where the Langue d'Oc (Occitan) predominated.[30] As the idiom of the ecumene, the Parisian variant of the Langue d'Oïl was destined to become the ultimate form of French to be used across modern France. However, in the mid-nineteenth century, French was a foreign language for roughly half of the country's population, with many speaking no French at all.[31] By the turn of the twentieth century, the situation was quite different. Mass education, universal military service, and the spread of daily newspapers led to the creation of a truly national community in term of language, as well as habits and outlook.

A similar process was underway across Europe, including in the newly forged nation-states of Germany and Italy. The creation of large tariff-free zone through the establishment of *Zollverein* (German Customs Union) in 1834 laid the groundwork for the establishment of German state. As a single economic and mercantile space was established across the German provinces, inter-cultural communication between the various German peoples evolved into a common cultural continuum. After German unification under the leadership of Prussia's Otto von Bismarck, the process was accelerated through state-support, specifically universal education and new communication infrastructure. Italy's unification process, often called the "Risorgimento," is even more closely linked with the spread of mass media. The movement took its name from *Il Risorgimento* ('The Resurgence'), a liberal, nationalist publication founded by Count Camillo Benso di Cavour in Turin in 1847. Functioning as the movement's main propagandist, Cavour emerged one of the seminal figures of Italian unification, alongside Giuseppe Garibaldi and Giuseppe Mazzini. Once Italy was united, the conservative statesman Massimo d'Azeglio famously told the country's new king Vittorio Emmanuel II, "We have Italy; now we must make Italians." Lacking the resources of Bismarck's Germany, Italy's national project did not fare as well; however, the country did initiate an earnest program of Italianization among its Piedmontese, Sicilians, Sardinians, and Friulians, as well as its smaller communities of Greeks, Slovenes, and other non-Italic minorities.[32]

Within a few decades, a wave of nationalism would pour over Eastern Europe extinguishing the Ottoman, Habsburg, and Romanov empires in its wake. While these powers were undoubtedly guilty of various offences against their imperial subjects, their nature demanded tolerance of ethno-linguistic and sectarian diversity. Within the galactic configurations of nations that comprised Turkey, Austria-Hungary, and Russia, there was ample room for even the tiniest nation, from the Circassians of Anatolia to the Szeklers of Transylvanian to the Gagauz of Bessarabia. As a dozen nation-states emerged from the ashes of the Great War, unimaginable pressure was now placed on these small ethnies, or proto-nations. Hitherto constituent parts of kaleidoscopic empires, these groups now faced the full brunt of twin forces of change: modernization and nationalism. In each and every case, the newly independent states of interwar Europe pursued nationalizing strategies intended to promote their titular nationality at the expense of the various ethnic minorities that resided within their borders. According to Rogers Brubaker, a nationalizing state is one that is involved in a "compensatory" project aimed at elevating the interests of the indigenous nationality above the interests of other nationalities.[33] Such projects typically occur in a milieu where the titular nationality has historically been oppressed by another nationality, usually an imperial invader.

During the first half of the twentieth century, Poland and Czechoslovakia represented paradigms of this process, as they sought to expunge German influence in the wake of their independence from the Teutonic Hohenzollern and Habsburg empires. In effect, the state's goal to eradicate all legacies of imperialism, especially those which previously confined the majority nationality to positions of weakness. Much of this transformation occurs at a symbolic level (statues, street names, etc.) through the replacement of imperial symbols with native ones. The newly independent states of post-World War I Central Europe "against all evidence—understood themselves as ethnically homogenous nation-states," despite straddling the "belt of mixed populations" of Central and Eastern Europe.[34] This pressure was most keenly felt in the education system, the military, and the media. A reconstituted Poland aggressively Polonized its Ukrainians, Germans, Kashubians, and Tatars. Bucharest set about turning its Hungarians, Slavs, Saxons, and Magyarized Jews into good Romanians. In Czechoslovakia, Germans in the west were forced into becoming Czechs, while Rusyns in the east were transformed into "good" Slovaks. All of these examples stand as testament to the veracity of Ernest Gellner's definition of nationalism as the principle that the state and the nation should be congruent.[35]

In *Imagined Communities*, Benedict Anderson argues that the ascension of the newspaper as the dominant medium of information distribution—when combined with the spread of capitalism—facilitated a rise in nationalism among nations in the late nineteenth century.[36] (In the above-referenced cases of Eastern Europe, this situation was delayed several decades until the end of imperial control over the region.) Anderson's work focused on emergent nation-states which operationalized a program of nation-building which proved successful in Western Europe during the early modern period. With the deployment of cheap and ubiquitous national newspapers, such imagined communities could be created in a startlingly brief period of time in places like Malaysia, Venezuela, etc. As Alexander J. Motyl states, "Education, urbanization and industrialization create national elites, who, together with nations and states represent the necessary conditions of the actual striving for nation-states and self-government."[37] Statist political, commercial, and intellectual elites within states showed themselves to be exceptionally adept at manipulating national identity to bring the masses in line with the goals of state-sponsored nationalism. An insidious nexus between the state, nationalism, and national identity was a direct outgrowth of mass mediation in the late 1800s and early 1900s.[38]

These nationalizing policies proved especially ominous for minorities living in such states, whether in the geographically-dispersed stateless nations, small isolated ethnies, or immigrant diasporas. Johan Galtung describes the "cultural violence" which the state directed against these groups; this symbolic violence took the form of aggressive symbols and acts including "stars, crosses, and crescents; flags, anthems, and military parades; the ubiquitous portrait of the Leader; inflammatory speeches and posters."[39] While the transformation was slow, it was—according to Galtung—invariable leading to a state of permanence for a single, dominant, and exclusive culture (at the expense of other cultures, which were—at best—demoted to a second-class status).[40] Statist elites among the bourgeoisie articulated and drove nationalism through the domination of mass media—principally, newspapers. Benedict Anderson terms this process and its outcomes "print capitalism."[41] Skyrocketing literacy rates, the growth of universal education, and the implementation of centralized state-crafted curriculums provided a potent environment for these elites to sow the seeds of nationalism. Harold Innis framed the issue as such: "The mono-polies of knowledge based on language reinforced by mechanized communication led in turn to nationalism."[42] Typically, these forms of nationalism were exclusio-nary and supported the aims of the majority (or titular) nation within a given state.

Nationalists frequently portray national identity as monolithic, and based on a single culture—that of the core nationality; although as Gellner cautions that these cultures are in many cases "inventions, or modified out of all recognition."[43] The irony is that many "national" cultures borrow their ethnic costumes, folk songs, cuisines, and cultural quiddities from minority or regional populations who have been subsumed by the larger polity (often suffering statist denials of their existence or even exterminated in the process). In industrial Europe, the voices of many na-tional minorities went unheard or were drowned in a deluge of competing positions within the dominant communication and information platforms. In the not-so-distant medieval past, there was nothing but "cultures, shading into each other, overlapping, intertwined; units of all shapes and sizes."[44] As a consequence, there was room for cultural communities of all shapes and sizes. However, with the rise of print culture and what McLuhan calls the "typographic man," borders—cultural, linguistic, economic, and social—came to have very real, sometimes deadly serious, meanings. And in the modern industrial era, it was the state which set itself as the ultimate determiner such meanings.[45] The advent of new broadcast media (motion pictures, wireless, radio, television, etc.) did little to disrupt the statist elite's domi-nion over the forge of national identity. In fact, as novel forms of mass media emerged, they quickly came to be monopolized by those acting in the interests of the state or by the state itself.

By the turn of the twentieth century, the nation-state's use of the newspaper had grown to immense proportions. Anderson demonstrates how the domination of the primary media of the day, combined with universal education, made almost every resident of a given state a target for the messages intended to craft a single unitary and monolithic national identity. Countless examples exist in the history of the late nineteenth and early twentieth centuries that testify to the centrality of the newspaper and other mass produced media such as the placard (political poster) to crystallizing nationalist sentiment and assuring patriotism. The lead-up to inter-state wars served as the most fertile environment for media technologies to serve as the platform for external nationalism, but other types of historical events allowed for such activity to flourish as well.

Electrifying the Nation

Prior to the mid-nineteenth century, certain nation-states had clear advantages over others due to their size. Countries which were quite small had difficulty defending themselves from their larger neighbors; however, extraordinarily large countries were clearly disadvantaged when it came to developing national cohesiveness due to several inherent difficulties: the constant challenge of regionalism; a lack of cen-tralization; and a poor transportation, communications and trade infrastructure.[46] Until the 1900s, France was seen as the optimally sized nation-state. Communica-tion between Paris and the outer edges of France averaged five days or less which has been suggested to be optimal, as such size balanced the threat of territorial invasion against the difficulties of maintaining a vast, hyper-regionalized state. However, with the advent of telegraphic data transmission in 1837, messages were no longer constrained by the movement of living beings, either in the form of men or beasts. Telegraphy triggered a complete rethinking of geopolitics allowing states "control space," in order to benefit their economic and military positions.[47]

The telegraph greatly increased the capital's dominance of outlying portions of the nation-state (a similar process occurred in the system of empire more tightly binding the periphery to the metropole). Furthermore, the new system of communication allowed for strengthening of the concept of the nation in much larger states which had hitherto been retarded by geography and distance. According to Vincent Mosco, "[T]he telegraph established a pattern of development, generally reflected in subsequent technologies including the telephone, radio. And television, that actually increased the power and control of business and government, particularly the military."[48] With the telegraph, a state like Greece or Indonesia (consisting of both mainland and distant island components) could set about drawing together the nation and reducing regional differences that had historically been reinforced by geographic factors. Just as importantly, great land mass states like Australia, Russia, and the United States could now stitch together their far-flung cities, villages, and vast barren zones through new communications networks. No longer did France, Spain, and the United Kingdom possess the special recipe for creating strong national identity and state-wide nationalism—now the Australian in Perth, the Russian in Vladivostok, and the American in San Francisco was just as much a part of the national community as their compatriot in the capital. The use of the telegraph for promoting national identity was not confined to the Western world. In the 1880s, the deployment of a national telegraph network enabled statesmen like Li Hongzhang to promote a form of "telegraph nationalism" in imperial China.[49] Through electric communication linkages, Li hoped to prevent fractures in Chinese national identity and inoculate the nation against the threats posed by British, German, French, Russian, and Japanese imperialists, all whom were encroaching on the borders of the Middle Kingdom by the end of the nineteenth century.

The electrification of communication allowed states to bind together the nation in ways never before possible. Information became a commodity with equal value and relevance at the core and the periphery. National markets developed as prices became standardized across the country. As Paul Starr points out, those nations—like the United States—which invested heavily in a telegraph network laid the foundations for future productivity in other fields of mass media including telecommunication, motion pictures, and broadcasting.[50] News was no longer confined to the region, but became easily transmitted across mountains, rivers, and seas. Even modes of dress and speech were "nationalized" through the increasing interaction of communities once separated by distance and geography. The electrification of national information had a keen impact on regional and ethnic minorities which had hitherto been beyond the daily reach of the capital, literally out of sight and out of mind. With the laying of telegraphic lines to such localities, the state was able to exponentially expand its nationalization efforts vis-à-vis minorities. Furthermore, the bounded nature of telegraph networks—closely linked to the deployment of railway networks—hemmed in communication. Nearly instantaneous, electronic, intra-state flows of information were now privileged over slower, older, and less dependable transborder communication pathways. The telegraph thus served to extend and amplify national projects and further marginalize national minorities and marooned nationals beyond the borders of the purported nation-state.

In many ways, the linking of various national capitals via the telegraph internationalized nationalism as well. For the first time, nearly instantaneous communication on a global scale became possible and created a global community divided by parochial interests. The implications for nationalism and national identity were not trivial. The Crimean War (1853-1856) served as a watershed event for media technology and its relationship with nationalism. The dominant medium of the pre-electronic era—the newspaper—was instantly amplified by the telegraph, thus forever changing the nature of information distribution. Almost instantaneous reporting of events allowed national elites to craft their country's identity in a wholly different way. A cogent example is Piedmont-Sardinia's participation in the Crimean conflict. The reporting of the war in Russia allowed Italian irredentists to manipulate information in such a way as to encourage national pride. The Sardinian's modest contribution to the war effort on the side of the British, French, and Ottomans was turned into a cause célèbre from the Alto Adige to Mount Etna. Furthermore, the newly established telegraphic connections with other parts of the proto-Italian state assisted in the development of a semi-unified national identity.

While most European states saw the telegraph as a powerful tool for promoting nationalism and crafting national identity, the new invention did function as a double-edged blade for other countries. Speaking about the Polish uprising against Russia in January 1863, the American Confederacy's chief propagandist in Europe, Henry Hotze, noted:

> I can only say that the insurrection, however much of heroism and patriotic devotion it has subsequently embodied, appears to me to have been to a great extent artificially stimulated by a wonderfully dexterous management of the press and the telegraph and by a social machinery which no other nation than one of generations of illustrious exiles can command.[51]

Hotze clearly implicates the use of information and communication technology by a repressed national minority as the stimulus for the uprising. Within twenty years of Samuel F. B. Morse's demonstration of the viability of the electric telegraph to convey complex messages, a national minority had successfully adapted this new, transnational medium to support its counter-hegemonic aspirations. The telegraphically-inclined Poles, however, would represent a tiny minority moving forward as nationalizing states used successive advances in mass media to homogenize their respective national identities over the next century.

Broadcasting the Nation

As the twentieth century approached, mass media began to enter a period of rapid transformation. Reflecting and reinforcing the power of nation-states, emergent broadcast media such as motion pictures, radio, and television allowed for the projection of state-crafted narratives of national identity to ever larger audiences. Monroe Edwin Price compares the power of broadcast media to that of state churches, which were able to use their narrative force to shape economic systems, ideologies, and morality, all the while assuring loyalty to and identification with the state.[52] For more than seven decades, national governments would enjoy the benefits of these powerful new tools for reifying their respective imagined communities.

In the 1890s, the motion picture joined the telegraph as a tool for mass-mediating emergent national identities.[53] Film was not initially perceived as a particularly important innovation for the promotion of nationalism or national identity, due to the cosmopolitan nature of the content of early motion pictures. As a silent medium, different national audiences were able to interpret scenes, plots, and the actors' gestures using their own sets of beliefs and prejudices. However, realizing the powerful potential of the medium, national elites soon begin to employ the platform to deliver more contrived messages to their respective audiences. Regarding the advent of telegraphic media in the twentieth century, Price states, "Imagery affects loyalties: that has always been known."[54] The motion picture's incorporation of dialogue (initially with *The Jazz Singer* in 1927) made such a development more practical, while simultaneously circumscribing the distribution of most films to national markets.

During the interwar period, the nascent German filmmaking industry pioneered the art of promoting nationalism via celluloid. In particular, Leni Riefenstahl's larger-than-life *Triumph of the Will* (1935) still stands as the ultimate example of the nexus between national identity, ideology, and filmmaking. Adolf Hitler also commissioned Riefenstahl to film a four-hour epic on the Berlin Games entitled *Olympia* (1938) which served to further the German state's position on the supremacy of the nation through portrayal of the dominant Aryan-German race of athletic beautiful people. According to Ellen Cheshire, the lingering shots and ubiquitous presence of "Nazi insignia on flags, bells, and the athletes' shirts" and Riefenstahl's emphasis on the German victories combined "to create an emotional patriotic film which tips *Olympia* into the category of 'propaganda' rather than a straight 'documentary.'"[55] The Nazis later used overt and aggressive nationalism to promote their ideology in film. The concerted effort to demonize a national minority through film is laid bare in such race-baiting offerings as *The Eternal Jew* (1940), a film that characterized the Jewish as a global infestation akin to rats. Imagery, narration, and musical accompaniment in German film served to highlight a stark "us versus them" narrative in Nazi Germany, with the Jews, Gypsies, and other non-Aryan peoples on one side of the mental divide and "good" Germans on the other.[56]

While the Nazis attacked their ethnic others as part of their national identity project, the Soviet and the Americans lauded their own minorities. Soviet filmmakers, most notably Sergei Eisenstein, used film as an extremely powerful canvas to portray the challenge of creating a Soviet nation. Eisenstein's *Battleship Potemkin* (1925), *October: Ten Days That Shook the World* (1927), and *Aleksandr Nevsky* (1938) serve as immortal reminders of the vibrancy of this medium in the first half of the twentieth century. In his films—and Soviet propaganda more generally—ethnic difference was part of the nationalist narrative. The United States, lacking the Soviets' outright domination of media, used more subtle triggers to embolden the nation and promote nationalist sentiment. With about 100 million people viewing at least one motion picture a week by 1929, the opportunity to influence an exploding population of Americans—many of whom were first- or second-generation immigrants—proved almost irresistible. During the Second World War, feature-length films were preceded by carefully orchestrated propaganda pieces detailing the achievements of "our boys" or vilifying the enemy with footage captured abroad.

After these state-crafted messages were delivered via newsreels, audiences would lean back in their chairs to watch films that employed more subtle congeries of messages meant to activate nationalist feelings.

Hollywood served as Washington's mouthpiece during the war by writing, filming, and promoting nationalist fare at the box office. Frank Capra's *Why We Fight* series represents the paragon of the American motion picture industry's propaganda effort. As the Oscar-winning director of such films as *It Happened One Night* (1934), and *Mr. Deeds Goes to Town* (1936), and *You Can't Take it With You* (1938), Capra put his talents to work producing a series of pro-war documentaries including: *Prelude to War* (1943), *The Nazis Strike* (1943), *Divide and Conquer* (1943), *The Battle of Britain* (1943), *The Battle of Russia* (1943), *The Battle of China* (1944), and *War Comes to America* (1945) among other projects. A key element of these films was the United States' ethnic diversity (though often concurrent with a heaping dose of racial and ethnic stereotyping). In fact, Capra's films were often used as a didactic tool for promoting racial tolerance in American life, particularly the military. Like the Americans, the Germans also made effective use of the newsreel, known in Germany as *Deutschen Wochenschauen*. As war in Europe approached, the Nazi Party exerted ever increasing control of content over these short, but evocative tools for shaping public consciousness.[57]

Quick on the heels of the motion picture came another broadcast medium, though one which lacked the image-making capacity and semiotic influence of the motion picture: the wireless. As a transmission platform, the radio began its existence—much like the motion picture—relatively free of the shackles of national boundaries. The successive advances of the Serbian-American scientist Nikola Tesla, the Italian-Irish inventor Guglielmo Marconi, and other lesser credited individuals from Russia and India produced an international system of wireless communication by 1907. Initially, the wireless was an extension of the extant telegraph system. However, with Reginald Fessenden and Lee de Forrest's innovations in the first decade of the twentieth century, voice transmissions and music soon entered the airwaves.[58] The delivery of nationally-circumscribed content in the state language exerted a powerful centripetal force on radio listeners from its inception.[59]

The coming of the Great War resulted in the effective nationalization of radio frequency communications in the name of national security. In the interwar period, the arguments shifted to the discursive field of *regulation* as peacetime governments labored to control who had access to radio frequencies, an increasingly precious commodity. Literature professor Laurence A. Breiner sums up the double-edged nature of the medium stating, "The convergence of radio and nationalism evokes some stereotypical images: on the one hand the romance of pirated frequencies and insurgents seizing the transmitter, on the other hand the new central government's control of broadcasting to promote both nationalist ideology and standardized language."[60] However, as Breiner suggests, state control was the norm, not the exception, and the state's influence over the medium only grew as the storm clouds of war began to brew again in Europe.

Nazi Germany relied heavily on the developing technology of radio as their primary medium for promoting the National Socialist party's extreme nationalist agenda. In fact, Joseph Göbbels declared in 1933, "What the press was to the nineteenth century, the wireless will be to the twentieth." For the Nazis, policing of the receiver rather than the conduits proved to be the critical aspect of control. Göbbels introduced the mass production of a cheap radio set, the *Volksempfänger* or 'people's receiver,' so that nearly every German would have access to radio reception in their homes and places of work. By the outbreak of the war, 70% of all German homes sported a wireless receiver. Over time, simple possession of a radio proved insufficient for the National Socialist Party, compulsory listening was also introduced.[61]

The very existence of the *Volksempfänger*, a device which had been designed to prevent reception of foreign broadcasts and to deliver government propaganda, underscores the vital role of mass media in shaping the nation. Innis states, "The Second World War became to an important extent the result of a clash between the newspaper and the radio…the sudden explosion of communication [in the form of the radio] precipitated an outbreak of savagery paralleling that of printing and the religious wars of the seventeenth century, and again devastating the regions of Germany."[62] Germany was also willing to push the envelope with even more experimental media for mass communication. Berlin was the location of the first television broadcast in 1931 and, within a handful of years, the media platform became an integral part of the National Socialists' propaganda campaign. In 1936, the Germans pioneered the field of international broadcasting by transmitting the Olympic Games to a worldwide audience in an attempt to display the superiority of the German race.[63]

Under one-party systems, the management of media proved a manageable challenge for the state. Whether de jure (USSR, Nazi Germany, Francoist Spain) or de facto (Japan, Mexico), one-party domination of the political system usually guaranteed control of the primary and secondary forms of media, including newspapers, radio, and television. In totalitarian societies, art and music were even manipulated to deliver the party line. As media changed, the dominant paradigm remained remarkably familiar—each new media platform that emerged was quickly monopolized by the state or those acting in the interests of the state. Minority voices were silenced (or more likely, never given a broadcast platform to begin with). This trend was evident in both free and closed societies.[64] In the former, the market demanded that small groups be marginalized or assimilated into larger ones. In authoritarian societies, the minority represented a challenge to the established order. The outcome was the same in both societies. According to Oscar Wetherhold Riegel, "The importance of exploiting acceptance factors leads to coyness and timidity with respect to the ideas and opinions of minority groups which may disturb or unsettle the minds of mass listeners."[65] While authoritarian and totalitarian states held overt control over media platforms, democracies have been able to exert significant control over the content of mass media to serve the interests of the state. According to Price, "The first half-century of broadcasting—the period from 1915 to the mid-1960s—was the era, generally, of the nation in control of its radio and then television structures."[66] As television began to replace the motion picture and radio as the preferred media, the state once again was able to maintain some level of control over the content that was piped over the airwaves.

Historically speaking, broadcasting networks around the world are inherently "national" in their composition and content. Even "international broadcasters" like BBC (originally the British Broadcasting Company Ltd.) and CNN have decidedly national roots in the United Kingdom and the United States, respectively. However, the norm has been and remains a television market that is dominated by the broadcaster(s). In such environments, the government funds, and thus ultimately controls the content of television programming, including news and entertainment. In some cases, this control is overt, unvarnished, and even aggressive. In other environments, the state's influence is more subtle, but nonetheless effective in shaping national identity through the media.

Fredrick S. Siebert links mass media to the political environment in which they operate. Siebert's theoretical framework—or "four theories of the press"—appeared at the very apex of state influence over the media environment.[67] Satellite television had yet to emerge, the Cold War was at its global zenith, and a host of new nation-states were emerging on the world stage as a result of decolonization in Asia and Africa. During this period, television, radio, and print media were all heavily influenced by state actors; however, Siebert identified four discernable strategies for states to influence media content: authoritarian, libertarian, social responsibility, and Soviet Communist. While these concepts are dated simply by the anachronism of the latter model, Siebert's analysis is helpful in understanding the historical conditions of media in the mid-twentieth century and still provides value in understanding the current media environment.

The authoritarian system is rooted in Europe's monarchic past, specifically the period of Absolutism. In this system, the press is not allowed to print or broadcast content that might undermine the established authority or give offense to the accepted ideology of the state. In the words of Peter J. Humphreys, truth is the "property of power" in such systems.[68] Ex post facto punishment may be meted out for an infraction, or press seizures may occur before the news in question is published or broadcast (assuming the state possesses a surveillance capacity to affect such interdiction). Paragons of such a system during the era in question included Portugal under António de Oliveira Salazar and Spain under Generalissimo Francisco Franco y Bahamonde; however, France during the Algerian War also bore some resemblance to this model. As Martin Harrison states, freedom of information became "one of the earliest casualties of the Algerian war," with press seizures becoming a common tool of the Fourth Republic.[69] In such an environment, there are certain "red lines" that cannot be crossed. As it relates to national or ethnic minorities, both France and Spain used the prerogatives of the authoritarian media system to limit the expression of their national minorities, specifically the Basques and Catalans in Spain and the indigenous—that is Muslim—populations of Algeria (it should be remembered that Algeria was not a colonial possession, but an integral part of France during the Fourth Republic).

The second system is the libertarian model, which is market-centric. The main goals of media under such conditions are to "inform, to entertain, and sell copy,"[70] though not necessarily in that order. An outgrowth of the Enlightenment and the *laissez faire* policies of the United States and Great Britain, the libertarian system permits criticism of the government's policies. In fact, such attacks are fully accepted and even encouraged as long as they do not call for a violent overthrow of the system itself. Ostensibly, libertarian media regimes place no restrictions on import or export of media messages across the national frontiers and journalists and editors are meant to have full autonomy within the media organization. In reality, however, most successful broadcast networks tend towards favorable portrayals of the state in order to guarantee access to the government. As Price suggests, "Even in democratic societies…the necessity for generating and maintaining a narrative of community is a universal occupation. Governments are virtually compelled to generate or favour images that reinforce the relationship between their subjects and themselves."[71]

Lacking overt controls over media production, the libertarian state engages in subtler forms of manipulation of content related to national identity. Journalists' constant "indexing" of important political actors (presidents, MPs, high court judges, etc.) as primary sources for the vast majority of news content demands fealty to the state.[72] Furthermore, media corporations themselves tend to be run by economic elites who seek to market their product to the largest audience possible. Speaking of radio and motion pictures in the 1930s, Riegel stated, their "primary, and virtually only, business is entertainment, and entertainment of a popular character that will hold the loyalty of mass audiences. Both industries therefore show a desire to avoid controversial topics and deny any obligation to change, criticize, or oppose the symbols representing the least common denominator of popular acceptance."[73] Not surprisingly, content on television—like radio and the newspaper before it—is most cost effective when it targets the largest single audience, assures those in power it means them no harm, and ultimately flatters the nation.

It is helpful to employ the Gramscian paradigm of "cultural hegemony" to conceptualize the role of mass media and communications technologies within the web of values and network of institutions utilized by intellectuals to support the goals of the state. According to Italian political theorist Antonio Gramsci, the governmental-coercive apparatus cannot function solely through the use of force—consent must also be present.[74] Through the media, national elites and representatives of the state acquired consent through contrived messages which were transmitted on a regular basis via the dominant forms of media. Thus, at least during the 1960s, catering to minority ethnic or religious groups within a larger "national" market was not cost effective. Even without the overt intervention of the state (as discussed in the authoritarian media examples above), over-the-air broadcast television continued to serve the nation-building project of statist elites even in libertarian media environments.

Siebert's third model—the social responsibility theory—can be contrasted with both the authoritarian and libertarian system in that it offers the potential for a diverse media environment. In reaction to the horrors of World War II, certain Western European states implemented a media regime that valued political pluralism and was community-centric. The social responsibility theory is based on that assumption that market forces alone are not sufficient to ensure that press freedom will result in truthful reporting and deliberative democracy. Consequently, it is the job of the state to ensure that the media live up their obligations to society. In such environments, informativeness, objectivity, and balance are highly valued, and the media are encouraged to reflect the diversity of society, as well as provide access to various points of view. Minorities—whether they are political, economic, social, ethnic, or religious—are given access to the public sphere. Under such a system, ethnic minorities are endowed with some privileges denied to them in other societies; however, prior to the advent of effective narrowcasting options in the late twentieth century, market factors continued to dampen the willingness of media organizations to invest too deeply in "minority media." Television presented the most obvious case where the demands of the market overrode those of the "socially responsible" system. Due to the limited nature of frequency for distribution of television signals, regulators were compelled to balance the needs of the "nation" with those of far less numerous minorities. In nearly every instance, the former won out over the latter.

Only in cases where the overall national identity is tied to a minority language or preservation of a regional culture, do we see enthusiastic support of national elites for such programs.[75] Eire, or the Republic of Ireland, is a prominent example of this trend. According to Iarfhlaith Watson, "As mass media in general, and television in particular, are viewed as having the dual ability to both threaten and defend a 'culture,' the Irish government, soon after independence, attempted to use radio to defend the new 'Irish identity'" and would later use television programming to do likewise.[76] During the twentieth century (as is the case today), Irish speakers were generally confined to a peripheral area of the country and commanded little economic influence; yet despite this, the government funneled significant funds into promoting their identity, language, and mores. This was a singular situation based on the historical marginalization of the Irish language under British rule. Given the peculiarities of the Irish case, such an outcome was rather rare during the zenith of national broadcast media; however, such policies provide a harbinger of things to come in the current era of rising regionalism and political devolution.

The last model, Soviet Communism, is a party-centric media regime in which mass media serve the interests of the revolution or dominant ideology. In the 1960s, this system was confined to governments which espoused Marxism-Leninism; today, we might refer to this media system as totalitarian.[77] Under this system, media messages are crafted by the government as a form of propaganda. In extreme cases, mass media goes beyond information distribution and simple entertainment, they also have a "more complex and socially critical function: to organize and mobilize the population for defined tasks."[78] There is no private ownership of the media, and the state controls all production facilities and distribution channels. When diversity exists, it is one of two forms: manufactured diversity or sanctioned diversity. In the case of manufactured diversity, there are competing media outlets catering to particular groups (workers, students, etc.) that offer distinction, but not difference in their content. Sanctioned diversity occurs when the central government permits seemingly contradictory positions by different actors; however, the positions are carefully policed to ensure that they do not impugn to the regime. Reflecting the totalitarian nature of these societies, external media is strictly prohibited (either through jamming or threat of prosecution), thus creating an almost hermetically-sealed media environment.

Ironically, this media environment was most friendly to the interests of minorities during the second half of the twentieth century. Since media in such countries as the USSR, the People's Republic of China, and the Socialist Federal Republic of Yugoslavia operated under a command and control economic system, they were beyond the scope of market dynamics. This freed up resources for transmission of media products in small languages and to miniscule markets, assuming the interests of the Party were at stake. As part of the revolutionary platform of Marxism-Leninism, ethnic minorities were granted the "right" to media and education in their own languages in most of the Second World.[79] Sorbs (Lusatian Serbs) in the Democratic Republic of Germany, the Albanian Kosovars under Josip Broz Tito in Yugoslavia, and dozens of peoples—large and small—within the Soviet Union benefited from such policies. In fact, Moscow made the creation of national languages and the foundation of mass media a major part of its cultural policies in Soviet Central Asia, the Caucasus, Siberia, and the Russian Far East. From 1922 to 1991, the Soviet state spent untold amounts of money building ethnic minority media outlets and subsidizing content in languages such as Evenki, Karakalpak, and Lezgian. Despite the linguistic cornucopia of media options, the substantive content of such offerings was mind-numbingly similar (such programming was officially described and subversively decried as "national in form, socialist in content," reflecting that all ethnic groups received the Kremlin line, though in their own languages). Ethnic minorities—like their majority counterparts, the Russians—suffered under a media regime where Communist Party doublespeak and censorship negated any notions of media freedom.

Television emerged at a critical juncture for nation-building and the formation of national identity in the developing world. As a mass medium, television had generally been confined to Europe and North America during the 1930s and 1940s. However, by the late 1950s, television was making inroads into colonial outposts and newly independent states such as Southern Rhodesia, the United Arab Republic of Egypt and Syria, and India. Broadcasting became an integral part of both the national liberation struggle and the attempt to craft unified national identities after independence. The 1960s—the apex of national media—saw a flurry of new nations gaining their freedom from European imperial powers, and the introduction of the television In 1960, the following countries African countries declared their independence: Cameroon, Togo, Senegal, Mali, Madagascar, Zaire (Congo), Somalia, Benin, Niger, Upper Volta (Burkina Faso), Côte D'Ivoire (Ivory Coast), Chad, Central African Republic, Congo (Brazzaville), Gabon, Nigeria, and Mauritania. Within a decade, most would also launch television networks to help develop cohesive national identities that superseded linguistic, religious, ethnic, tribal, and clan-based affinities. According to Joseph D. Straubhaar, television represented a central plank in these new governments' attempts to build a common national market, promote loyalty among the citizenry, and develop a sense of military security based on new borders.[80] The image-making capacity of television allowed new state symbols (flags, seals, monuments, etc.) to craft a narrative of national unity, which in some cases was extremely tenuous as many of these "new nations" were simply the result of European imperial power grabs and cartographic expediency. In such environments, "Television becomes a crucial medium to unify geographically and ethnically dispersed peoples into a sense of nationhood."[81] As a didactic tool, television easily outstripped its mass media rivals in terms of national identity production.

Ironically, the increasing demand for televised content would ultimately undermine the value of the television as a national medium. In 1963, news of U.S. President John F. Kennedy's assassination was reported almost simultaneously around the world via the Telstar satellite. A year later, the Tokyo Olympics were relayed via satellite from Japan to the United States. By the end of the decade, an estimated 724 million people simultaneously heard astronaut Neil Armstrong's declaration "That's one small step for a man, one giant leap for mankind" upon his crew's successful moon-landing. Television, once a gift to insular regimes, increasingly began to resemble a Trojan horse of globalism, allowing the penetration of ideas from the outside world into the homes and minds of their citizenries. Fortunately for regimes intent on curtaining regional, sectarian, and/or minority media revolts against the national machine, the market dynamics of satellite television is not conducive to such projects. Furthermore, despite the introduction of new media like satellite TV and novel information technologies such as the fax machine during the 1970s, state boundaries retained a great deal of importance. The state still had a number of tools at hand, including outlawing certain technologies, prohibitive pricing, fear of surveillance, etc. However, as the new world order envisioned by Allied policymakers at the Bretton Woods conference in 1944 slowly became a reality, the globalization of media technologies accelerated, ultimately producing a world linked by an "ever-thickening network of communications systems, extending its reach in a capillary-like structure to every nook and cranny of the planet."[82] While the United States' culture industry was the most immediate beneficiary of this phenomenon, other countries benefited as well, including India, which saw its Bollywood fare exported beyond its borders, the UK with the spread of BBC news and entertainment across the Anglophone world, and the international popularity of Mexico's nascent telenovela industry.

The years between the Reformation and the Golden Age of Television were characterized by a state-domination of media platforms and significant elite control over content manufacture. Distribution could be limited to exclude those who challenged the interests of the state, while content could be massaged to foster increased loyalty to the state and shape identities. The media came to play a central role in the creation of nation-states and marginalization of those ethnic, cultural, linguistic, or religious groups whose lifeways did not correctly fit the mold of the national project. Cheap novels and plays made Frenchmen out Bretons, Occitans, Corsicans, and Basques. Newspapers crafted a British nation out of Scots, Manx, Cornish, Welshmen, and Englishmen. Radio and television made Italians out of Sardinians, Lombards, Tyroleans, Sicilians, and Greeks. While there were certainly numerous cases of the media being put to use by minorities, counter-culture groups, and seditious elements, the dominant paradigm during the modern era was undoubtedly one of state control. However, this monopolistic system began suffer its first clefts in last quarter of twentieth century as technological aspects of Marshall McLuhan's "global village" began to emerge.[83]

Notes

1. James Curran, "Communications, Power and Social Order," in Michael Gurevitch, Tony Bennett, James Curran and Janet Woollacott, *Culture, Society and the Media* (London and New York: Routledge, 1990), 223.
2. The dominance of Caesaropapism in the Byzantine Empire and other parts of Eastern Europe did little to promote a significantly different milieu, despite the existence of comparatively more openness to foreign ideas and influences.
3. While many scholars of nations and nationalism tend to view nations as primordial, I believe much of their analysis to be retro-fitted to support their own arguments. Greeks, Jews, and Armenians figure prominently in such analyses, but their "national" identities were patently religious in the pre-modern past. I believe the nation be to a direct outcome of the age of industrialization, dependent on the advent of communications and commercial networks which bound geographically-disparate communities together.

4. While Hebrew, Greek, and even Arabic were known to some, few outside the Church possessed fluency in these tongues.

5. In regards to the latter, a speaker's dialect would after a few days of travel become almost unintelligible to those he encountered.

6. The elite (barons, nobles, kings, *et al.*) might also be considered a separate community with which the mass maintained direct, albeit limited and infrequent, contact.

7. In fact, Chae Yun-eui invented the first iron printing press in Korea around 1234, over 200 years ahead of Gutenberg; however, the Korean variant failed to achieved significant social change within East Asia unlike Gutenberg's printing press.

8. Karl Deutsch, *Nationalism and Social Communication: An Inquiry into the Foundations of Nationality* (Cambridge: The Technology Press of the Massachusetts Institute of Technology, 1953), 23.

9. According to Deutsch, an *ecumene* is that part of country or region which is well peopled and sits on a convergence of transportation (and thus, communication) links: "Typical examples of key areas are harbors or river mouths which may dominate much larger river valleys in matters of trade and transportation. Control of such areas by members of one nationality gives them power over the lives of other peoples in the hinterland"; see Deutsch, *Nationalism and Social Communication*, 23.

10. A few examples of village-sized nations continue to persist even in the modern era, especially in the Caucasus; see, for instance, Yo'av Karny, *Highlanders: A Journey to Caucasus in Quest of Memory* (New York: Farrar Straus Giroux, 2000).

11. Marshall McLuhan, *The Gutenberg Galaxy: The Making of Typographic Man* (Toronto: University of Toronto Press, 1962), 130.

12. Indulgences offered atonement in the afterlife for sins which might otherwise bring about eternal punishment. While intercession of a Christian martyr on behalf of another has its origins in early Christianity, the practice of forgiving sins for good works or remuneration given to the Church began to be abused in the late Medieval Period as "professional pardoners" (*quaestores*) capitalized on the increasingly profitable market for personal salvation.

13. Ronald J. Deibert, *Parchment, Printing and Hypermedia: Communication in World Order Transformation* (New York: Columbia University Press, 1997), 67.

14. Deibert, *Parchment, Printing and Hypermedia*, 71.

15. Harold A. Innis, *Empire and Communications* (Toronto: University of Toronto Press, 1972), 170.

16. For more on the "cartographic revolution," see P. D. A. Harvey, *Maps in Tudor England* (Chicago: University Of Chicago Press, 1994).

17. Anthony Smith, *National Identity* (Reno: University of Nevada Press, 1991), 173.

18. David W. Anthony, *The Horse, the Wheel, and Language: How Bronze-Age Riders from the Eurasian Steppes Shaped the Modern World* (Princeton. Princeton University Press, 2007), 9.

19. Ferdinand Tönnies, *Community and Society* (Mineola, NY: Dover Publications Inc., 2002); originally published in German, 1887.

20. Marshall McLuhan, "Effects of the Improvements of Communication Media," *Journal of Economic History* 20, no. 4. (December 1960): 566-575.

21. See Deibert, *Parchment, Printing and Hypermedia*, McLuhan, *The Gutenberg Galaxy*, and Innis, *Empire and Communications*.

22. Panikos Panayi, *An Ethnic History of Europe since 1945: Nations, States and Minorities* (Harlow: Longman, 2001), 7.

23. Ernst Gellner, *Nations and Nationalism* (Ithaca, NY: Cornell University Press, 1983), 11.

24. Edward Said, *Orientalism* (New York: Vintage Books, 1979), 331-2.

25. Lynn Hunt, *Politics, Culture and Class in the French Revolution* (Berkeley: University of California Press, 1984), 56.

26. Paul Starr, *The Creation of the Media: The Political Origins of Modern Communications* (New York: Basic Books, 2004), 69.

27. See Hunt, *Politics, Culture and Class.*

28. Starr, *The Creation of the Media*, 68.

29. Napoleon Bonaparte's conquest of continental Europe spread the ideals, diction, and methodologies of nationalism, while simultaneously triggering virulent reaction against French hegemony.

30. The two tongues are quite closely related, both being Latinate languages within the Gallo-Romance sub-family. In their nomenclature, the respective glosses for 'yes' are highlighted as a shibboleth, with northerners using *oïl* (pronounced [wil] or [wi]) and southerners using *oc* for 'yes.'

31. Eugen Weber, *Peasants into Frenchmen: The Modernization of Rural France, 1870-1914* (Stanford: Stanford University Press, 1976), 67.

32. Italian identity has been, and continues to be, fractured; however, the advent of ubiquitous mass media in the form of national television networks has somewhat decreased regional linguistic and cultural divisions between the north and south since 1945. There is a strong separatist movement among the self-styled Padanians (affiliated with the secessionist Northern League) who have even embarked on an Internet campaign to support their aims; see Rohan Jayasekera,"Waiting for the Kingdom: Nations in Cyberspace are No Substitute for the Real Thing," *Index on Censorship* 29, no. 3 (May/June 2000): 140-145.

33. Rogers Brubaker, *Nationalism Reframed: Nationhood and the National Question in the New Europe* (Cambridge: Cambridge University Press, 1996), 5-6.

34. John Torpey, *The Invention of the Passport: Surveillance, Citizenship and the State* (Cambridge: Cambridge University Press, 2000), 126.

35. See Gellner, *Nations and Nationalism*, 1. It is worth noting that two of the principle thinkers in the field of 20th century nationalism—Ernest Gellner and Karl Deutsch—were native German-speakers, born and educated in Habsburg Prague, and naturalized as Czechoslovak citizens upon the country's independence from Austria-Hungary. Both later emigrated to the United states during World War II.

36. Benedict Anderson, *Imagined Communities: Reflections on the Origin and Spread of Nationalism* (London: Verso, 1991). In fact, historian Mark Poster critiques Anderson's very usage of the term "imagined" to describe national communities. Recognizing the central role of media, he argues that we should instead refer to nations as "mediated communities"; see. Mark Poster, "National Identities and Communications Technologies," *Information Society* 15, no. 4 (October-December 1999): 235-240.

37. Alexander J. Motyl, "The Modernity of Nationalism: Nations, State and Nation-States in the Contemporary World," *Journal of International Affairs* 45, no. 2 (Winter 1992): 311-323.

38. See Michael Billig, *Banal Nationalism* (London: Sage Publications, 1995) and John Breuilly, *Nationalism and the State*, 2nd ed. (Chicago: University of Chicago Press, 1994).

39. Johan Galtung, "Cultural Violence," *Journal of Peace Research* 27, no. 3 (August 1990): 291-305.

40. Galtung, "Cultural Violence," 294.

41. Anderson, *Imagined Communities.*

42. Innis, *Empire and Communications*, 167.

43. Gellner, *Nations and Nationalism*, 56.

44. Gellner, *Nations and Nationalism*, 49.

45. One should point out that the situation in the Americas, Australia, and certain other "settler colonies" is somewhat different since *jus soli* ('right of territory') of rather than *jus sanguinis* ('right of blood') tends to be the determining factor in national identity. The United States for example, does not officially exclusively rely on either, and instead declares that civic ideals trump both. The letter that naturalized citizens receive when granted citizenship

reads: "Our country has never been united by blood or birth or soil. We are bound by the principles that move us beyond our backgrounds, lift us above our interests, and teach us what it means to be citizens. Every citizen must uphold these principles."

46. Richard Langhorne, *The Coming of Globalization: Its Evolution and Contemporary Consequences* (Houndmills: Palgrave, 2001).

47. Peter J. Hugill, *Global Communications since 1844: Geopolitics and Technology* (Baltimore: Johns Hopkins Press, 1999), 36.

48. Vincent Mosco, "Communication and Information Technology for War and Peace," in Colleen Roach, *Communication and Culture in War and Peace* (Newbury Park: Sage, 1993), 42.

49. Erik Baark, *Lightning Wires: The Telegraph and China's Technological Modernization, 1860-1890* (Westport, CT: Greenwood, 1997), 174.

50. Starr, *The Creation of the Media*, 15.

51. Cited in John F. Kutolowski, "Mid-Victorian Public Opinion, Polish Propaganda, and the Uprising of 1863," *Journal of British Studies* 8, no. 2 (May 1969): 86-110.

52. Monroe Edwin Price, *Television, the Public Sphere, and National Identity* (Oxford: Oxford University Press, 1995), 16.

53. In the interim, Alexander Graham Bell introduced the telephone. However, as a medium that was primarily designed for one-to-one communication, we need not explore the role of the telephone in these pages.

54. Price, *Television, the Public Sphere, and National Identity*, 3.

55. Ellen Cheshire, "Leni Riefenstahl: Documentary Film-Maker or Propagandist?" 2000, http://www.kamera.co.uk/features/leniriefenstahl.html (2 November 2003).

56. R. C. Raack, "Nazi Film Propaganda and the Horrors of War," *Historical Journal of Film, Radio and Television* 6, no. 2 (January 1986): 189-195.

57. Roel Vande Winkel, "Nazi Newsreels in Europe, 1939–1945: The Many Faces of UFA's Foreign Weekly Newsreel (*Auslandstonwoche*) Versus German's Weekly Newsreel (*Deutsche Wochenschau*)," *Historical Journal of Film, Radio and Television* 24, no. 1 (Fall 2004): 5-34.

58. Music, as a nation-independent entertainment form, encouraged radio consumption across borders, a fact that worried many governments bent on policing the national identity of their peoples.

59. Irving Fang, *A History of Mass Communication: Six Information Revolutions* (Boston: Focal Press, 1997), 89.

60. Laurence A. Breiner, "Caribbean Voices on the Air: Radio, Poetry, and Nationalism in the Anglophone Caribbean," in *Communities of the Air: Radio Century, Radio Culture*, edited by Susan Merrill Squier (Durham, NC: Duke University Press, 2003), 95-96.

61. Z. A. B. Zeman, *Nazi Propaganda,* Second ed. (Oxford: Oxford University Press, 1973), 49.

62. Innis, *Empire and Communications*, 167.

63. An event highlighted in Carl Sagan's *Contact* (1985) which portrays an extraterrestrial intelligence's act of re-transmitting the broadcast back to earth as a sign of their existence along with the willingness and capacity to communicate.

64. An important exception is Canada, where multiculturalism became enshrined through the dominant media system; see Lorna Roth, *Something in the Air: The Story of First Peoples Television Broadcasting Canada* (Montreal: McGill-Queen's University Press, 2005).

65. Oscar W. Riegel, "Nationalism in Press, Radio and Cinema," *American Sociological Review* 3, no. 4. (August 1938): 510-515.

66. Price, *Television, the Public Sphere, and National Identity*, 5.

67. Fredrick S. Siebert, Theodore Peterson, and Wilbur Schramm, *Four Theories of the Press: The Authoritarian, Libertarian, Social Responsibility, and Soviet Communist Concepts of What the Press Should Be and Do* (Chicago: University of Illinois Press, 1963).

68. Peter J. Humphreys, *Mass Media and Media Policy in Western Europe* (Manchester: Manchester University Press, 1996), 8.

69. Martin Harrison, "Government and Press in France during the Algerian War," *American Political Science Review* 58, no. 2 (June 1964): 273-285.

70. Humphreys, *Mass Media and Media Policy*, 9.

71. Price, *Television, the Public Sphere, and National Identity*, 234.

72. See Lance Bennett, *News: The Politics of Illusion*, Seventh ed. (New York: Longman, 2007).

73. Riegel, "Nationalism in Press, Radio and Cinema," 513.

74. Antonio Gramsci, *Selections from the Prison Notebooks* (New York: International Publishers, 1999).

75. In the Western Hemisphere, Canada provides a representative example, with its large and influential French-speaking minority, which enjoys linguistic and cultural representation even the boundaries of Quebec.

76. Iarfhlaith Watson, "The Irish Language and Television: National Identity, Preservation, Restoration and Minority Rights," *British Journal of Sociology* 47, no. 2 (June 1996): 255-274.

77. The Nazi media system could not be adequately described using this model as the German government did allow private ownership of the press during the late 1930s and early 1940s.

78. Ellen Mickiewicz, *Media and the Russian Public* (New York: Praeger, 1981), 51.

79. A few key exceptions include the Hungarians in Romania during the reign of Nicolae Ceauşescu, Roma (Gypsies) under certain East European regimes, and Bulgarian Turks in the latter years of communist rule.

80. Joseph D. Straubhaar, *World Television: From Global to Local* (Los Angeles. Sage Publications Inc., 2007), 69-70.

81. Straubhaar, *World Television*, 61.

82. Poster, "National Identities and Communications Technologies," 235.

83. See McLuhan, "Effects of the Improvements of Communication Media."

Chapter 2
Media Unbound: The Internet, Cyberspace, and Nationalism on the Web

With the introduction of the printing press, Europe experienced four centuries of history in which mass media served to promote loyalty to the state and reified the notion of monolithic nations based on unique and unadulterated cultures. From the late eighteenth century onwards, newspapers came to be read by ever increasing numbers of citizens, creating national information spaces based on the mass-mediated, daily ceremony of news consumption.[1] In the mid-1800s, the telegraph expanded the scale and the scope of these information satrapies by allowing large states like Canada, Russia, the United States, and Australia to knit together far flung peripheries to the core. It also allowed smaller states to solidify their control of information and more effectively police the construction of national identity. This process accelerated during the era of "national mass media," which lasted from the late 1800s until the mid-1960s. In the first few decades of this period, new broadcast media such as motion pictures and radio added imagery and sound to the national projects.

In the twentieth century, as a host of new nations emerged on the world stage as a result of the waves of decolonization that followed the two World Wars, the tight linkage between information and communications technologies and nationalism spread beyond confines of Europe and its settler state offspring (Canada, the United States, Australia, and the Latin American creole republics). The end result was the global ascendancy of identity based on collective membership in the nation-state. In most cases, this phenomenon trumped pre-existing loyalties forged in religion, class, gender, or other characteristics. Just as new nation-states developed their own militaries, economies, bureaucracies, and education systems, they developed their own media spaces. This trend reached its apex in the aftermath of World War II. However, with the advent of satellite television, quickly followed by the rise of the Internet and emergence of cyberspace, mass media entered a new phase of development. From the 1970s onward, media steadily experienced a deterritorialization of content, an expansion of authorship, and a revolution in the scale and scope of its distribution. Today, it has been argued, the Internet assumes the role of print media in the previous century.[2] In this chapter, I explore the evolution of cyberspace and its impact on the creation and maintenance of virtual communities, particularly those groups linked through common ethnicity.

The Internet: A New Medium for a New Millennium

The Internet, like many major post-World War II technological innovations, is a direct outgrowth of the public-private partnership between the U.S. military, large American corporations, and the country's premier universities, often referred to as "Big Science." Owing to such origins, the Internet—even from its earliest days—has been politicized. What we today refer to as the Internet is based on a conceptual framework put forth in Vannevar Bush's 1945 paper "As We May Think." Bush, who managed the U.S. atomics program in the early years of WWII, prophesied a "memex" machine that would allow information to be stored and then retrieved via associated links. He identified the need for a proto-Internet as such:

> The difficulty seems to be, not so much that we publish unduly in view of the extent and variety of present-day interests, but rather that publication has been extended far beyond our present ability to make real use of the record. The summation of human experience is being expanded at a prodigious rate, and the means we use for threading through the consequent maze to the momentarily important item is the same as was used in the days of square-rigged ships.[3]

Bush then eerily describes a typical instance in which a user of this as-yet-unrealized memex would search its records for information related to twelfth century warfare—specifically comparing the English longbow to its short, more effective Turkish counterpart. The user's "search" then "branches off on a side trail which takes him through textbooks on elasticity and tables of physical constants. He inserts a page of longhand analysis of his own. Thus he builds a trail of his interest through the maze of materials available to him. And his trails do not fade."[4] In that moment, Bush conceived of a new information space in which the consumer was simultaneously a producer of knowledge. Even though broadcast media would remain the dominant paradigm for another half century, Bush foresaw a world where media transmission would no longer be a one-way street.

While Vannevar Bush personified the intellectual wellspring of the Internet, J.C.R. Licklider actually began the process of building the Net more than a decade later. His paper "Man Computer Symbiosis," written in the late 1950s, discussed the "mechanically extended man" who would emerge through the symbiosis of computer-generated and maintained data on the one hand, and human thoughts, actions, and desires on the other. In subsequent papers, Licklider fleshed out his idea of "galactic network of thinking centers" that would nebulously correlate and coordinate human knowledge across time and space.[5] His bold predictions of a deterritorialized information superhighway have only been realized quite recently, despite more than forty years of steady advance. However, the root structure of the future Internet was completed by the end of the decade. Since that time, the original network of distributed computing has simply grown in terms of users, applications, and usability.

Licklider's tenure as the first head of computer research at the U.S. Defense Advanced Research Projects Agency (DARPA), the agency that would build the first intranet through its Information Processing Techniques Office (IPTO), proved instrumental in the development of the proto-Internet. A direct outgrowth of both the space race and the Cold War, the Kennedy administration had created the IPTO in 1963 with the expressed intent to introduce systems that would improve command and control of the United States' defensive capabilities. The new agency's charge included developing improved techniques of analysis, new man-computer languages, and better computer hardware. Under his leadership, Licklider focused on advanced human-machine interaction with the goal of large scale intellectual resource sharing via a network of geographically-dispersed, but digitally-connected databases.[6] Licklider's work, while visionary, failed to solve the problem of data transmission. That issue was tackled by Massachusetts Institute of Technology (MIT) researcher Leonard Kleinrock, who was instrumental in developing the packet-switching theory.

Packet switching revolutionized data transmission by parsing the transmission up into small units and then reassembling these back into their original form prior to reception. The name itself comes from the parallel work being done by Donald Davies in the UK. Davies had been particularly sensitive to the international implications of his nomenclature; in fact, he only settled on the term after having linguists confirm the existence of cognates in other tongues.[7] Working with the ideas of both these Internet pioneers, Lawrence G. Roberts, an MIT researcher, realized that packet-based switching over long distances was feasible. He soon set about experimenting with the sending of packets of data across the current telephone network. In 1965, Roberts successfully tested the first wide area network (WAN) computer system, which linked a computer at MIT's Lincoln Labs, known as the TX-2, to System Development Corporation's Q-32 computer in California.

Overnight, Roberts became the premier force in networked computing. In 1966, Roberts assumed Licklider's position at DARPA (then known simply as ARPA) and began the development of ARPANET: the nucleus of the modern Internet. The core of Licklider's galactic network boasted a modest four computers in its early days. Robert's found it difficult to persuade researchers to share their "personal" computers with others despite the promise of collective benefits through resource sharing and networked computing. Not known for his charisma, Roberts did prove to be an effective manager, and pursued the networked strategy as a pragmatic solution to the growing demand for access to the rare and expensive computers of the day. Although Roberts was not necessarily concerned with building a decentralized information system as a bulwark against complete data loss in the event of a nuclear exchange, he was influenced by RAND researcher Paul Baran's papers on the necessity of a decentralized computer network. Baran's 1964 memorandum, "On Distributed Communications," in particular, focused on the use of "redundancy as one means of building communications systems to withstand heavy enemy attacks" and laid of the requirements for the survivability of an all digital, distributed data network in the event of a nuclear exchange between the Cold War superpowers.[8] In 1968, Baran was brought in as a consultant on the project adding more grist to the Cold War mythology of the early Internet. His ideas were not, however, deluded by paranoia. Baran's notion of decentralized neural nets, digitization to ensure against degradation, and "bursty" streams of data all eventually became integral to the Internet's global success.

In the autumn of 1969, ARPANET began as linked nodes connecting computers at UCLA, Stanford Research Institute, University of California at Santa Barbara, and the University of Utah. A year later, the consulting firm of Bolt Beranek and Newman (BBN), which had been commissioned to develop the Information Message Processors (IMPs) at the universities, installed a fifth node at their headquarters in Cambridge, Massachusetts making ARPANET a transcontinental network. Over the next 24 months, the network quadrupled in size. While BBN worked on the hardware, a small coterie of computer engineers under Kleinrock's direction developed systems for allowing the computers to interface with one another. Vinton Cerf, the so-called "father of the Internet," was a leading figure in this new Network Working Group (NWG). Concurrently, ARPA funded an alternative project in the Pacific: ALOHAnet, a now defunct University of Hawaii-based network sharing system. Using radio-like transmissions of data, ALOHAnet moved information very slowly, but laid the groundwork for future Ethernet technologies. Like many incipient information and communication technologies, ALOHAnet was designed to overcome inherent geographically barriers to communication; in this case, it was the challenges posed by communicating across an archipelago. ALOHAnet thus became the world's first wireless packet-switched network and provided the ultimate viability of satellite-based computer communication, which would ultimately link even the most remote areas of the global to the information superhighway.[9] A host of similar networks would soon follow. However, it is interesting to note that the last American state admitted to the union—and one with a decidedly different ethno-historical legacy than its mainland counterparts—emerged as a world leader in distributed communications.

Lawrence Roberts' tenure at the IPTO saw ARPANET evolve from an idea into a genuine information sharing platform. In 1971, file transfer protocols (FTP) were established to allow the sending and receiving of electronic documents over the network. A year later, Ray Tomlinson, a consultant at BBN, developed the earliest form of electronic mail (e-mail) as an ad hoc system for improving communications between the users of the network. Almost immediately, Roberts recognized the viability of the new communication medium and developed an email management program to coordinate transmission and reception of messages sent over the network. The seductively simply interface gave users the ability read, file, forward, and respond to messages, thus making it one of the fastest growing applications of the late twentieth century. In October, Bob Kahn, the future director of IPTO, introduced ARPANET to the public at the International Conference on Computer Communications; at the time, ARPANET boasted connections to some forty computers. The following year saw the internationalization of ARPANET with connections to the University College of London (England) and the Royal Radar Establishment (Norway). With this expansion of the network, the development of a global, deterritorialized communications network was underway. Yet, the early Net remained the domain of the U.S. military-industrial complex and was thoroughly ensconced in the Anglophone world. This monopoly would be short-lived, but the early dominance of such interests would linger on for a generation.

As ARPANET expanded, Vinton Cerf, now head of what was deemed the Inter-Networking Group (INWG), continued to advance ARPANET's connection and transmission protocols. While his own network was growing rapidly, Cerf also recognized a new phenomenon: the proliferation of alternative networks existing independently of ARPA funding. Shortly after the public demonstration of ARPANET, he and Bob Kahn began developing protocols for inter-network communication. In 1974, the two delivered their paper "A Protocol for Packet Network Intercommunication." They called their man-computer language "transmission-control protocol" (TCP) and designed it to "accommodate variation in individual network packet sizes, transmission failures, sequencing, flow control, and the creation and destruction of process-to-process associations."[10] The name was later changed to TCP/IP, integrating Internet Protocol into the name itself. This breakthrough provided the building blocks of the modern Internet. Despite ARPANET's cloistered status, Cerf and Kahn were looking ahead to an open information environment when they declared their goal to "allow conversion between packet switching strategies at the interface, to permit interconnection of existing and planned networks."[11] As the decade progressed, the world witnessed the spread of a new wide area networks using satellite, radio, and other technologies. With the tools provided by Cerf and Kahn, these informational satrapies now could be linked together in an expansive digital empire through the lingua franca of TCP/IP.

The most important of these new networks was Usenet, described by its inventors as a "poor man's ARPANET." Established by two Duke University graduate students in 1979, Usenet's popularity stemmed from its openness. Usenet benefited from ARPANET's limited scope of subject matter, as well as continuing challenges to piercing the "iron curtain" of security clearances necessary to become a user of ARPANET. Until the advent of Usenet and other competitive networks, only government employees and members of those academic departments with U.S. Department of Defense funding could access to proto-Internet. Stephen Daniel, one of the first Usenet programmers, stated:

> I don't remember when the phrase [poor man's ARPANET] was coined, but to me it expressed exactly what was going on. We (or at least I) had little idea of what was really going on on the ARPANET, but we knew we were excluded. Even if we had been allowed to join, there was no way of coming up with the money. It was commonly accepted at the time that to join the ARPANET took political connections and $100,000. I don't know if that assumption was true, but we were so far from having either connections or $$ that we didn't even try. The poor man's ARPANET was our way of joining the Computer Science community and we made a deliberate attempt to extend it to other not-well-endowed members of the community.[12]

Usenet also employed a novel software that allowed for distribution of news (Newsnet), as well as emails and file sharing. Usenet became a place where individuals could communicate about anything and everything from illicit drugs and government conspiracies to perennial gardens and family recipes. By creating a hierarchical environment based on particular topics, e.g., science, social issues, computers, recreation, etc., Usenet shaped the emergent geography of information and precipitated the diversification of "computer-supported social networks" or

CSSNs. These groups formed the first virtual communities based on real or imagined linkages between "kindred souls" for the purpose of "companionship, information, and social support."[13]

In effect, members of the evolving Internet society (*Gesellschaft*)—who had been artificially thrown together through their adventures in cyberspace and whose ties were relatively self-interested, transitory, and impersonal—were now looking to create intimate, organic, and cohesive online communities (*Gemeinschaften*).[14] The Usenet ethos was forged in an environment where users (consumers) of information were also required to be providers (producers) of content. According to essayist Douglass Rushkoff, "The Internet's unexpected social side effect turned out to be it incontrovertible main feature. Its other functions falls by the way side. The Internet's ability to network human beings is its very lifeblood. It fosters communication, collaboration, sharing, helpfulness, and community."[15] In these early days, the network's code of conduct developed rapidly. For example, "lurking," or reading without posting, was defined as anti-social behavior.

Internet historian Michael Hauben coined the term "netizen" to describe those responsible users of networked bulletin boards he first encountered in 1985. "netizens...contribute towards the nurturing of the Net and towards the development of a great shared social wealth."[16] Reflective of its origins "outside" of the secret garden of ARPANET, Usenet tended to cultivate a fairly counter-culture, anti-authoritarian esprit among its users. As discussed in the previous chapter, central control of content is the mainstay of most forms of mass media; however, unlike television and other forms of broadcast media, the content posted on Usenet was controlled by its audience rather an elite group of information producers. "The very nature of Usenet promotes change. Usenet was born outside of established 'networks' and transcends any one physical network. It exists of itself and through other networks. It makes possible the distribution of information that might otherwise not be heard through 'official channels.' This role makes Usenet a herald for social change."[17] Given the large number of foreign-born technology workers in Silicon Valley and other high technology hubs, it not surprising that disgruntled émigrés soon began to gravitate to the Usenet to discuss and debate their home countries' policies. Over time, other ethnic communities begin to identify themselves in the Newsnet with the hope of establishing diasporic links in the new digital geography of the network of networks.

As the network of networks expanded, consumption and production of information became inextricably linked in this new universe of bits and bytes. Access to Usenet, unlike ARPANET, was egalitarian and soon technology enthusiasts flocked to the new network—a phenomenon that was aided by the growing use of the personal computer during the early 1980s.[18] In an idiosyncratic parallel to the invention of the printing press roughly half a millennium earlier, the personal computer and printer gave the individual the ability to produce a nearly limitless amount of documents.[19] Steve Jobs and Steve Wozniak pioneered the affordable personal computing device with the introduction their Apple II in the late 1970s. Shortly after the turn of the decade, computer giant IBM introduced their own version of the "home computer," the IBM PC. Connecting that PC to the burgeoning Internet allowed transmission of information in ways that Johannes Gutenberg could have never imagined, and ushered in a new era of self-publishing that is still in its early stages.

In 1981, Usenet and ARPANET were linked significantly widening the access of grassroots groups to portions of cyberspace which had hitherto been restricted to a relatively small number of DARPA-vetted researchers. A year later, the U.S. military cordoned off access to certain sensitive sites and placed them with the domain of MILNET, a decision that allowed for ARPANET to be further opened to unvetted users.[20] In 1983, ARPANET shifted from its older protocols to TCP allowing true interactivity with other, non-governmental intranets. Over the next decade, ARPANET would become obsolete as the U.S. government opted instead for proprietary networks and other users moved on to what was to becoming the Internet.[21] The structure of this Internet lent itself to the creation of both narrow and broad epistemic communities from its early days. One-to-one and one-to-many communication pathways were established through the first emails and electronic mailing lists (Listservs).

Initially, all content pages in this new digital space were identified by their Internet Protocol (IP) addresses, a series of four binary octets punctuated by periods that uniquely identified a particular location where data is stored.[22] By 1984, however, domain names were introduced which allowed for alpha characters to be employed. Internet sites thereafter were located through a universal resource locator (URL), i.e., a unique alpha-numeric address rather than an IP address. Rather than having to remember or catalogue the 32-digit addresses of sites, users could now use words and names in conjunction with a top level domain name (.com, edu, .gov, etc.). This innovation ultimately allowed for states to make their presence felt in the hitherto un-annexed space of data flows generated by the Internet. The "nationalization" of Internet space came with the introduction of geographic determinates for many sites located outside the United States. Foreign sites soon came to include domain names with their country of origin embedded at the terminus of the URL, e.g., .uk (United Kingdom), .fr (France), and .jp (Japan). As Robert Kitchin points out, the spread of Internet use created a new social space that existed beyond the formal constraints of geographic space, however, this new world was also rooted in "real-world spatial fixity."[23] This paradox increasingly shaped the development of the Internet from the mid-1980s onward.

Cyberspace: Exploring and Expanding the Digital Frontier

Just as states were making their presence felt in this new geography of Internet space, William Gibson coined the term "cyberspace" in his dystopian tale of hackers and transnational crime syndicates: *Neuromancer*. In the cyberpunk novel, Gibson spoke of cyberspace's "unthinkable complexity, lines of light ranged in the nonspace of the mind, clusters and constellations of data."[24] Today, the term has become a catchall for the digitized space created and maintained by connections and communications which run over the Internet. Cyberspace is not simply a medium like television or radio; instead, it is a new form of all-enveloping media (that is, multiple mediums of transmission) in which one can escape what is going on in the world rather than embrace it. As postmodern scholar Tony Myers points out, Gibson also uses the concept of the *matrix* to discuss this space, "a word that finds its etymology in 'womb'—the paradigmatic topos of container and contained."[25]

Despite his prescient ruminations, the cyberspace of the mid-1980s had far from realized its full potential. Yet, Gibson recognized—earlier than most—the powerful effects that adventures in virtual space had on identity, politics, and human affairs in the "real world." According to literary critic Benjamin Fair, "William Gibson's *Neuromancer* allows new forms of identity. Within that cyberspace, the self can be called into question, decentered, split apart, and rendered unknowable."[26] In this respect, when returning to the non-cyberworld, one brings some of that experience with him or her. But it is important remember that, as Internet law expert Julie Cohen contends, "Cyberspace is not, and never could be, the kingdom of mind; minds are attached to bodies, and bodies exist in the space of the world."[27] As such, it is prudent to view cyberspace through the lens of French sociologist Henri Lefebvre's conceptual triad of spatiality: the conceived, the perceived, and the lived spaces.[28] It is a utopia where imagination rules, it is an isotopia constructed to mirror existing places, and it is a mixed zone where these two spaces interconnect and "reality" is the result of interplay between the utopia and isotopia.[29]

In terms of its etymology, it is coincidental that Gibson chose to adopt the affix "*cyber-*" rather than "*hyper-*" for his construct. While both words are of Greek origin, there meanings are decidedly different. Hyperspace—the term preferred by some scholars and used in some continental European languages—suggests something *beyond* or *above* given its Classical Greek gloss 'over.' However, "cyber-" is derived from the Greek *kubernetes* ('governor' or 'steersman'), and is thus linked to the Latin *gubernator*.[30] By linking the use of cyber in English to the Internet, Gibson guaranteed—even if only at the subliminal level—that power, governance, and politics would be intrinsically linked to very concept of the Net.

Coincidentally, the year 1984 also witnessed the Soviet Union's first connection to the Internet. While the spread of the Internet would remain tightly constrained under the Soviet regime, the insidious spread of cyberspace into the Second World did portend important structural changes in the flows of data in the global marketplace of ideas. The proliferation of information and communications technologies across the communist bloc has been cited as a significant component of the weakening of the one-party system and, by extension, the ultimate collapse of the USSR.[31] Until the institution of Soviet premier Mikhail Gorbachev's institution of the policy of *glasnost*, few people had been allowed access to personal computers, fax machines, or Xerox machines for fear that they would use the one-to-many communicative capabilities of these devices to undermine the system. Historically speaking, Soviets had been fairly comfortable with "traditional" twentieth-century broadcast media as an invaluable extension of the power of the state. Moscow had even welcomed certain elements of "new media," especially the advent of satellite television, when they could be harness to expand rather than wither the power of the Communist Party of the Soviet Union over its fifteen republics which spanned eleven time zones. In fact, the Soviet Union became a pioneer in the field becoming the first country to deploy a national satellite TV network, Orbita, in 1967. Just over a decade later, Moscow again led the world with the first nationally-available direct-to-home satellite broadcasting system, Ekran. Unlike the U.S. and Western Europe where private satellite programming flourished in the late 1970s, "Programming content was monitored by the KGB, and the military and defense ministries controlled the development, allocation, launch, and uses of communications satellites."[32]

By the 1980s, the Soviet Union and its eastern European satellites had begun to suffer from an information technology gap. This was partly driven by fear of the distributive power of ICT, but also by a lack of need for the labor and payroll savings provided by data processing application.[33] While Japan, Germany, and the U.S. scrambled to free their workers from the mundane activities that consumed their day in the 1950s and 60s, Soviet enterprises strived to keep superfluous staff occupied. Gorbachev's introduction of *perestroika* attempted to streamline industry by dismantling counterproductive bureaucratic structures and encouraging freer flows of ideas within and across Soviet institutions. ICT slowly became a key measure of this process.[34] However, as the *New Republic* pointed out in a 1989 article on ICT in the communist bloc communication technologies, "TV is not intrinsically a technology of the individual," but the personal computer is "fundamentally democratizing."[35] As has been demonstrated by a number of scholars, the spread of personal ICTs does have impact on the development of liberal pluralism.[36] While the impact of the Internet on the USSR was infinitesimal, its rise does reflect creation of a new social space for discussion of non-sanctioned ideas, what might be called a virtual *samizdat* space.

While cyberspace provided a vast new reservoir for digital content, the Internet's ability to impact interpersonal communication remained evolutionary rather than revolutionary until the end of the 1980s. Email, as useful as it might be, offered few advantages to the increasingly popular fax machine until the introduction of Internet Relay Chat (IRC). In 1988, Jarkko "WiZ" Oikarinen of Finland's University of Oulu introduced IRC—a technological platform which allowed geographically distributed users to converse with one another in real time. Bulletin board-type communication was instantly transformed into something much more robust, by allowing users to communicate messages back and forth across incredible distances. For those with access to the technology, issues of cost were marginal. IRC demonstrated the emergence of what public intellectual Eugene Volokh has labeled a proliferation of "cheap speech" in cyberspace.[37] With IRC, the world enjoyed its first "party line" for chatting about a variety of topics from the banal to esoteric. The growth of the new platform in its first year was explosive. In the summer of 1989, IRC provided vital channels of unfiltered communication, allowing the outside world to learn about China's brutal crackdown on the Tiananmen Square protests in record time. The popularity of IRC as a tool for tracking political events in 1989 served as a harbinger of the increasingly politicization of cyberspace. In 1991, as a failed Soviet coup d'état and a war in the Persian Gulf gripped the imagination of the world, the global IRC community grew by leaps and bounds.

While the number of netizens increased at an exponential rate during the 1980s, the Internet remained a preserve of the technologically savvy. It was not until 1990 when Tim Berners-Lee, a British scientist working in Switzerland, developed a browser for navigating cyberspace that the Internet began its transition to a mainstream technology. In addition to the browser, he also introduced hypertext, or digitally-linked content. Hypertext, in conjunction with the Graphic User Interface (GUI) and the increasingly ubiquitous computing mouse, produced a system that allowed Web users to simply click on embedded links in text in order to access other, typically related, Web pages. Berners-Lee's innovations enabled Internet users to navigate a new, user-friendly world he termed the World Wide Web (WWW). The use of images, hypertext links, and Web pages created an aesthetically pleasing human-computer interface. Speaking of his work, Berners-Lee noted, "My vision was a system in which sharing what you knew or thought should be as easy as learning what someone else knew.... The system should not constrain the user; a person should be able to link with equal ease to any document wherever it happened to be stored.... If everyone on the Web could do this, then a single hypertext link could lead to an enormous, unbounded world."[38]

With this series of innovations, we can begin to date the emergence of something akin to a "people's cyberspace." The Web's technical, social, and knowledge-based barriers to entry began to crumble with the introduction of subsequent innovations by new users of the Web. As the 1990s progressed, user-friendly search engines aided navigation by providing Web "surfers," coined in 1992 by librarian Jean Armour Polly, with lists sorted by relevance related to the items they for which they were searching.[39] Consequently, users could now access information relevant to individual interests and build new communities without regard for propinquity. New and improved Web browsers like Netscape Navigator in 1994 allowed novices to surf the Web quite successfully in search of information and later iterations of the Web browser enabled Internet users to download various data such as music, video clips, and other dynamic content furthering the utility and attractiveness of the platform. The spread of the Internet in the 1990s resulted in a precipitous increase in people on the Web (over one billion), a mindboggling number of email correspondence (around 200 billion sent daily), and an explosion of Web pages (rapidly approaching five billion). Venerable netizens and technorati were now forced to rub virtual elbows with greenhorn users of the Web, so-called "newbies." With this influx of users, came a cacophony of new issues being introduced into the virtual public sphere of cyberspace. The Web was quickly turned into a global agora where anyone with an opinion and a modem could make their case. This new order began to challenge long-held conception of space, governance, and regulation as it quickly became evident that cyberspace did not recognize territorial borders.[40]

Although initially confined to industrial, academic and security communities, the commercial sector became increasingly involved in the use of and development of applications for the Internet after the ban on conducting business transactions online was lifted in 1991. Tom Holland describes the process as such, "From being the plaything of libertarians and techno-shamans, the Internet had gone on to become the largest wealth generator in history, all within the space of five heady years."[41] The introduction of a commercially-driven search engine, Lycos, in 1994 marked a major turning point in the evolution of the Web. As commercial interests begin to take notice and the home PC grew in popularity, the use of the Internet skyrocketed in the developed world and even made its way to large parts of the developing world. However, the uneven spread of adoption and the deployment of vital transport infrastructure created a so-called digital divide between the developed and developing worlds. In recent years, the spread of wireless technologies has allowed certain countries to "leapfrog" to higher levels of Internet access among their populations; however in the first decade of the Web (1990-

1999), wealthy, northern states led the world in Internet access and English was the lingua franca of cyberspace.

During the World Wide Web's second decade, a new suite of innovations added to its allure, making it a multifaceted communications and information platform. Moving beyond basic emails and simple Web pages, there are now a host of tools and functions available for users of the Internet including: video and voice emails; streaming media beamed worldwide from inexpensive webcams; and countless chat rooms on every conceivable subject. As a communications platform, the Internet has greatly benefitted from a convergence with satellite, landline, and wireless telephony enabled by the Digital Revolution. The emergence of cyberspace combined with the communicative power of the Internet has resulted in a lowering of the threshold for information distribution and access in modern society. The control over content and domination of the channels of distribution previously held by nation-states has significantly devolved in the past quarter century. As increasing numbers of Internet users began to enter cyberspace to cheaply, anonymously, and instantly communicate with their Web-enabled peers, the patterns of production and consumption of mass media began to change. While there have been many evolutionary advances in global media since World War II (the emergence of satellite television, the proliferation of a global network of fax machines, etc.), the convergence of the Internet with new media technologies such as the wireless phone and handheld computing devices represents a truly revolutionary development. The difference is a result of the scale and scope of media power provided by cyberspace, a genuinely unique, ubiquitous, and unlimited terrain for the production, consumption, and—importantly—preservation of media products.

More than twenty years after it was published, William Gibson's *Neuromancer* now seems surprisingly modest in its futurism, given the novel's rather modest predictions for cyberspace. The growth in computing power, the evolution of access devices, the increase precipitous in users, and the proliferation of interlinked applications has created a robust conceptual universe that dwarfs Gibson's "world of wires." Whereas access to the Internet was once the sole domain of academic researchers and government employees with security clearance, the Web can now be accessed by nearly everyone everywhere. Benedictine monks log on to eBay from Alpine cloisters; Indian farmers use government-financed Internet kiosks to check weather forecasts; Estonians download government forms on to their wireless laptops while sipping espresso at their local coffee shop; trans-oceanic adventurers maintain blogs detailing their voyages using satellite Web-phones; and potential mates troll digital chat rooms, despite being separated by tens of thousands of miles and vastly different cultures. Every day, the social changes wrought by the expansion of cyberspace become clearer.

Moore's Law—the empirical observation that the complexity of an integrated circuit, with respect to minimum component cost, will double in about 24 months—has resulted in a steady shrinking in the physical size of computers, an increase in their capacity for data processing, and plummeting prices over the past several decades. As such, Internet-capable computers no longer fill a room; conversely, they barely fill up a shirt pocket. Privatization of communications networks, increased competition, and evolving technologies have also played their part to make ubiquitous, high-speed Internet access a reality across large parts of the globe. Desktop computers are quickly being displaced as the primary platform for accessing the Internet. Handheld wireless devices are increasingly used to get online, especially in developing countries, many of which lack entrenched landline telephony networks. Widespread Internet use in the new industrialized countries (NICs) of the world is an accepted fact. Japan and the Asian Tigers (South Korea, Singapore, Taiwan, and Hong Kong) are dependent on the Internet for their banking industries and logistics. In North America and Europe, the Internet is rapidly displacing television as the primary source of media and news, with youth almost totally reliant on the Web for their news content.[42] This is in great part due to the growing ubiquity of the Internet in daily life. In industrialized countries, access to the Internet is found at home, school, airports, libraries, and has become indispensable in the workplace. Internet cafes abound, and one just needs to look around any major metropolitan center in the developed or the developing world to see people accessing the Web from their mobile phones and converged devices.

Despite the persistence of global digital divide, public and private partnerships have pushed the Internet into poorer parts of the world as well. Microsoft, Cisco Systems, Lockheed Martin Telecommunications and other large transnational corporations have ploughed huge sums of money into wiring developing countries. Organizations such as Internet guru Nicholas Negroponte's One Laptop Per Child provide sturdy, crank-powered WiFi-enabled laptops to children in developing countries for as low $100 per unit. State governments have also been keen to promote Web usage among their various populations. Even dictatorial and oppressive regimes have seen value in promoting "information societies" to advance their respective countries' economic well-being. The leaders of Uzbekistan, the People' Republic of China, and Burma have all made concerted efforts to expand Internet use, despite the increased dangers such freedom of expression poses to the current regimes.[43]

The rapid and widespread adoption of the Internet can be partially attributed to its unique nature. As stated earlier, the Internet completely replicates all previous mass media platforms. Perhaps more importantly, the migration into digital space has allowed these older platforms to evolve in new, exciting, and sometimes disturbing ways. The agora has found a new life on the Web in the form of blogs, chat rooms, usenets, and countless other variations of one-to-many and many-to-many platforms. The Internet has allowed the staid newspaper to be reborn. Local dailies are now consumed by expatriates on distant continents, while national papers now have the capacity to provide local content. Independent publishers have seen their entire business model revolutionized by new media as minuscule audiences no longer preclude profitability.

The expansion of talk radio into cyberspace allowed for ever more incendiary discourse to reach global audiences. Music and entertainment programs have also migrated onto the Web, and found themselves having to compete with Internet-only broadcasts which began to spring up in the early 1990s. Online radio providers like Last.fm and Live365 even allow individuals to broadcast their own formats which often tend to the esoteric, but such software is also used to broadcast ethno-national programming. The lowering of economic and regulatory barriers for radio broadcasting has allowed hundreds of ethnically-driven radio stations to flourish online, from localized minorities such as the Breton station An Tour Tan and Norway's Sámi Radio to Public Radio of Armenia and The Yiddish Voice, which deliver a variety of content directed at their respective diasporas.

Film and television have likewise made their way into cyberspace. Ripping of DVDs and the posting of the content on transient Web sites and through peer-to-peer file-sharing services like Kazaa and LimeWire has provoked a global response by international media corporations bent on preserving their intellectual property around the world. Web sites like IFILM provide world-wide access to American television shows, British advertisements, and homemade combat footage from Iraq. As media delivery platform, the Internet has progressed at a breakneck pace. The worldwide popularity of video-sharing sites such as YouTube has enabled everyone from disgruntled teenagers to Tibetan human rights activists to deliver content to millions of viewers without the filter of government censors and without regard for political borders.[44] For indigenous peoples and national minorities, this demonopolization of information and power is enabling a "shift from that of 'cultural subject' to that of nation 'media citizens'" with a voice of their own.[45] Video programming, untethered by the development satellite television networks and YouTube re-broadcasting capacity, is now truly transnational.

The Internet has also radically expanded local, national, and global communication capabilities. According to Kurt Mills, a scholar of online movements, "Territorial boundaries are rendered meaningless as bits and bytes, electrons, data, faxes, and images speed along fiber optic cable, up and down satellite links, and through the matrix of cyberspace."[46] Mobile device such as Apple Computer's iPhone allow individuals to access the Internet via cellular and wireless signals, thus cutting the cord to the desktop computer. The ubiquity of Internet messaging (IM) and microblogging has reduced the communication time between continents from months to milliseconds. The migration of phone traffic onto the Internet has most directly affected international calling which was once beyond the reach of most. Today, calls around the world can be made using relatively inexpensive and increasingly available technology that circumvents the control once exercised by national governments and telecom monopolies. International migrants were the earliest and most enthusiastic adopters of this technology owing to the fact that these calls cost a fraction of traditional landline connections. Internet protocol telephony providers such as Skype provide free or nearly free voice services to users around the globe making calls between immigrants and their homelands—once an impossible luxury—a daily occurrence, and video messaging is making telepresence—once a science fiction fantasy—a reality. The plummeting costs of Internet access and the proliferation of devices for surfing the Web have made the Internet a truly global phenomenon, despite lingering issues of the digital divide.

Email—the Internet's first "killer application"—has likewise revolutionized modern communications by allowing fast and (nearly) free correspondence across towns, states, countries, continents, oceans, and even extraterrestrial space. Attachments such as photos, video, documents, and sound files have increased the attractiveness of the communication platform. Instant messaging, first developed by Israeli entrepreneurs under the name ICQ, has added a unique complement to email messaging by allowing GUI-based, real-time correspondence between Web users anywhere in the world. Webcams which allow videoconferencing have further expanded the communicative capabilities of the Internet; other services such as Internet-based faxes, blogs, chat rooms, etc. round out the communicative functions of the Web. Together, these technologies have, according to geographer Rickie

Sanders, made the twenty-first century into an era of "concentrations, of juxtaposition, of the near and far, of the side-by-side, and the dispersed."[47]

The increasing convergence of mobile telephony and the Internet has wrought new realities regarding human interaction. Many wireless phone now come with video-recording technology which allow users to make permanent, easily distributed records of the things which shape their lives. Government crackdowns in China are now taped and sent out to technology-savvy dissidents in the West for global transmission. British hooligans have begun to videotape attacks on unsuspecting victims with their mobiles and then post to the Web or email them to friends in what is sardonically called "happy slapping."[48] And spies and terrorists alike have adapted the technology to record images of sensitive information and potential targets respectively. The evolution of the Internet and cyberspace continue to shape the marketplace, commercial networks, and work patterns around the world. Reliable, high-speed digital networks allow telecommuting for countless workers in the developed world. The global communication network also facilitates the outsourcing of customer service and other information services from North America and Europe to transitional and developing economies such as India, Russia, and the Philippines. E-commerce—not only the buying and selling of goods over electronic networks, but also inter-company and intra-company functions such as marketing, project management, supply chain and logistics, and online collaboration—has sparked a massive increase in worker productivity and increase in global trade and interdependence. Multinational corporations never need to sleep as their workforce on some part of the globe is always engaged and connected through the Internet. Global monetary networks have also changed the nature of work by allowing guest workers to instantly and verifiably make remittances to their families in the developing world though Web-based services such as Western Union.

The structure of the Web allows for alternative approaches to information. Unlike novels, newspapers, motion pictures, satellite TV, etc., "cyberspace is not a broadcast medium with a few producers and many consumers, but rather a decentralized communication system where individuals are both the consumer and the producers… cyberspace is interactive; users can choose what information they receive and send."[49] Ronald Deibert identifies this as a large–scale shift in the modes of communication towards new media like the Internet as a *distributional change* that is leading to a *world order transformation* on par with the shift from parchment to printing in the waning days of the medieval period.[50] Such changes have enormous potential for altering political authority. As law professor Christoph Engel affirms, "Governments lose the possibility of collective amnesia. They can never be sure when a search engine will once again reveal a bad deed committed at the beginning of a legislative period."[51]

The Internet provides the means to bypass and circumvent traditional state sovereignty and transcend geographically bound entities, thus allowing Web-enabled communities a great deal of latitude in the way that they confront issues of gender, class, political affiliation, etc.

All states have suffered a diminution of both internal and external authority in the face of the pressures of the global communications revolution, brought about by the magic combination of telephones, orbiting satellites and computer. The overlapping webs of human activities which have resulted have served to erode the spiritual and practical bases upon which the nation state was predicated.[52]

The Internet is extremely effective in creating apertures in the propaganda blankets which have been established through state domination of traditional mass media (newspapers, radio, and television). In the words of Victoria Bernal, "The Internet can be seen as decentralized, participatory, unregulated, and egalitarian in operation compared to mass media such as newspapers, radio, or television where communication is largely one way and consumers have very little opportunity to be producers of content."[53] Correspondingly, the Internet allows its users to circumvent (if they so choose) the corporatist messaging of mass media which is prevalent in wealthy, developed societies—though as I will point out, the Web is itself increasingly corporatist in its orientation.

Regardless, the Internet enables its users to access an extreme diversity of views based on either push or pull methods of receiving information, news, and other forms of content. It is important to remember, however, that older power structures are so embedded in traditional space that they will make their presence felt in cyberspace—in fact, the Internet often serves to reinforce existing hierarchies or becomes a tool of those wishing to re-conquer lost authority.[54] As Saskia Sassen puts it, "Digital space, whether public or private, is partly embedded in actual societal structures and power dynamics: its topography weaves in and out of non-electronic space."[55] In fact, informatics researcher Alexander Halavais demonstrated that national borders continue to play an important role in shaping the digital terrain of cyberspace.[56] However, if we look at cyberspace as a geography, it becomes readily apparent that nation-states are vastly underrepresented in virtual space versus real space.

Internet-based communications and political activity conducted within and across state borders have highlighted the increasing porousness of the state in the postmodern, postinternational age. As Jim Falk states, "The communication space of the Web has the potential to be simultaneously more universalistic and more particularistic, and this mirrors a world in which national boundaries are becoming more permeable."[57] Through existing structures of communication and new computer-mediated forms of interaction, Internet-enabled elites have begun to ignore, circumvent, and even contest the state's domination of identity production which has traditionally been maintained through control of the media and a monopoly on the education system. As intercultural researchers Laura B. Lengel and Patrick D. Murphy state, "the Internet is dramatically redefining the nature of social relationships between nations and challenging cultural sovereignty by creating an increased sense of borderlessness."[58] With the creation of virtual communities based on epistemic, social, and ethno-linguistic commonalities, the preeminence of national borders in shaping identity is waning.

Cybernations: The Ultimate Virtual Communities

Critics of the Internet often demonize it as a homogenizing force that eradicates differences among peoples and threatens cultures creating what professor of global sociology Jan Nederveen Pieterse calls a "creolized global mélange."[59]

Paradoxically, cyberspace also offers great promise for the preservation of identity and national culture. Through computer-mediated communication, nations have the ability to maintain and reinforce their identity in new and compelling ways. Anthems, legends, genealogies, histories, photographs, manuscripts and other tangible assets of national culture are being protected, distributed and accessed in cyberspace. The Internet in conjunction with other information technologies such as satellite television and inexpensive mobile phones has significantly contributed to the so-called "death of distance," thus lessening the need for individuals or communities to have face-to-face contact in order to build and maintain strong ties. These technological advances have been especially welcome among stateless nations, ethnic minorities, and dispersed immigrant communities who have historically lacked access to many of the tools possessed by elites acting in the name of nation-states.

Beyond cyberspace's role as reservoir for the preservation of digitized representations of national identity and a platform for increased communication, it also functions as an agent for change. The unique nature of Internet allows dispersed peoples to (re)create the bonds of community without regard for propinquity.[60] Geographer Rob Kitchin argues, "Cyberspace thus offers us the opportunity to reclaim public space and recreate the essence and nature of community on-line."[61] In addition to the dissemination of cultural and artifacts and creation of transborder communities, new media allow for communication with local and global non-governmental organizations and international government organizations and enhancement of communal education.[62] According to sociologist Mary Chayko, "The modern world has seen electronic technology bring *simultaneity* to communication across distances and with it another revolution in social connectedness. Now people who are spatially separated can actually share an experience at the same time, which makes the connection even more direct, more vivid, and...more *resonant*."[63] This resonance has undoubtedly aided ethnic entrepreneurs in their various campaigns to revive flagging or even dormant minority identities and digerati among the world's diasporas who seek to bind far-flung ethnic communities.

Through its ability to knit together these distant communities of common interest, cyberspace thus enables the creation of cybernations. In the words of cultural studies professor Abril Trigo, "A cybernation constitutes a national virtual community realized in cyberspace through the performance of the ritual sharing of memories. The virtual space of this imagining community is moulded through the recollection of remembrances, the telling of stories and practice of distinct dialectical variance."[64] The cybernation represents the epitome of the virtual community since it shares a genuine heritage, common set of symbols, and cultural values that other ad hoc Internet-based communities typically lack.[65] Kurt Mills states, "Given that all communities are imagined, constructed in the minds of the members, it thus not surprising that such communities could appear or be strengthened in cyberspace."[66] The drivers of this revolution are Internet-enabled elites with significant access to and influence within their offline communities.

Nations are, of course, composed of living, breathing individuals that inhabit actual space in "real" countries. However, national identity is on the whole a mental construct which is just as at home in the digital corridors and cul-de-sacs of cyberspace as it is in an Irish pub, an Armenian church, or the Arab street.

According to postmodern political theorist Homi K. Bhabha, "Nations, like narratives, lose their origins in the myths of time and only fully realize their horizons in the mind's eye."[67] Cyberspace is thus a powerful new environment which enables national identity projects to flourish under even the most restrictive "real-world" regimes, assuming that participants in such projects have reliable access to the Internet. Likewise, cyberspace is becoming a battle ground for nations. In his writings on "e-nationalism," political scientist Evgeny Mororov states: "Blogs and social networks have proved to be splendid platforms for mythmaking, spitting out visceral imagery and edgy slogans that quickly embed themselves in the national consciousness."[68] Because of its unique structure, the Internet makes it possible to experience identity as "a sheer construction with no other point of sustenance than pure and simple desire."[69]

While the Internet offers revolutionary new possibilities for the revitalization of national identities, it does not necessarily provide an environment which is conducive to such (re-) constructions. Like all technology platforms, the Internet is—at its roots—neutral, in terms of its politics. Linda Leung states that Web is a "site of both resistance (by ethnic minorities) and power (of dominant forces)."[70] However, as I argue throughout this text, once patterns of use and interaction begin to evolve, media become charged with life-altering properties. Les Back, a scholar of online movements, states, "A particular technology, be it pop music or the Internet, has no inherent ideological orientation. Rather, the relationship between form and content is found at the interface between particular technologies and their utilization."[71] Therefore, the effect of media like the Internet is *not* neutral. The absence of face-to-face contact surely alters the ways in which national identity projects evolve. Cyberspatial nation-building allows for a more fluid relationship with the nation, e.g., one can be railing against the imperialist policies of the titular majority on one Microsoft Explorer screen and be shopping for computer parts on another. Such tacking back and forth from nationalism to the banal may certainly retard serious commitment to Web-based national projects. It is perhaps better to think of the Web as an extension and amplification of previous media rather than some transformational meta-structure (despite the latter interpretation being en vogue among many communications theorists).

In his essay "The Meaning of the Web," Jim Falk discussed the critical distinctions between "robust" and "ephemeral" communities and how the Web tends to create more of the latter.[72] Members of robust communities will invest significant personal and professional resources into the community because they consider it to be stable, growing, supportive, and effective. If a calamity befalls the community, its members will rally in support of the group because of a collective belief in the community's long term viability. In contrast, ephemeral communities are unstable and transitory and rarely satisfy more than handful of their members' needs. This is particularly true of cyber-communities where identities are often constructed with little regard to reality.[73] Often members of these communities have very different world views on topics not related to the immediate issue which has brought them together. Consequently, these groups tend to break down quickly during times of strife or external threat. For cybernations, the "real-world" cohesiveness of the unit is thus more important than the contours of cybernationalism.

Regardless, the Internet has proved a powerful tool of empowerment for minority nationalities with access to the Web since it represents a *terra nullius* where readily accessible "virtual archives" of alternative histories can be constructed and maintained.[74] As scholar of multinationalism Frank Louis Rusciano points out, the Internet endows marginalized groups "the ability to 'tell one's story' [and] affect one's political conditions."[75] Communications professor Leda Cooks argues that the Internet has had a powerful effect on identities among diaspora communities, especially in relation to the concepts of state and nation. However, the peculiarities of identity formation in cyberspace does not "erase the hierarchies or annihilate the old markers of membership" among ethnic groups.[76] Such actions are part of a larger shift in political action in the postmodern world.

The Web has also become a tool of expression, coordination and mobilization for minorities completely isolated within individual states. In both cases, Internet-enabled elites are staking out claims of authority in cyberspace attempting to "speak for the nation," or as Mary Chayko frame it, "Technological mediators act as 'bridges' between separated people, facilitating their joint mental orientation."[77] States attempting to create homogenous statist identities (typically focused on the "core" nation or titular nationality) are thus facing unforeseen challenges as they attempt to implement new or maintain older national projects in the form of new Internet-enabled elites who stand as potential impediment to such actions.[78]

The Web—a decentralized, global, anonymous platform with all the functionality of print, radio, and television media—has become a shadow space which the state has little ability to impact. Intellectual polymath Ziauddin Sardar concludes that the Internet has prompted the emergence of a "new civilisation (sic)...through our human-computer interface and mediation," which he deems *Cyberia*.[79] Challenges of distance and politics that once prevented the dispersed Ruthenian, Kurdish, and Armenian nations (discussed in later chapters) from communicating across state borders have almost completely evaporated as new virtual relationships develop which are "uninhibited by conventional notions of political territory and national sovereignty."[80] As a result, the Internet is an invaluable tool for generating social capital among marginalized communities, particular diasporan groups. Jennifer Brinkerhoff argues that cyberspatial community building is translating into tangible political benefits, the spread of liberal values, and strengthened (hybrid) identity among groups such as Afghan-Americans, Eritreans in Europe, and others.[81] While In cyberspace, the Internet has enabled a new public sphere upon where national identity is being recast on an almost daily basis. This evolution is still in its infancy, but it is clear that the ramifications of the Internet for nations, identities, and national identities are substantial.

It is perhaps better to think of the Web as an extension of media than some transformational meta-structure which is often *en vogue* among communications theorists. As Marshall McLuhan so famously stated, "the media is the massage" (although he is even more famously misquoted as saying "the media is the message").[82] In other words, the delivery system shapes and molds the ways in which the information is processed. This is certainly true when one considers the corporatist structures of the modern Internet which is littered with the detritus of consumerism—a form of consumerism which tends to use the lowest-common denominator in order to reach the largest audience possible. Despite the emergence of tightly-bound (occasionally bordering on xenophobic) epistemic communities in cyberspace, the overall structure is built to be inclusionary rather than exclusionary.

When questioned, increasing numbers of young people around the world tend to suggest that the proliferation of corporatist messaging which is transmitted through "global media" platforms such as the Internet, music videos, Hollywood, *manga*, and lifestyle magazines significantly contribute to their desires and self-image. As global communications scholar Tehri Rantanen states, "Globalization challenges the process of national identity building by producing competing identities."[83] Thus, the mental space which might have previously been reserved for national identity is now being encroached upon by Benetton, U2, *The Matrix*, LG, and Microsoft. Travel and personal contacts with people outside their local, ethnic, and national communities tend to reinforce transnational commonalities, thus fueling globalized (or at least denationalized) identities. Despite such trends, the Internet is and most likely will remain a place where blood-based nationalism, racial hatred, and sectarian diatribes proliferate. As stated previously, the medium itself is neutral—it is only through the actions of its users does the Internet emerge as social space.

While certain scholars are quick to suggest that the Internet poses a threat to national sovereignty,[84] there is little evidence to suggest that access to the Internet overrides the roles played by territory, habits, institutions, etc. which are key to the "living" of national identity. The "imagining" of national identity is certainly affected deeply by the new conceptual universe of bits and bytes, but it is important to contrast this with real world behavior. The absence of real world interaction (work, shopping, face-to-face leisure activities, etc.) is a serious impediment for the building of true, nation-based communities. Experiences in cyberspace often ring hollow when compared to real life events, emotions, and responses. Utilizing the tool of Henri Lefebvre's previously referenced conceptual triad of spatiality (the conceived, the perceived and the lived spaces), the conceived and perceived are quite viable in cyberspace but "living" there is, as yet, an unrealized goal. One cannot experience the heat of the jubilant crowd, the eerie sense of connection that comes from a thousand voices chanting in unison, or the smell of one's homeland on a spring morning on the Internet—in other words the lived is still the exclusive property of real space.

This being stated, the Internet does offer ethnic entrepreneurs the potential of mobility and economic transformation on a personal (rather than national) level and it in this arena where I discovered the most profound impact on conceptualizations of community and identity. The "infinite, boundless, limitless virtual world" of cyberspace may provide a temporary narcosis from the daily "raced, gendered, classed" travails of minority status for Russians in Latvia, Kurds in Turkey, or Tamils in Sri Lanka, it does not re-write the rules of daily life.[85] Thus, the Internet does not necessarily override reality, but like a drug, it offers a temporary escape from it. On the other hand, the Web does connect individuals to opportunities abroad. And while these new opportunities entail significant challenges, they typically to do not carry the institutional barriers to personal promotion which are endemic to life as a residual imperial minority in a nationalizing state.

In his seminal work *Modernity at Large: Cultural Dimensions of Globalization*, Arjun Appadurai identified the insidious influence of information and communications technologies (ICT) on global diasporas and the role of mass mediation in crafting *transnational* identities.[86] Appadurai points out that technology tethers transnational elites to their homeland and, in fact, changes the political and social environment for those who leave as well as those who stay. Javanese-Australian cultural researcher Ien Ang has pointed to the emergence of *transnational nationalism* "based on the presumption of internal ethnic sameness and external ethnic distinctiveness. Unlike nationalism of the nation-state, which premises itself on a national community which is territorially bound, diasporic nationalism produced an imagined community that is deterritorialized, but that is symbolically bound nonetheless."[87] Extrapolating from Ang and Appadurai's work, I focus on the impact of ICT (specifically the Internet) and mass mediation on national minorities, i.e., groups which are to some extent "trapped" in states which do not give them the same level of rights conferred upon their neighbors who are seen as part of the "core nationality." In today's postmodern world, the evolving identities of national minorities, unlike those among Appadurai's global diasporas, do not reflect mobility, but a lack thereof.[88] Thus, I am therefore hesitant to use the term transnational which at its root implies some level of movement. However, like those scholars who look at transnational phenomena, I am concerned with the role of the state in its relation to identity.

Rather than transnational, I have instead adopted for the use of *postnational identity* which I believe better represents the situation among challenged nations within nationalizing states. As Homi Bhabha points out, the addition of "post" attached to various notions—feminism, modernism, etc.—signifies "beyond" rather than any sequential marker. "'Beyond' signifies spatial distance, marks progress, promises the future" but we need a thorough understanding of the present and the past to understand such differences.[89] For German philosopher Jürgen Habermas, postnational identity grew out of Germans' difficult embrace of their own past in the wake of the Holocaust.[90] As the European Community grew into a robust socio-economic—and ultimately juridical and quasi-political—framework for late twentieth century Europeans, the ability to embrace simultaneously cosmopolitan and local identities rapidly eroded the need to invest one's national identity solely within the vessel of the nation-state. By using the term postnational, I am highlighting the nation-state's decaying monopoly on loyalties, allegiances, and power,[91] which in my view demands an updated view of national identity and the liminal space in which it inhabits. Nowhere is this transformation more profound than among ethnic minorities who are no longer shackled by the restrictions on communication that defined an earlier age. In the subsequent chapter, I will explore the political backdrop that has multiplied the efficacy of this communications revolution's impact on minority identity.

Notes

1. Benedict Anderson, *Imagined Communities: Reflections on the Origin and Spread of Nationalism* (London: Verso, 1991).

2. Candan, Menderes and Uwe Hunger. "Nation Building Online: A Case Study of Kurdish Migrants in Germany," *German Policy Studies* 4, no. 4 (2008): 125-153.

3. Vannevar Bush, "As We May Think," *Atlantic Monthly* 176, no. 1 (July 1945): 101-108.

4. Bush, "As We May Think," 107.

5. J.C.R. Licklider, "Man-Computer Symbiosis," *IRE Transactions on Human Factors in Electronics*, HFE-1 (March 1960): 4-11.

6. See Chigusa Ishikawa Kita, "J.C.R. Licklider's Vision for the IPTO," *IEEE Annals of the History of Computing* 25, no. 3 (July-September 2003): 62-77.

7. Katie Hafner and Matthew Lyon, *Where Wizards Stay Up Late: The Origins of the Internet* (New York: Touchstone, 1996), 67.

8. Paul Baran, "On Distributed Communications: I. Introduction to Distributed Communications Networks," Memorandum RM-3420-PR, prepared for the United States Air Force Project RAND. Santa Monica: RAND Corporation, 1964, http://www.rand.org/pubs/research_memoranda/2006/RM3420.pdf (22 February 2008).

9. Franklin F. Kuo, "ALOHA Packet Broadcasting System," in Fritz E. Froehlich and Allen Kent, *The Froehlich/Kent Encyclopedia of Telecommunications* (Boca Raton: CRC Press, 1991), 108.

10. Vinton G. Cerf and Robert E. Kahn, "A Protocol for Packet Network Intercommunication," *IEEE Transactions on Communications*, COM-23 (May 1974): 637-648.

11. Cerf and Kahn, "A Protocol for Packet Network Intercommunication," 638.

12. Cited in Michael Hauben and Ronda Hauben, *Netizens: On the History and Impact of Usenet and the Internet* (Hoboken: Wiley — IEEE Computer Society Press, 1997), 40.

13. Barry Wellman, Janet Salaff, Dimitrina Dimitrova, Laura Garton, Milena Gulia and Caroline Haythornthwaite, "Computer Networks as Social Networks: Collaborative Work, Telework, and Virtual Community," *Annual Review of Sociology* 22, no. 1 (1996): 213-238.

14. See Ferdinand Tönnies, *Community and Society*, English ed. (Mineola, NY: Dover Publications Inc., 2002 [1887]).

15. Douglas Rushkoff, "The People's Net," *Yahoo! Internet Life* 7 (July 2001): 78-84.

16. Hauben and Hauben, *Netizens*, x-xi.

17. Hauben and Hauben, *Netizens*, 54-55.

18. Richard Langhorne, *The Essentials of Global Politics* (London: Hodder Arnold, 2006).

19. Hauben and Hauben, *Netizens*, 12.

20. Roy Rosenzweig, "Wizards, Bureaucrats, Warriors, and Hackers: Writing the History of the Internet," *American Historical Review* 103, no. 5 (December 1998): 1530-1552.

21. Langhorne, *The Essentials of Global Politics*.

22. Aden Evens describes IP as "a four-part number that, something like a street address, identifies each node on the Internet, including each attached computer....The four parts of the IP address specify the location pointed to by the link in a hierarchy that hones in on the intended node. The message sent also includes a return IP address, so the responding server knows where to send the data back to"; see Aden Evens, "Concerning the Digital," *Differences: A Journal of Feminist Cultural Studies* 14, no. 2 (Summer 2003): 49-77.

23. Robert M. Kitchin, "Towards Geographies of Cyberspace," *Progress in Human Geography* 22, no. 3 (September 1998): 385-406.

24. William Gibson, *Neuromancer* (London: Gollancz, 1984), 51.

25. Tony Myers, "The Postmodern Imaginary in William Gibson's *Neuromancer*," *Modern Fiction Studies* 47, no. 4 (Winter 2001): 887-909.

26. Benjamin Fair, "Stepping Razor in Orbit: Postmodern Identity and Political Alternatives in William Gibson's *Neuromancer*," *Critique* 46, no. 2 (Winter 2005): 92-103.

27. Julie E. Cohen, "Cyberspace as/and Space," *Columbia Law Review* 107, no. 1 (January 2007): 210-256.

28. Henri Lefebvre, *The Production of Space* (Cambridge: Blackwell, 1991).

29. Cohen, "Cyberspace as/and Space," 214.

30. Barnabas D. Johnson, "The Cybernetics of Society: The Governance of Self and Civilization," Jurlandia web site, 2004, http://www.jurlandia.org/cybsoc.htm (27 February 2008).

31. See David R. Henderson, "Information Technology as a Universal Solvent for Removing State Stains," *Independent Review* 4, no. 4 (Spring 2000): 517-523.

32. Gladys D. Ganley, *Unglued Empire: The Soviet Experience with Communications Technologies* (Westport: Ablex Publishing, 1996), 5.

33. Donald MacKenzie, "Perestroika and Parallelism: Advanced Information Technology and the Soviet Union," *Technology Analysis & Strategic Management* 1, no. 2 (June 1989): 145-156.

34. MacKenzie, "Perestroika and Parallelism," 153.

35. "Our Chip Has Come In," *New Republic* 200, no. 24 (June 1989): 7-8.

36. See, for instance, Shanthi Kalathil and Taylor C. Boas, *Open Networks, Closed Regimes: The Impact of the Internet on Authoritarian Rule* (Washington: Carnegie Endowment for International Peace, 2003); Zixue Tai, *The Internet in China: Cyberspace and Civil Society* (New York and London: Routledge, 2006); and Chang Woo-Young and Lee Won-Tae, "Cyberactivism and Political Empowerment in Civil Society: A Comparative Analysis of Korean Cases," *Korea Journal* 46, no. 4 (Winter 2006): 136-167.

37. Cited in Cohen, "Cyberspace as/and Space," 220.

38. Tim Berners-Lee and Mark Fischetti, *Weaving the Web: The Original Design and Ultimate Destiny of the World Wide Web by Its Inventor* (San Francisco: Harper, 1999) 34.

39. Langhorne, *The Essentials of Global Politics.*

40. Stanley D. Brunn, "Towards an Understanding of the Geopolitics of Cyberspace: Learning, Re-Learning and Unlearning," *Geopolitics* 5, no. 3 (Winter 2000): 144-149.

41. Tom Holland, "Nothing Will Ever Be the Same Again. Or Will It?" *New Statesman* 128, no. 4463 (November 1999): 33-35.

42. David T. Z. Mindich, "The Young and the Restless," *Wilson Quarterly* 29, no. 2 (Spring 2005): 48-53.

43. See Shanthi Kalathil, "Dot Com for Dictators," *Foreign Policy* 135 (March/April 2003): 42-49.

44. Moisés Naím, "The YouTube Effect," *Foreign Policy* 158 (January/ February 2007): 103-104.

45. Lorna Roth, *Something in the Air: The Story of First Peoples Television Broadcasting Canada* (Montreal: McGill-Queen's University Press, 2005), 17.

46. Kurt Mills, "Cybernations: Identity, Self-determination, Democracy and the 'Internet Effect' in the Emerging Information Order," *Global Society* 16, no. 1 (January 2002): 69-87.

47. Rickie Sanders, "The Triumph of Geography," *Progress in Human Geography* 32, no. 2 (April 2008): 179–182.

48. See Robert A. Saunders, "Happy Slapping: Transatlantic Contagion or Home-Grown, Mass-Mediated Nihilism?" *Static* 1 (Autumn 2005), http://static.londonconsortium. com/issue01/saunders_happyslapping.html.

49. Robert M. Kitchin, *Cyberspace: The World in Wires* (Chichester, UK: John Wiley and Sons, 1998), 74.

50. Ronald J. Deibert, *Parchment, Printing and Hypermedia: Communication in World Order Transformation* (New York: Columbia University Press, 1997).

51. Christoph Engel, "The Internet and the Nation State," in Christoph Engel and Kenneth H. Heller, *Understanding the Impact of Global Networks in Local Social, Political and Cultural Values* (Baden-Baden: Nomos Verlagsgesellschaft, 2000), 122.

52. Richard Langhorne, *The Coming of Globalization: Its Evolution and Contemporary Consequences*. Houndmills: Palgrave, 2001), 81.

53. Victoria Bernal, "Diaspora, Cyberspace and Political Imagination: The Eritrean Diaspora Online," *Global Networks* 6, no 2 (April 2006): 161-179.

54. Ziauddin Sardar, "alt.civilizations.faq: Cyberspace as the Darker Side of the West," in Ziauddin Sardar and Jerome Ravetz, *Cyberfutures: Culture and Politics on the Information Superhighway* (New York: New York University Press, 1998).

55. Saskia Sassen, "The Impact of the Internet on Sovereignty: Unfounded and Real Worries," in Christoph Engel and Kenneth H. Heller, *Understanding the Impact of Global Networks in Local Social, Political and Cultural Values* (Baden-Baden: Nomos Verlagsgesellschaft, 2000), 198.

56. Alexander Halavais, "National Borders on the World Wide Web," *New Media & Society* 2, no. 1 (March 2000): 7-28.

57. Jim Falk, "The Meaning of the Web," *Information Society* 14, no. 1 (November 1998): 285-293.

58. Laura B. Lengel and Patrick D. Murphy, 2001. "Cultural Identity and Cyberimperialism: Computer-Mediated Exploration of Ethnicity, Nation and Censorship," in Bosah Ebo *Cyberimperialism?: Global Relations in the New Electronic Frontier* (Westport, CT: Praeger, 2001), 187.

59. Jan Nederveen Pieterse, *Globalization & Culture: A Global Mélange* (Lanham, MD: Rowman & Littlefield, 2003), 70.

60. Engel, "The Internet and the Nation State."

61. Kitchin, *Cyberspace*, 11.

62. Michael Dahan and Gabriel Sheffer, "Ethnic Groups and Distance Shrinking Technologies," *Nationalism & Ethnic Politics* 7, no. 1 (Spring 2001): 85-107.

63. Mary Chayko, *Connecting: How We Form Social Bonds and Communities in the Internet Age* (Albany: SUNY Press, 2002), 14.

64. Abril Trigo, "Cybernation (Or, *La Patria Cibernetica*)," *Journal of Latin American Cultural Studies* 12, no. 1 (March 2003): 95-117.

65. Dahan and Sheffer, "Ethnic Groups and Distance Shrinking Technologies," 102.

66. Mills, "Cybernations," 70.

67. Homi K. Bhabha, "Narrating the Nation," in Vincent P. Pecor, *Nations and Identities: Classic Readings* (Malden, MA: Blackwell Publishers, 2001), 359.

68. Evgeny Morozov, "A Melting Pot It's Not," *Foreign Policy* 171 (March/April 2009): 26.

69. Trigo, "Cybernation," 110.

70. Linda Leung, *Virtual Ethnicity: Race, Resistance and the World Wide Web* (Farnham, UK: Ashgate, 2005), 48.

71. Les Back, "Aryans Reading Adorno: Cyber-culture and Twenty-first Century Racism," *Ethnic and Racial Studies* 25, no. 4 (July 2002): 628–651.

72. Falk, "The Meaning of the Web."

73. Lisa Nakamura, *Cybertypes: Race, Ethnicity and Identity on the Internet* (London: Routledge, 2002).

74. Maja Mikula, "Virtual Landscapes of Memory," *Information, Communication & Society* 6, no. 2 (June 2003): 169–186.

75. Frank Louis Rusciano, "The Three Faces of Cyberimperialism," in Bosah Ebo *Cyberimperialism?: Global Relations in the New Electronic Frontier* (Westport, CT: Praeger, 2001), 15.

76. Leda Cooks, "Negotiating National Identity and Social Movements in Cyberspace," in Bosah Ebo. *Cyberimperialism?: Global Relations in the New Electronic Frontier* (Westport, CT: Praeger, 2001), 234.

77. Chayko, *Connecting*, 42.

78. See Rogers Brubaker, *Nationalism Reframed: Nationhood and the National Question in the New Europe* (Cambridge: Cambridge University Press, 1996).

79. Ziauddin Sardar and Jerome R. Ravetz, "Introduction: Reaping the Technological Whirlwind," in Ziauddin Sardar and Jerome Ravetz, *Cyberfutures: Culture and Politics on the Information Superhighway* (New York: New York University Press, 1998), 1.

80. Bosah Ebo, *Global Relations in the New Electronic Frontier* (Westport, CT: Praeger, 2001), ix.

81. Brinkerhoff, Jennifer M. *Digital Diasporas: Identity and Transnational Engagement* (Cambridge: Cambridge University Press, 2009).

82. Marshall McLuhan and Quentin Fiore, *The Media Is the Massage: An Inventory of Effects* (London: Penguin Books, 1967).

83. Terhi Rantanen, *The Global and the National: Media and Communications in Post-Communist Russia* (Lanham: Rowman & Littlefield, 2002), 7.

84. See, for instance, Dahan and Sheffer, "Ethnic Groups and Distance Shrinking Technologies"; Langhorne, *The Coming of Globalization*; George Bugliarello, "Telecommunications, Politics, Economics, and National Sovereignty: A New Game," *Technology in Society* 18, no. 4 (December 1996): 403-418; Mark Poster, "National Identities and Communications Technologies," *Information Society* 15, no. 4 (October-December 1999): 235-240; and Paul Spoonley, Richard Bedford, and Cluny Macpherson, "Divided Loyalties and Fractured Sovereignty: Transnationalism and the Nation-State in Aotearoa/New Zealand," *Journal of Ethnic & Migration Studies* 29, no. 1 (January 2003): 27-46.

85. Sanders, "The Triumph of Geography," 181.

86. Arjun Appadurai, *Modernity at Large* (Minneapolis: University of Minnesota Press, 1996).

87. Ien Ang, "Together-in-Difference: Beyond Diaspora, into Hybridity," *Asian Studies Review* 27, no. 2 (June 2003): 141-154.

88. In her definition of transnationality, Aihwa Ong suggests that "trans-" denotes both moving through space and across lines; see Aihwa Ong, *Flexible Citizenship: The Cultural Logistics of Transnationality* (Durham: Duke University Press, 1999), 4.

89. Homi K. Bhabha, *The Location of Culture* (London and New York: Routledge, 1994), 5-6.

90. See Jürgen Habermas' "Citizenship and National Identity: Some Reflections on the Future of Europe," in Ronald Beiner, *Theorizing Citizenship* (Albany: SUNY Press, 1995) and "The European Nation-State—Its Achievements and Its Limits On the Past and Future of Sovereignty and Citizenship," in Gopal Balakrishnan, *Mapping the Nation* (London: Verso, 1996), as well as *The Postnational Constellation: Political Essays* (Cambridge: MIT Press, 2001).

91. Richard Rosecrance, "The Rise of the Virtual State," *Foreign Affairs* 74, no. 4 (July/August 1996): 45-61 and Jessica T. Matthews, "Power Shift," *Foreign Affairs* 76, no. 1 (January/February 1997): 50-66.

Chapter 3
New World (Dis)Orders: National Identity and Ethnic Politics in the Global Era

In 1989, the Berlin Wall—an instantly recognizable symbol of the Cold War—was torn down by jubilant Germans, a single people once again. Yet, as one nation was reunited, the seeds of ethnic separatism, political violence, and civilizational clashes were planted across the Eurasian continent. With the end of the Iron Curtain, the effects of globalization rushed into Eastern Europe and, soon, the former Soviet Union.[1] The increased movement of people, ideas, money, information, goods, and technology across national borders opened new doors to community building, cultural autonomy, and even the possibility of independence for certain aspirants.[2] In this new milieu, civil society flourished, submerged identities exploded, and transnational links grew. Operating in a unipolar world where the global hegemon (the United States) was preoccupied with its own domestic concerns, global religious movements, intergovernmental organizations (IGOs), non-governmental organizations (NGOs), transnational social and environmental movements, international criminal syndicates, and multinational corporations all saw their power grow. The evaporation of the colossal struggle between Washington and Moscow also had important ramifications, including an "abandonment of Africa" and a reorientation of foreign policy away from ideological outcomes. In the ensuing years, the nation-state's withering monopoly on power grew more evident as a host of phenomenon—from failed states to the spread of hybridized cultures to the proliferation of supranational economic unions—reshaped international politics.

Taken together, these important years since the fall of communism marked a watershed for the coming of globalization.[3] The process, however, had been underway since the end of World War II, when the Allied nations crafted a global system intended to promote free trade and self-determination for all peoples. During the Cold War, American and Soviet political concerns resulted in haphazard and sometimes unpredictable manifestations of these primary goals. With the opening of post-Soviet Eurasia to the world, the marketization of the People's Republic of China and India, the democratization of most of Latin America, and the spread of neoliberalism across generous swaths the developing world, the world entered into a new period of globalism in which the wartime aims of the U.S. and its allies were more fully realized. In this comparatively anarchic environment, resurgent national identity among minorities has been one of the most important drivers of this global transformation. In the chapter, I trace the recent history of national movements that attack the status quo, as well as the impact of these movements on global politics.

The Coming of Globalization

On 11 March 1985, the Communist Party of Soviet Union (CPSU) elected its first General Secretary born after the 1917 Bolshevik Revolution. Less than five years later, Soviet domination of the Eastern Bloc had collapsed and the USSR was hurtling towards disintegration. After a quiet start to his premiership, Gorbachev launched three new policy directions at the Twenty-Seventh Congress of the CPSU: *glasnost* ('openness'), *perestroika* ('restructuring'), and economic *uskorenie* ('acceleration'). The introduction of these reforms allowed the underpinnings of globalization to creep into the USSR. Collectively, these policies and their outcomes are viewed as bringing an end the Cold War, the viability of Marxism-Leninism, Russia's domination of Eastern Europe, and the Soviet Union itself. The collapse of the Bolshevik state serves as a suitable analogy for the rapid and far-reaching changes which have gripped the world since the mid-1980s.

As the USSR opened up itself to societal criticism, restructured its bureaucracy for the contemporary international realities, and accelerated its embrace of technology, global flows of commerce, and new economic policies, it faced momentous challenges to its authority. Ensconced in a cocoon of its own making, the socialist superpower had isolated itself from the coming globalization for several decades.[4] While citing any single event invites historiographical criticism, it is plausible to date the initiation of the current era of globalization with the signing of the Atlantic Charter in 1941. A beleaguered Winston Churchill and an buoyant Franklin D. Roosevelt set out a common policy which called for the all nations, large or small, to have "access, on equal terms, to the trade and to the raw materials of the world which are needed for their economic prosperity" and sought "to bring about the fullest collaboration between all nations in the economic field with the object of securing, for all, improved labor standards, economic advancement and social security." While the U.S. was not yet at war, the document was meant to help shape the post-fascist world order. Echoing Woodrow Wilson's idealistic Fourteen Points of some two decades earlier, the charter proclaimed free trade, self-rule, and the expectation of material advancement for all peoples to be the guiding principles of the post-war order. For Britain, this meant the eventual dismantling of its empire and sacrificing its long-held position as global hegemon. For the Americans, the Atlantic Charter represented the apotheosis of its century-old pursuit of "open doors" to overseas trade, and validation of its deeply-held anti-tyrannical tradition. It was hoped, somewhat vainly, that the Joseph Stalin would subsequently commit his country to its tenets as the recent victim of an unprovoked Axis invasion earlier that summer.[5]

As the Anglo-American Alliance emerged victorious from the carnage of the Second World War, the two partners set about constructing an international regime which would achieve the goals of the Atlantic Charter. Even as Britain was foregoing its role as master of the seas, it was able to maintain a strong position in global trade due to America's rising power in global affairs. However, it was clear that the nineteenth century's *Pax Britannica* had given way to a new era, that of the *Pax Americana*. Despite frequent differences on tactics, these two allies instituted a highly successful strategy for the new era of global trade. Sometimes called the Bretton Woods system, this global economic order benefitted its authors (US, UK, and other industrialized nations) through the stabilization of globalized marketplace.[6] Via the Marshal Plan, NATO, and other economic and military schemes, the U.S. invested massive amounts of money in and guaranteed the security of dozens of states across Western Europe, the Pacific Rim, and portions of the Middle East to secure unfettered access to the markets and resources necessary to promote global economic advancement and ever higher levels of trade (at least within its own sphere of influence).

France, the Benelux countries, Italy, Germany, Japan, and America's other allies—both large and small—were forced into relationships based on "shared sovereignty" to take part in this new order.[7] Concurrently, the U.S. and the UK were likewise forced to open up to the flows of people, goods, and ideas which resulted from the policies of openness, restructuring, and economic acceleration which defined the post-war era in what came to be known as the West, an ambiguous concept which included, for example, Japan, but not Czechoslovakia. As decolonization took root across Africa and Asia, new independent countries were forced to choose between remaining economically (and thus, by default, politically) linked to their old imperial masters (Britain, France, Belgium, etc.) or embracing the revolutionary ideals of Marxism-Leninism and Moscow's sometimes suffocating tutelage. Some countries opted to steer a neutral course, opting for what some deemed Third Worldism. Irrespective of the Cold War-era alliances they forged, all countries in the developing world understood the necessity of engaging in global trade: Nasser's Egypt grew dependent on Russian arms, Algeria needed markets for its oil, Congo sought foreign direct investment to develop its mineral resources, etc. This restructuring of trade effectively destroyed the remnants of the incendiary "national economies" that had characterized international political economy in the wake of the Great Depression. These global flows of trade—some of them mirroring imperial core-periphery routes while others were totally novel—became the hallmark of the new era of globalization.

Just as was the case during previous eras of globalization (Sinic, Roman, Mongol, or British), the movement of goods soon translated into the spread of people, information, and ideas, deeply affected the communities touched by such flows. According to historian of globalization William H. Mott, "Modern economic globalization transformed an expanding materialism into a social obsession with prosperity and growth and the conviction that economic prosperity deserved first priority among people's many social concerns....globalization implied restructuring not lonely political and economic relationships but also cultural perspectives."[8] Such effects were felt in the international arena as well as domestically, as certain groups benefited from the economic upheavals of globalism. Decolonization and economic prosperity in Europe brought guest workers, students, dissidents, and refugees to the UK, France, Germany, the Netherlands, Belgium, and Portugal. Hitherto homogenous communities adapted to and benefited from post-war cosmopolitanism, a process which expanded national consciousness while simultaneously altering it. Expatriate communities in the West worked for political, social, and economic improvements in their home communities. Improving communication links began to compress the time-space continuum, allowing for evermore knowledge of distant places and peoples. Economic development in the non-communist portions of the Pacific Rim steadily encouraged a liberalization of the political cultures of these countries. Japan, Korea, Taiwan, Singapore, and other countries in East Asia moved from authoritarian systems towards democracy (though "Asian" in form). In the "Free World," i.e., the market-based economies of North America, Western Europe, Oceania, and East Asia, technological innovation emerged as the key driver of progress in from the 1970s onward for the global economic system. These new technologies connected rather than divided nations, states, and non-governmental organizations and endowed the capitalist states with new dynamics and encouraged greater levels of internationalism.

This economic dynamism was, however, dependent on freer and faster regimes of information. For the Soviet bloc, these developments were anathema. Moscow had directed its allies to avoid economic dependency on the West in the mid-1940s, lambasting the Marshall Plan as "dollar imperialism." Though the Kremlin established its own Eastern variant of a trans-regional economic scheme, COMECON, to mirror the benefits of the European Coal and Steel Community (the forebear of the European Union), state capitalism and Stalinist ideological constraints smothered any potential success for such programs. Worsening East-West relations, an embarrassing exodus of Eastern Europeans to the West, and societal upheaval in East Germany (1953) and Budapest (1956) forced Moscow to lock down the borders of its satellites, truly creating what Winston Churchill had so famously called an "Iron Curtain" in 1946. This barrier separated the economically-liberal states in the south, north, and west from the totalitarian ones in the east. Behind the Iron Curtain, Communist Parties exercised almost total control over information, media, and communications technology, a phenomenon which effectively de-linked the Soviet Bloc from the processes which were re-shaping the outside world.

Throughout the Cold War, the Soviet Bloc countries continued to pursue heavy industrial development often with spectacular successes, but generally failed to keep pace with technological innovation, especially in the field of information-centric technologies. Fear about the anonymous, fast, and free distribution of information which accompanied the computerization of the "Western" workplace prevented Warsaw, Leningrad, and Alma-Ata from emerging as hubs keeping up with developments in San Francisco, Dublin, and Seoul. Nikita Khrushchev's prediction that the USSR would surpass the developed economies of the West crumbled in last quarter of the twentieth century as European, North American, and capitalist East Asian economies implemented ever greater levels of technology into the workplace. This shift from heavy to light industry then into a post-industrial phase based on human capital and information rather than raw materials and super-factories left the Communist Bloc economies stuck in the past. This situation was only partially the result of self-imposed restrictions; in fact, Western countries' reticence to engage in technology transfer to the Communist Bloc also played a major part in the growing disparity.[9] Regardless of the cause, the socialist economies were hobbled by the dearth of high technology. A telling example is Poland, which had been the tenth largest economy in the world and had a rate of growth nearly equal to Japan's in the early 1970s, but quickly fell behind, nearly going bankrupt in the 1980s. The failure to keep up with changing industrial demands can be seen as key factor in this equation.

With Mikhail Gorbachev at the helm, the USSR began to open the floodgates to change in the second half of the 1980s. Gorbachev's greatest error was his gross miscalculation of the Soviet system's ability to simultaneously cope with the intertwined challenges that emerged from a tripartite reform policy of economic, structural, and social change. The People's Republic of China, for example, chose to implement a form of restructuring and acceleration at the end of the 1970s, but Beijing was always careful to prohibit the openness prescribed by Gorbachev. In hindsight, this moderation in reform seems to have been the necessary mechanism for preserving the communist party's monopoly on power. Gorbachev had unwittingly opened Pandora's Box. Despite half-hearted attempts to continue repressive policies of technology and information management, KGB surveillance, and ideological control, the virus of opposition spread through Soviet society, aided by the radical new networking technologies of the 1980s.[10] Information about the West, Stalin's crimes, and the weakness of the Soviet economy spread quickly just as the Kremlin had long feared it would. The emergence of comparatively free information spaces across the USSR and formerly communist Eastern Europe significantly aided the development of a long-retarded civil society, and made meaningful global coordination with diaspora communities and anti-communist organizations a reality. This change in communicative and informational structures became another catalyst for the collapse of the Soviet hegemony in Eastern Europe during the late 1980s and then the dissolution of the USSR itself in 1991.

A World Without Borders, But Still Obsessed By Them

Given the rapidly changing nature of the global affairs since the end of the Cold War, it is prudent to revisit some of the basic assumptions about the influence of ethnic minorities in world politics. Undoubtedly, the widespread and penetrating implications of the collapse of the USSR have prompted the revision of long-held truths in a number of fields from economics to sociology. The challenges of living in this world of powerful transnational, non-state actors, innumerable cross-border flows and viscid linkages of people, goods, information and finance, and decaying states have deeply impacted national identity. Traditional studies of nationalism and national identity in an environment where states were the preeminent actors in international affairs. It has been prudent, therefore, to question some of the dominant theories of nationalism since 1991. An increasing contingent of scholars is now revisiting the nation in the age of globalization and attempting to divorce their analysis from long-held Westphalian prejudices towards nations, national identity and nationalism.[11] National identity, according to such scholars, is not immune to the effects of the time-space compression brought about by the amorphous but undeniable phenomenon of globalization.

Currently, we are witnessing a radical reshaping in the ways in which human beings are constructing and maintaining communities while identities are shifting both upwards and downwards in much of the world. While there is nothing novel about identity shift, the extent to which it has seemed to accelerate in the latter decades of the twentieth century has prompted increased scrutiny in the social sciences. Globalization, regionalization, and localization are all happening concurrently; however, these processes are occurring unevenly around the globe.[12] Large scale regionalization of culture, economics, and education are emerging across the globe. The most obvious example is in Europe where the increasing mobility of continent's people, labor, capital, media, ideas, and goods has created a geo-political space where national borders are less relevant than at any time in the past four centuries. While the European common market remains the paragon, collective economic spaces are also emerging in sub-Saharan Africa, North America, and elsewhere, which are rapidly reducing the importance or international borders between the countries in these regions.

Technological unification, the spread of transnational organizations, regional integration, and qualitative changes in the Westphalian state system have all furthered this evolution. In twenty-first century Europe, Glaswegians retire to the rocky shores of Croatia, Latvians pick mushrooms in Eire, Deutsche Bank meetings are held in English, the Euro has replaced the drachma, Belgian chocolates are sold in Brno's hypermarkets, and the Anglo-Saxon economic model has been adopted by and then exported from Estonia. Such regionalization in not however confined to the European Union. In Asia, economic ties and cultural hybridity between the People's Republic of China, Japan, and South Korea are binding nations which once were diehard enemies.[13] Australia, driven by geographic and economic realities, is now whole-heartedly orienting itself towards Asia, and making political decisions which increasingly distance the country from its erstwhile Anglophone allies in Europe and North America.[14]

Diasporas are a large part of this process. Overseas Chinese have developed transnational identities and mobility across the Pacific Rim and, acting as economic and social elites, have created cultural continuums that bind San Francisco, Sydney, Taipei, Kuala Lumpur, Hong Kong, Seoul, Tokyo, Beijing, and Shanghai. Latino immigration has likewise begun to change American culture, as has North African and South Asian immigration to Europe. Gastarbeiter communities and established diasporas in the developed world are increasingly connected to their homelands through technology and more politically active than ever in their host societies bringing the controversies of distant states into the political mainstream of Canadian, British, US, and German politics.[15] Across the Middle East, transnational media products like Al Jazeera are influencing millions of people in dozens of countries and rebinding linguistic communities long separated by political boundaries. Likewise, the emergence of pan-Islamic religious parties like the Hizb ut-Tahrir (Party of Liberation) have quite successfully sought to reshape the discursive space in the Dar al-Islam or Muslim world regarding the importance (or lack thereof) of political boundaries separating Muslim peoples from the Maghreb to Mindanao, often using the Internet as a tool of such activities.

Benjamin Barber's prescient essay "Jihad vs. McWorld" identified two powerful forces that are tearing at the fabric of (post)modern society: globalism and tribalism.[16] As formerly national societies are being strung together by global markets, products, and media, they are simultaneously being ripped apart by parochialism often based on ethnic or religious differences. It is only natural that disaffected groups such as national minorities, religious fundamentalists, and other groups whose interests have been challenged rather than supported by the state system tend to reach for the tools at hand to perforate the once sacrosanct position of the state as the ultimate source of authority. According to international scholar Hedley Bull, the greater the "tyranny of existing concepts and practices," the easier it is for non-state actors to supplant part or all of the loyalties of a given subset of people.[17] It is not surprising that radical non-state actors have emerged as powerful and disruptive forces in countries where the state has doggedly pursued its own interests without the input of civil society. While this phenomenon is hardly new, the capacity of such actors to communicate and coordinate across national boundaries with ease and anonymity is rather novel. Global media, commercial networks, and transportation systems have coalesced in such a way that the challenges posed to states by non-state actors is significantly higher now than in at least the past few centuries.

Al Qaeda draws its members and support from Arab societies that have been cowed by decades of ossified rule by dictators of many stripes (theocratic, dynastic, socialist, nationalist, etc.), but also dependent on "rootless," second-generation immigrant Muslims in Europe, Russia, and North America who have been affected by a form of globalization that "provides an opportunity to dissociate Islam from specific cultures and develop a universal model that can work beyond cultural confines" and be used for violent purposes.[18] Moving identity politics in the opposite direction, stateless minorities from the Muslim world have also used the diasporic experience to make their voices heard on the global stage. The Palestinian diaspora has organized itself into a powerful, global force, as have Kurds in Germany, Baloch in Britain, Berbers in France, etc. Identity politics have been untethered from their homelands by the various processes of globalization. According to political scientist Rey Koslowski, "Jet airlines, international telephone service, satellite television, fax machines and the Internet have made it easier for emigrants to maintain contact with their homelands and participate in homeland politics. Increasing international migration, the information revolution and democratization have propelled a globalization of domestic politics of many states similar to the globalization of national economies."[19]

The trends of globalization and tribalism feed off one another and create a witch's brew of instability in transitional states.[20] Eastern Europe and the former republics of the Soviet Union have emerged from decades of communist domination only to grapple with pernicious questions of ethnicity and identity that were once thought confined to the dustbin of history. The cataclysmic collapse of communism was compounded by a turbulent entrance into a world community defined by global flows of people, capital, information, and goods. This rapid succession of events exacerbated the complex situation faced by post-communist countries. The violent ethnic fractures in Yugoslavia, neo-Nazism in Russia and East Central Europe, and violent Islamism in the Caucasus and Central Asia represent just a few of the manifestations of reduced state authority, increased mobility, and access a free and often biased media that shape Western perceptions of Eastern Europeans and former Soviet citizens.

Ethnic separatism—though overshadowed and even co-opted by Islamist struggles—continues to grow on a global basis. Zbigniew Brzezinski, former National Security Advisor to U.S. President Jimmy Carter, has identified what he calls the "Global Balkans"—a continuum of fracturing and fractious states which spans the World Island of Africa, Europe, and Asia.[21] Building on his late 1970s identification of a "arc of crisis" in the Muslim world, Brzezinski continues to identify the band of territory from the Suez Canal to Xinjiang as the future danger zone as local and global conflicts converge. Few countries in the swath of territory which stretches from East Africa through southern Eurasia and into Southeast Asia do not face either separatist insurgents or threats from international purveyors of violence. In the Philippines, Thailand, Uzbekistan, India, Afghanistan, Russia, and Israel— the two forces are often combined. In the words of historian Jerry Z. Muller, "Whether politically correct or not, ethnonationalism will continue to shape the world in the twenty-first century."[22] Such a powerful conflation of identity bodes ill for the future of strong, unitary states based on the now almost passé model of one nation, one country.

New Countries, Resurgent Regions, Failing States, and Globalized Struggles for Independence

The decade from 1989 to 1999 witnessed an explosion of new states onto the world stage. These new countries are part of what can be called the "Third Wave" of states to gain independence during the twentieth century.[23] In the wake of the Great War (1914-1918), the demise of the Ottoman, Habsburg, and Romanov empires launched a host of new nations onto the world stage including Iraq, Czechoslovakia, and Latvia. After World War II, decolonization nearly doubled the number of internationally-recognized states adding Ghana, Algeria, and Indonesia among others. In the most recent manifestation of this ongoing process, the dissolution of the federal states of the USSR, Czechoslovakia, and Yugoslavia produced twenty-two new countries. In the 1991, the Soviet Union's fifteen socialist republics—Russia, Ukraine, Belarus, Moldova, Estonia, Latvia, Lithuania, Georgia, Armenia, Azerbaijan, Kazakhstan, Uzbekistan, Turkmenistan, Kyrgyzstan, and Tajikistan—gained independence. Each of these political entities had existed as Soviet Socialist Republics (SSRs) within the Soviet Union. This represented the highest echelon of autonomy within the federation. Despite a number of factors that bound these states together, ethnic and cultural differences that had been nurtured by Stalin's national delimitation and the Soviet Union's "affirmative action" empire made it easy for elites to play the national card once the shackles of the Communist Party's domination of the system were broken.[24]

In the post-totalitarian Europe, myriad nationalities have sought to establish their own voices since the Soviet Union's collapse. While certain ethnic diasporas attempted to maintain contact with their co-nationals during the Cold War, the Soviet-imposed Iron Curtain tended to ensure that such contact had little meaningful impact on the political development of socialist societies. In less than a decade, the cultural, communicative, economic, and informational barriers that had been so assiduously maintained by Moscow fell away. The vast geopolitical space which stretched from Brandenburg to Vladivostok was quickly opened up to the forces of economic, commercial, and cultural globalization. The successor states to the USSR spanned a wide range of political structures from pluralistic Lithuania to authoritarian Turkmenistan. Yet in each every case, there has been a tendency in post-Soviet states for non-state actors to make their voices heard. Unlike the decades of Soviet rule, subnational and transnational groups function as interstitial powers, capable of shaping policy and the development of society. The USSR was not the only post-communist fatality. Czechoslovakia's peaceful dissolution in 1993, the so-called "Velvet Divorce," added two more independent countries to the map of Eastern ·

Europe: the Czech and Slovak Republics. All but two of the Socialist Federal Republic of Yugoslavia's six constituent republics declared independence beginning in the 1990s. Slovenia and Croatia went first in June 1991, with Macedonia declaring independence a few months later. Bosnia and Herzegovina followed the next year. (In 2006, Serbia and Montenegro parted ways, followed two years later by Kosovo's declaration independence from Serbia.)

As these multi-ethnic federations abandoned the one-party system, national elites in the periphery leveraged changes in the global system to promote their own interests. Estonians, Latvians, and Lithuanians used glasnost to rewrite Soviet histories of the homelands. Along with Georgia, these recalcitrant republics pushed for independence from the Soviet Union, ultimately triggering similar centrifugal movements across Soviet Eurasia. As part of the "new" Europe, Slovaks employed the newly-accessible democracy to separate themselves from the paternalistic oversight of their Czech neighbors. In the most extreme case, Croats and Slovenes took up arms against their own federal army to gain independence, a decision which set off a decade of wars across the west Balkans. Communist-era leaders from Khrushchev to Josip Broz Tito had struggled to "keep the lid on" ethnic tensions. Part of this process meant constructing convoluted federative structures which guaranteed some level of cultural—if not political—autonomy to national minorities. Ironically, in the wake of communism's purported collapse, many of these ostensibly prophylactic delineations became fault lines and even conflict zones, as entry into the global marketplace triggered competition for resources which in turn acted as a magnifier of ethnic grievances.[25] While many authors have attributed the ethnic violence that spread across the region to "ancient hatreds" and "tribalism," the immediate causes of the conflicts stemmed from competition rooted in modernity, and—in some cases—postmodernity. According to Tim Heleniak,

> Suppressed ethnic grievances and territorial claims have come into the open as the result of the end of the cold war and the liberalization that contributed to the breakup of the Soviet Union, Yugoslavia, and Czechoslovakia. As new states seek to correct these grievances or assert claims, other ethnic groups are excluded. The response of many has been to migrate back to what they perceive to be their ethnic homelands. This massive, unplanned, and chaotic ethnic unmixing has had a negative impact on development and has led to increased poverty at a time when the states are also transforming their economies away from the centrally planned models they used for decades.[26]

In this environment of resurrected identities, the obsession with gaining international recognition, guaranteeing economic independence, and asserting uncontested sovereignty became the most pervasive issues among national minorities in postcommunist Europe after 1989. In each case mentioned above, the *national* triumphed over other considerations such as class, gender, etc.; however, in all cases, recognition of the changing structure of world economic markets, international transportation and communication networks, and global governance was evident.

In Western Europe, the resurgence of sub-state (and transborder) national identities was no less noticeable, but differed greatly from those of post-communist Europe. Under the aegis of NATO protection and aided by the common economic space afforded by the European Community, Hedley Bull's prognostication of a neo-medieval Europe began to reach fruition in the 1980s and 1990s. This trend was most noticeable in the larger and wealthier states of Western Europe: Britons rediscovered themselves as Scots, Welsh, and English; French re-manifested as Bretons, Occitans, and Alsatians; Spaniards reemerged as Basques, Catalans, and Gallegos; and Italians re-identified as Piedmontese, Sicilians, and Tyroleans. These fledgling identities have been complemented—rather than challenged by—the increasingly meaningful mantle of "European."

While the late 1960s and 1970s had seen the proliferation of separatist terror groups operating in the UK, France, Italy, and Spain, the success of the European project sapped support of such violent actors. In fact, the 1990s also saw significant progress on settling long simmering issues between regional separatists and their metropole adversaries. Waning support for regionalist terrorist groups can be partly attributed to changing economic and political conditions across the continent. The European Community's 1992 Maastricht Treaty pushed Europe closer towards a political and economic union, and created a milieu where regionalism could be promoted though legal and peaceful means (rather than by the gun or the bomb).

Regionalism has become a natural outgrowth the "loosening of the state framework" in European political space as more authority is granted to the various mechanisms of the European Union.[27] As regions accrue greater levels of autonomy, long–suppressed ethnic identity have flourished from Cornwall to the Basque Country to Lapland. Consequently, the "Europe of Regions" phenomenon has developed as fairly effective remedy against economically, politically, and socially disruptive self determination movements.[28] The "Europe of Regions" paradigm, rather being a formal politico-economic structure within European governance, is instead a conceptual device and an alternative political agenda driven by the notion that "sub-national entities have little by little acquired greater protagonism in the political, economic, social and cultural arenas to the detriment of nation-states."[29] In describing the situation in Western Europe, interdisciplinary sociologist Gerard Delanty states: "Regions are emancipating themselves from the tutelage of the nation-state, whose sovereign status has been much diminished by both the transnational processes over which national governments have little control and by bottom-up demands for new forms of subnational autonomy."[30]

Over the past several decades, the increasing mobility of Europe's people, labor, capital, media, ideas, and goods has created a geo-political space where national borders are less relevant than at any time in the past four centuries. Technological unification, the spread of transnational organizations, regional integration, and qualitative changes in the Westphalian state system have all furthered this evolution.[31] Today, Germany's *Länder*, Catalunya, Padania, and Scotland are all exercising their strength in a new environment more friendly to regional aspirations than has been the case since the Middle Ages. The "Europeanization"—a regionalized manifestation of the oft-used, yet conceptually ambiguous notion of globalism—of (western) Europe has triggered a reactive embrace of local values, languages, and identities. Across the continent, advocates of long-suppressed regional tongues, national minorities, and transborder communities are putting the new possibilities of European integration to work in defense of their own agendas. Whereas regionalists once operated singularly within the space of the nation-state, forced to play by the often arbitrary rules imposed on them from the metropole, these movements are now able to act in concert with one another, often making use of various structural mechanisms that encourage subsidiarity across the European Union.

The end of the Cold War also precipitated a relative new problem in international politics: the proliferation of failing and failed states. In part, this phenomenon resulted from the evaporation of the global ideological struggle for worldwide dominance that characterized the American-Soviet rivalry from 1948-1989. While the connection to the resurgence of national identity on the global scale may not be readily apparent, the role of sub-state nationalism cannot be ignored when discussing such phenomena. Political scientist Jean-Germain Gros defines failed states as "those in which public authorities are either unable or unwilling to carry out their end of what Hobbes long ago called the social contract, but which now includes more than maintaining the peace among society's many factions and interests."[32] In some cases such as Somalia, Chad, and Haiti, the failure of the state is a pernicious problem that afflicts nearly all parts of the country. However, in other cases, governments are denied the ability to exert influence over certain portions of their territory. Often, these areas are inhabited and dominated by ethnic and/or religious groups who view the central government as a threat to their interests.

In post-Soviet space, a number of states have been unable to extend sovereignty over their own territories. Over the last fifteen years, Azerbaijan, Moldova, and Georgia have failed to reincorporate lands lost before and after the breakup of the USSR. In Azerbaijan, Nagorno-Karabakh exists as a de facto independent republic as the result of an interstate war between Armenia and Azerbaijan which lasted from 1998 until a ceasefire in 1994. Today, Armenians represent about 95 percent of the population. This numeric domination result from an Azeri exodus from the region during the conflict in the early 1990s. Nagorno-Karabakh is not recognized by any foreign state (including Armenia), but possesses all other attributes of sovereignty. In neighboring Georgia, the situation is even more complicated. In the early 1990s, a civil war erupted pitting the Muslim Abkhaz in the country's northern Black Sea region against the majority Christian Georgian population. The Abkhaz were supported by their Circassian ethnic cousins and co-religionists from across the Russian border. The Abkhazian forces ultimately handed the Georgian military a stinging defeat and, since that point, Abkhazia has functioned as an independent state under Russian tutelage (though without formal recognition by Moscow of its independence). Wartime ethnic cleansing and subsequent Georgian emigration ultimately resulted in the Abkhaz establishing a plurality in the region.

In the north of Georgia, the Ossetians—an Indo-European people ethnically distinct from the Caucasian-speaking Georgian majority—have established the South Ossetian Republic which like Abkhazia functions as a de facto nation-state under Russia's protection. There is strong support among the population for accession to the Russian Federation and unification with the Republic of North Ossetia-Alania.[33] On the western shores of the Black Sea, another frozen conflict with its roots in the Gorbachev era continues to fester. Slavic-dominated Transnistria, known officially as Pridnestrovian Moldavian Republic, does not recognize the authority of the central government in Chişinău. Like Nagorno-Karabakh, Abkhazia, and South Ossetia, Transnistria has a government, parliament, military, police and postal system, as well as a constitution, flag, national anthem, and coat of arms, all distinct from Moldova's. Moscow likewise supports Transnistria and maintains a consulate in the capital, Tiraspol; however, as is the case with other breakaway republics, the Kremlin has not yet extended full diplomatic recognition.

Interestingly, Russia—a strong supporter of such de facto republics—expended a great deal of blood and gold in the North Caucasus in an attempt to extinguish its own separatists' efforts at independence. Inspired by the devolution of power from Moscow to the SSRs at the end of the 1980s, the Chechens—a Muslim Caucasian people who were violently incorporated into tsarist Russia in the nineteenth century—unilaterally declared the creation of the Chechen-Ingush Republic in 1990 hoping to ultimately gain independence from the Soviet Union. A year later, the Chechen political leadership dissolved its Soviet parliament and declared an independent Chechen Republic of Ichkeria. Moscow—fearing a second round of decolonization which might free Tatarstan and other integral parts of the newly-formed Russian Federation from its control—rejected Chechnya's declaration of independence as illegal. After 1991, Chechnya held an ambiguous status; the country possessed de facto sovereignty without international or Russian recognition of its independence.[34] The uncomfortable union lasted until 1994 when Boris Yeltsin, in a risky gamble, sent in troops to reintegrate the breakaway province. After two years of destructive war, a ceasefire allowed for Chechen self-rule without formal independence. Upon his ascension to power, Vladimir Putin renewed the conflict, ostensibly to prevent a spread of ethnonational and inter-religious conflict across the Caucasus (the late Chechen guerilla leader Shamil Basayev had provoked Moscow by conducting forays in the oil-rich, neighboring republic of Dagestan). Through military might and rule by proxy, Russia effectively reestablished authority over Chechnya, but continues to allow the region extensive autonomy. Importantly, as part of his greater "war on terrorism" within the Russian Federation (with the Chechen conflict at its heart), Putin was able to successfully reverse his predecessor's policies of "asymmetrical federalism." During his administration, Putin sapped the countries many ethnic republics of their autonomy and effectively restored centralized power in Russia reversing the dominant trend of increased ethnic autonomy across Europe and post-Soviet Eurasia.[35]

In other parts of the world, failing and failed states have also spurred a rise in minority ethnonationalism. Iraq represents the paragon of this phenomenon. Since the 2003 US-led invasion, the country has effectively devolved from a unitary state into a tripartite political entity. In the north, Kurdistan is almost completely disconnected from the rest of the country and behaves (though it is not recognized) as a sovereign actor on the world stage. As such, ethnic Kurds, a group that has long existed as a minority under Arab, Persian, and Turkish rule, now enjoy a quasi-independent nation-state to call their own. In the rest of Iraq, sectarian conflict between the minority Sunni Arabs and the majority Shiites has resulted in a functional split of the country along religious lines with separate police force, militaries, and economies. A similar division currently exists in Lebanon with Shi'a in the south living under de facto Hezbollah governance, while Sunnis and Christians in the north governing their own affairs under the nominal protection of the central government.

The current war in Afghanistan (2001-present) also unveiled lingering issues of the Pakistani state's failure to control its own territory. As many Taliban quit Afghanistan in the wake of the US-led invasion of the country, they fled to the tribal areas of Pakistan where their co-ethnics, the Pashtuns, form the majority. Generally beyond the reach of the Pakistan military, these areas effectively became a Pashtunistan mini-state, comprised of Afghan and Pakistani citizens. Regional instability also spurred on regional separatists in Pakistan's Baluchistan region as well as Kashmiri separatists across the border in India. Journalist Jeffrey Goldberg predicts the splintering of the current state system across the Muslim world in the coming decades with upwards of a dozen new ethnic and/or religiously defined states from the eastern shores of the Mediterranean to the Indus River. "[S]ince 9/11 America's interventions in the region—and especially in Iraq—have exacerbated tensions there, and have laid bare how artificial, and how tenuously constructed, the current map of the Middle East really is."[36] Goldberg's predictions for the greater Middle East echo those of Brzezinski, one in which waves of Balkanization lead to smaller and weaker states even more prone to conflict than the current array of regimes.

On the African continent, Sudan has been wracked by decades of civil war based on its ethnic diversity. Arab Muslims who control the central government in Khartoum fought southern separatists who were predominantly black African Christians and animists. More recently, the Arab *Janjaweed* militias—backed by the government—have engaged in an internationally recognized genocide against black Muslims in the Darfur region in the east of the country. Some Darfuri rebels, including the Darfur Liberation Front, advocate for secession of the region along territorial and ethnic lines. In central Africa, Rwanda was the scene of a massive genocide in the 1990s as the majority Hutus slaughtered some 800,000 ethnic Tutsis, people of mixed ancestry, and Hutus who tried to stop the carnage. The Tutsi victory over their Hutu enemies prompted a mass exodus of the latter to surrounding countries igniting the Second Congo War (1998-2003), also known as Africa's World War due the large number of state and non-state belligerents. The war in Africa's interior ignited many long-simmering ethnic rivalries, which had been ignored or even stoked during the decades of post-colonial rule. As the social contract between the state and its people withered, loyalties based on imagined ties of the nation, ethnic group, and clan filled the gap, creating what Robert Kaplan has described as "a pre-modern formlessness" akin to the situation that existed in medieval Europe.[37]

Even prosperous East Asia has not escaped the effects of a recent global resurgent in national liberation struggles; however, the increasingly global nature of domestic politics is more to blame than the failure of states. In the People's Republic of China, the effects of globalization have directly impacted its internal cohesion. Tibet, reincorporated into China shortly after the Communist Revolution, has become a magnet for democracy advocates in the West. Buttressed by the support of high profile international celebrities such as the Prince of Wales, the Brooklyn-based rap group The Beastie Boys, Icelandic songstress Björk, and American actors-turned-Buddhists Richard Gere and Steven Seagal, China's human rights record in Tibet has emerged as an international *cause célèbre*. This issue has been particularly supported by Western youth who have gravitated to the amorphous "Free Tibet" movement associated with the independence/autonomy campaign of the region's exiled spiritual leader, the Dalai Lama, but also use the issue as a sort of consumerist badge of youthful activism similar to the ubiquitous wearing of a Che Guevara T-shirt. Communications scholar Michael Santianni has further argued that the "movement" is a latter day example of Orientalism, which allows Westerns to construct their own imaginaries of the "utopian East" as a mechanism for condemning the spiritually bankrupt "West."[38]

In western China, another minority movement is underway, that of the Uyghurs, a Muslim, Turkic people who are historically and ethnically linked to Central Asia. Like the Tibetans, this ethnic group experienced their reduction to minority status in their own homeland. Over the past few decades, Han Chinese have settled in the Xinjiang Uyghur Autonomous Region in large numbers, outstripping the indigenous Uyghurs. According to Joshua Kurlantzick, "Worried about growing Uyghur separatism, Beijing tightened its control of Xinjiang, turning the region into the death-penalty capital of the world."[39] China's draconian measures against the assertion of Uyghur national identity radicalized many young people, a good number of who fled to Afghanistan where they gained terrorism training before returning to fight for independence from China. Generally ignored for most of the twentieth century, the Uyghurs have recently emerged as an important ethnic minority with global implications, a result of their Muslim faith, cultural ties to Afghanistan, and tenuous links between separatist organizations and transnational Islamist groups. After 9/11, the U.S. and other governments quickly complied with Beijing's request to label Uyghur separatists groups as "terrorist organizations," thus paving the way for even greater Chinese suppression of local activism. Under the umbrella of the surprisingly weak and ineffectual East Turkestan Islamic Movement, young radicals and China's over-reaction to the threat have effectively globalized the campaign for an independent Xinjiang and opened a new front in the Huntingtonian "clash of civilizations" between the Islamic world and its neighbors.[40]

The global "war on terror" and its blowback in the Muslim world have fueled ethnic separatism in other parts of Asia as well. In Thailand, a Pattani separatist movement reemerged with new vigor in 2001. While the current iteration of the movement has a Islamist patina, it remains at its core a reaction to long-term Thai economic and cultural imperialism directed at the Malays of the country's deep south, as well as the bifurcation of their ethnic community by international borders. As David Brown points out, the Malay-Muslims are still widely referred to as *phuak khaek* ('strangers' or 'visitors') in their own country.[41] In the Philippines, the nationalist aspirations of the various Moro peoples have taken even greater impetus from the post-9/11 restructuring of global politics. While *moro* ('Moor') was an exonym applied to all Muslims in the Spanish-ruled Philippines, the mantle has been adopted as collective identifier of nationhood by roughly a dozen ethnicities in the archipelago's southern islands. While the central government established an Autonomous Region in Muslim Mindanao in 1990, separatists have been agitating for an independent Bangsamoro ('Moroland'). Over time, the struggle has been slowly Islamicized, with the mainstream Moro National Liberation Front (MNLF) losing members to the Moro Islamic Liberation Front (MILF) and, more recently, to the Islamist terrorist group Abu Sayyaf. Abu Sayyaf has taken up the cause of an independent Bangsamoro as part of larger caliphate across southern and southeastern Asia. According to Filipino intellectual E. San Juan, Jr., "With the MILF's temporary suspension of its secessionist agenda, the Abu Sayyaf is the only Moro group that can claim to be the agency for realizing an independent Islamic state for the Moro nation."[42] Furthermore, after 2001, U.S. military support of the Philippine army against the group has hardened attitudes in the region, and stimulated transnational Islamist support for the organization.

Conceptualizing Minorities in the New World Disorder

Recognizing the radical local and transnational challenges to the accepted norms of national identity, this second portion of this text attempts to provide a theoretical and empirical salvo with hope of adding to the burgeoning understanding of the new realities of nationalism in the current century. In order to do so, it is necessary expand on the understanding of national minority identity in the post-Cold War environment before moving on to discrete case studies.

Using my own typology of contemporary minorities, I employ the following categories: archipelago nations, isolates, and diasporas.[43] Members of this first category, *archipelago nations*, can be subdivided into state-holders and stateless variants. The first group possesses an internationally-recognized nation-state to speak in their interests; however, a significant portion of the nation resides outside this political territory (typically in states which border the "ethnic homeland"). In some cases, these nationalities might be post-imperial minorities such as Serbs in Croatia, Hungarians in Romania, or Swedes in Finland. In other cases, this category is represented by some group that lacked political dominance in their historic homelands, such as the Albanians in Macedonia, the Slovenes in Italy, or the Uzbeks in Kazakhstan. Given the existence of an established nation-state, these groups often embrace irredentism and/or are used as pawns by both their state of residence and their ethnic homeland.

In contrast to these groups, there are also stateless archipelago nations. Such nationalities are the predominant group in a particular region, but lack a state to call their own. As is the case with Ruthenes (Rusyn), Lapps (Sámi), and Basques (Euskaldunak), these people may live in a contiguous space that overlaps multiple states. For instance, the Rusyn live in Transcarpathia, a region that includes parts of Poland, Slovakia, and Ukraine; the Sámi inhabit Sápmi, a region which includes parts of Norway, Sweden, Finland, and extreme northwestern Russia; and the Basques live in Euskal Herria which includes parts of northwestern Spain and southwestern France.[44] In other cases, an ethnic population may be widely scattered over multiple states, failing to form a majority in any given area in which they live. The Roma (Gypsies), Assyrians, and Aromanians (Vlachs) represent paragons of this type of minority. Roma live in every European country (and many non-European states), but do not form a majority in an region; Assyrians are a dwindling minority population in Iraq, Syria, and other Middle Eastern states; Aromanians live in small communities in Greece, Albania, and other Balkans countries.

Besides archipelago nations, there are also localized minorities which I often refer to as *isolates*. These groups inhabit comparatively small geographic areas within a single state, e.g., the Sorbs (Lusatian Serbs) of eastern Germany, the Bretons of western France, the Frisians of northeastern Holland, and the Romansch of the Switzerland. The Russian Federation lays claim to dozens of such nationalities, especially in Siberia and the North Caucasus, including the Nenets, Chuvash, and Nogai. Within this grouping, it is also prudent to mention the vast array of indigenous peoples in the "New World" from North America's First Nations to the Amerindian nations of Latin America to the Aborigines of Australia. The fate of such isolates varies widely, from the extremely successful situation of Catalans of Mediterranean Spain to the near extinction of the Finno-Ugric Livonians of Latvia, who numbered less than fifty in 1990. It is helpful to distinguish these groups from the two stateless transborder archipelago groups mentioned above because of political relationship between the minority and its state of residence generally falls within the framework of domestic politics. Although in some cases, diasporic activism or attention from the international community may globalize the issues at stake as is the case with Tibet (People's Republic of China) or Chechnya (Russian Federation).

The last category, *diasporas*, includes those immigrant communities that have settled in large numbers outside their ethnic homeland, but consciously maintain strong communal, ethnic, and linguistic identities in exile. While the term derives from the dispersal of Greeks and later Jews across the Mediterranean Basin, it has more recently come to be used by sociologists and political scientists to describe any group that resides in multiple countries, left their ancestral lands either involuntarily or as the result of some compelling motivation, and maintains some contact with the homeland through institutionalized networks of exchange and communication (Choi 2003: 11).[45] The largest groups in Western Europe are South Asians in Great Britain, North Africans in France, and Turks, Kurds, and Yugoslavs of various ethnicities in Germany. A number of Eastern European states now possess reasonably-sized communities of economic migrants, mostly from formerly socialist countries in Africa and Asia. The Czech Republic, for example, has a modest diaspora of Vietnamese, while the Russian Federation has an increasing number of Chinese immigrants, especially in the Russian Far East, as well as millions of Russophone immigrants from other former Soviet Republics.

In the Gulf States, there are significant communities of Palestinians, South Asians, and Southeast Asians, who live semi-permanently in the region. In the United States, Latino immigrants from Mexico, Cuba, Central America, and parts of South America represent the largest diasporic group, but sizeable numbers of Chinese, Indian, and Eastern European immigrants are also present. In addition to recent immigrants, there are also tightly-bound communities of co-ethnics around the world who sustain links to their kin in the ethnic homeland and third countries. In this category, we find overseas Chinese, Armenians, and Jews, as well as non-assimilated South Asians in parts of the British Commonwealth (South Africa, Guyana, Malaysia, etc.). In such cases, these communities tend to live in ethnic ghettos and retain their linguistic, cultural, and religious attributes from generation to generation, thus forming distinct and visible minorities within the larger national community, despite having full citizenship rights and often strong economic interests in their country of residence.

Until recently, all of these groups faced significant challenges to their community-building or sustaining efforts. As discussed earlier, the state's monopoly over the education system and mass media served as a powerful tool for marginalizing minority populations and/or encouraging assimilation.[46] Today, however, the dynamics of communication and consumption on the Internet has broken the state's monopoly on information distribution and disrupted the political, cultural and economic elite's—that is those representing the "core nationality"—ability to dominate thought, common sense and everyday assumptions within societies.[47] Mark Poster argues that the nation-state's ability to inculcate a monolithic national identity into beings within its borders was characteristic of the analog media system, and is no longer guaranteed in the digitized communications milieu of today.[48] In fact, the advent of ethnic broadcasting in countries like Canada during the late 1970s presaged the massive changes we are witnessing in the current "digital revolution."[49]

Cultural, national, and state identities are no longer exclusively in the hands of few authors, instead the power has shifted to multiple nuclei resembling a galactic configuration rather than a solar system.[50]

Internet-savvy elites among national minorities have stepped into the breach seeking to gain influence and capture some of the authority that has been wrenched from the state. In other cases, the Web has functioned as a stopgap measure for those national minorities which have been denied state-support or have seen their control of the state wither. In post-totalitarian space, this effect has been especially acute. For example, Lusatian Sorbs enjoyed significant state support by the German Democratic Republic (DDR) during its existence, but since German reunification in 1990 the Slavic residents of the Saxony and Brandenburg suffered from a sharp diminution of such aid. Across the former USSR, newly independent republics have abandoned the promotion of once-favored minority groups (Karakalpaks in Uzbekistan, Gagauz in Moldova, etc.) as part of their efforts to raise the status of the titular or "core" majority. For such groups and their diasporas, the Internet offers some consolation for the loss of Moscow's protection. The Web has also been used to prevent the dissolution or promote the resurgence of certain Communist-era identities, such as the Yugoslav nation or the East German nation. Yugonostalgia and *Ostalgie* have both benefited from cyberspace, which allows Internet users to access long-lost TV commercials, blog about the "good old days," and meet like-minded.[51]

While the classroom and the daily newspaper remain the engine of national identity production, the Web has opened up some new possibilities for cultural proselytizing. Representatives of all the different categories detailed above have begun utilizing the Web to mobilize their respective nations and diasporas. Such mobilization can be as banal as the mass distribution of ancestral recipes to more ominous actions, such as fund-raising efforts for arms purchases and Web-based coordination of terrorist activities. For those state-holding archipelago nations mentioned above, the Internet provides a powerful medium to connect distant "islands" of the nations with the ethnic homeland. State-supported Internet efforts combined with increasing numbers of Internet users in the ethnic homeland can be used to coax distant pockets of co-nationals into the mental space of the nation, and reestablish broken or weakened connections to the homeland. For example, Web-enabled schools in Macedonia are using the Internet to connect with ethnic Macedonian schoolchildren in Albania, thus bringing together portions of the nation who have not had regular contact for decades. Russia has similarly developed distance-learning programs that use cyberspace to connect ethnic Russians in the Republic of Kazakhstan with their "co-fatherlanders" in the Russian Federation. Non-governmental organizations representing the interests of minority co-nationals living outside the ethnic homeland are using the Web to collect information about the economic, social, cultural, and political conditions of their countrymen across Europe and Eurasia. Ultra-nationalists in the former Yugoslavia have even employed cyber-terrorism (Internet-based attacks on governmental Web sites and information resources) in support of their aims for independence or autonomy for their ethnic brethren "trapped" in hostile states.

Stateless dispersed peoples, have found solace in the Internet as a means of tying together powerless, though often numerically large, groups who reside in many states, but have none to call their own. Take for instance, the Assyrian Web site

"'Nineveh On-Line" which has now become the lifeblood for an endangered nation that has been cast about the globe over the millennia.

> Today, Assyrians are one of the most widely scattered indigenous peoples. Most Assyrian families in the U.S. generally have relatives in Australia, Sweden, Lebanon, Iraq, or Canada. For such a small nation scattered throughout the world, the Internet is a dream come true....Today, "Nineveh On-Line" is home to over 100,000 visitors per month....Now, the global community can learn a great deal about our traditions, language, and history on the Internet...The web pages presented by the U.S.-Assyrian community are well organized and offer plenty of information about the Assyrian culture and our activities. These pages have been developed by individuals, as well as organizations and links have been established between most of the pages. Beyond presentations on the church organization, our faith, and our history, we also see web pages with a focus on our ethnic background that refer to Assyrians, Arameans, and our language, "Syriac."[52]

The Web site of Assyriska (http://www.assyria.se/), an Assyrian-immigrant football team which is based in Södertälje, Sweden, has also proved to be a powerful tool in uniting the global Assyrian diaspora through the combined media of spectator sports, fandom, and Internet communication. Other stateless peoples have likewise adapted their political, cultural, and economic mobilization efforts to the postmodern era by employing cyberspace to partially accomplish long-held goals of linking the nation across state borders and gaining international and local recognition of their communities' rights. Through Internet-based communication and organization, these nations which have been long divided by international borders are now realizing some level of conceptual contiguity.

For isolates, cyberspace is an exciting new realm where members of small and often ignored nations can meet and exchange information about culture, history, and politics. The minimum requirements for launching a nation into cyberspace are modest. A single advocate for the nation, e.g., a college student with an interest in their nation's history and political situation, merely needs to gain access to the Web on regular or semi-regular basis. In today's world of user-friendly Web services, even a novice can produce a comprehensive site in a matter of hours. Countless Web sites exist on Yahoo's Geocities and other free Web hosting services that expound the values, mores, and attributes of tiny nations from Oceania to the Caucasus to the Amazon. A few examples include the Karelians of the Russian Federation, the Crimean Tatars of Ukraine, and the Gallegos of northwestern Spain.[53]

The Internet's capacity for the resurrection of dead or maintenance of moribund languages has been especially welcome by members of such nations. "Many smaller languages, even those with far fewer than one million speakers, have benefited from state-sponsored or voluntary preservation movements. On the most informal level, communities in Alaska and the American northwest have formed Internet discussion groups in an attempt to pass on Native American languages to younger generations."[54] Cornish, Manx, and other languages that are only a generation or two in the grave have seen new interest from Web-based advocates. Scots, the Germanic language prevalent in the Scottish lowlands until the seventeenth century, has benefited from the emergence of instant messaging which provides new learners with a private domain to practice their skills without the fear of humiliation that comes with learning a new language—especially one, which in the case of

Scots, was driven out of existence because it was seen as "socially inferior." Even in face of almost certain annihilation, the Web stimulates action quixotic national identity building projects, e.g., the previously mentioned Livonians have a Web site for almost every surviving member of their linguistic community.[55]

While few analysts expect the Web to keep these endangered languages from falling out of daily use, there is optimism that they will be permanently preserved in cyberspace, thus differentiating the dead languages of today and tomorrow from those countless tongues lost forever in the past. Roughly a third of the world's 6,000 languages have 1,000 or fewer speakers left and many of the younger generation are failing to learn these languages from the parents and grandparents.[56] It is expected that upwards of 80 percent of the world's languages will be dead or moribund by the end of the current century. Much of the blame can be laid at the feet of imperialism which promoted the use of conqueror's language as lingua francas across diverse linguistic spaces. As a result, a small number of "conquering" languages replaced myriad "conquered" languages in Central and South America (Spanish), in North America and Australia (English), and elsewhere. State languages have also been a factor, with Hindi, Bahasa, and Russian respectively eclipsing the languages of ethnic minorities in India, Indonesia, and the Russian Federation. Today, global capitalism keeps the pressure on small languages as the young tend to spend more time on studying English (or another commercial language such as Mandarin or Swahili) than on maintaining their ancestral language. However, the Internet makes distance learning and inter-generational contact possible for those members of the nation willing and able to maintain their ancestral tongues.[57]

The impact of global media is most perceptible among immigrant diasporas and *Gastarbeiter* ('guest worker') communities. During the last major wave of American immigration (1890-1910), communication between immigrants and their homeland could take as long six months if not more and information provided through newsletters and newspapers were meager at best. Conversely, contemporary industrialized countries with large immigrant populations have witnessed an explosion of satellite and cable consumption among its immigrant population over the past two decades. Internet-based remittances, combined with text messaging through mobile phones and Internet access to local as well as national media content in the homeland, has radically lessened the emotional demands placed on immigrant communities. The advent of the Internet allows distant expatriates to maintain daily contact with their homeland though local news Web sites, email, instant messaging, even weather and religious news. Salaam.co.uk, for example, provides tens of thousands of British Muslims with information about the beginning of Ramadan, Islam's holiest month when Muslims are required to fast from sunup to sundown.

Today, communication is nearly instantaneous and generally reliable when compared to previous methods of information transmission. Additionally, the dynamics of the Internet allow information to "pulled" by rather than "pushed" to immigrants as they are able to decide what types of information they want and when. Thus, the socio-geographic conditions which encouraged the development of tight ethnic ghettos in previous decades and centuries have lessened.[58] Today, an immigrant can use a combination of e-commerce, instant messaging, satellite TV, and Web-based news sources to create a conceptual, micro-universe of the homeland which is superior to that available to earlier generations.[59] Web-based broadcasting of ethnic media can now be accessed in Juneau, Alaska as easily as in Los Angeles, CA—the epicenter of ethnic broadcasting in the United States with stations for the Armenian, Persian, Filipino, Korean, and other diaspora communities. Furthermore, children born in diaspora can now use the Web for connecting to their peers in their ethnic homeland, as an educational resource, and for other identity-building purposes. According to Abril Trigo, the contingency of *migrancy* (the dual challenge of geographic displacement and downward socio-economic mobility) is the "black hole where the nation fails,"[60] but migrant communities can avoid such failure through nation-building efforts based on frequent and sustained communications and cultural exchange over the Internet.

The Internet can even serve to provide context to pan-national movements. A good example is the proliferation of pan-Turkic and pan-Turanian sites which attempt to reconstruct the lost (or—according to some linguists—completely imaginary) bonds between the Uralic (Finno-Ugric) and Altaic (Turkic, Mongolic, and Tungusic) peoples of the world from Helsinki, Finland to Istanbul, Turkey, to Almaty, Kazakhstan to Ulan Bator, Mongolia. In addition to promoting cultural links, the sites often attack the policies of "imperial states" in Inner Asia, especially the People's Republic of China, the Russian Federation, and the United States. Modern pan-Turkism demonstrates striking similarity to an earlier iteration of this internationalist ideology, which relied on newly-popularized mass media of newspapers such Ismail Bey Gaspıralı's *Tercüman* ('The Interpreter') and Yusuf Akçura's *Türk Yurdu* ('Turkic Motherland'). These newspapers were published across the Turkic information space from the Balkans to Western China. The *lingua franca* of the time was a simplified form of spoken Turkish used by the Tatars of southern Russia; today it is most often English (the language the elites from Anatolia, the Caucuses, Central Asia, and Xinjiang tend to share more than any other, although Russian is still the prevalent mode of inter-ethnic communication for those Turkic peoples from the former Soviet Union). Similarly, pan-Arab, pan-Slav, and other pan-ethnic elites have launched into cyberspace attempting to use the Web for political and/or cultural mobilization. Given the real world contemporary and historical issues that separate these peoples, it is like that these "empires of forgetting" will only exist in cyberspace.[61]

In addition to above mentioned groups, there are even contrived nations being created on the Internet. Michael Dahan and Gabriel Sheffer call these groups "purely virtual" national communities.[62] Communities such as Freedonia, Nova Arcadia, the Republic of Melchizedek along with other virtual nations are not based on any specific territory, but which model their cyberspatial activities in such a ways to appear as if they truly represent a nation. "These groups are often based on a singular political ideology, such a libertarianism or various forms of monarchism, or on either honest or fraudulent enterprises" and do not typically aspire to create independent states, although a few do in fact argue for realization of some form of territorial acquisition.[63]

The use of the Internet by challenged nations parallels similar political actions conducted by countless interest groups across the globe. By utilizing ever more powerful search engines that scour the World Wide Web for content, individuals are now able to virtually connect with millions of people who share their interests, ideas, and even prejudices. As Jim Falk states, "Communicating through the Web is a distinctive experience. The use of hypertext-embeddable addresses enables browsers to create almost seamless pathways from one piece of information to another, wherever the information sites may be located on the Net."[64] Furthermore, the Web allows groups who have been targeted by the state to circumvent traditional restraints on their ability to communicate with one another. According to Maya Raganathan, "The potential of the Internet to outperform other media lies in its capacity to reach those persons physically far removed from the area of publication. It is the only unregulated medium requiring minimal equipment that transgresses physical space and reaches across countries and continents...Communities that fear persecution are using the Internet not only to reach their members spread far and wide but by doing so manage to evade the power and authority of the perceived oppressor."[65] In many ways, cyberspace thus represents the perfect refuge for minority media.

The ramifications of selective consumption and community-building for national minorities, previously at the mercy of statist elite-dominated media platforms, are substantial. As Thomas Hylland Eriksen points out:

> Seen together, the increased mobility of people and the rapid spread of new communication and information technologies contribute to creating new conditions for collective identity management....Both tendencies have the potential of liberating individuals from place-bound identities embedded in myth and kinship; and, at the macro level, of breaking up the nationalist alloy of place, language, ethnic identity, state, culture and nationality into constituent components, leaving many options open and few identities questioned.[66]

The Internet, unlike its technological forebears, has eliminated the barriers of distance and time between widely dispersed ethnic groups creating conceptual contiguity among members of these groups. This, in turn, enables the creation and maintenance of virtual nations in cyberspace by elites with Internet access. The emergence of political active and Internet savvy elites among national minorities has some important ramifications for the future of state sovereignty. There has been a widening and a deepening of the community of authors with the proliferation of the Internet.[67] Furthermore, the entire relationship between producers/authors and consumers/readers has been changed by the advent of the computer-mediated communication. The time/space compression of cyberspace allows for a vast range of new activities.[68]

> [National minorities can now] systematically construct national and cultural identities over time. The other media of communication are constrained by the lack of space and time. A newspaper can contain only so many pages and a radio or television programme can run for only so many minutes/hours, whereas material on the Internet, at least in principle, can remain forever. This allows for the slow and careful construction of material, especially that relating to a community's historical and cultural antecedents.[69]

In cyberspace, minorities can virtually coalesce with their co-nationals, leaving behind the harsh realities of marginalization in a state dominated by an "alien" nation. The Internet, as stated earlier, is a mass media platform which replicates the television, newspaper, and radio, and thus tends to fill in where such media are unavailable or inaccessible for whatever reason.

In my own research, I have found that there are few truly novel methods of creating/maintaining the nation in cyberspace. Instead, I have witnessed Internet-enabled elites using the Web to fill gaps, optimize information consumption, and save time and money when trying to keep up contacts with the nation (whether it is in the form of friends and family, political developments, economic interaction, etc.). There have been and always will be alternatives to mainstream media—something that every ethnic entrepreneur is clearly aware of. The Internet is merely an evolutionary development for such elites to take advantage if they so choose. Cyberspace does not substantively alter the realities of daily life in London, Moscow, or Beijing, but it does offer those individuals who have access to it another realm of existence for a brief period of time. It also expands opportunities and horizons—it is in this nexus that we find the Web's truly revolutionary capacities. While the Web may alter perceptions, we must be careful not to overestimate the importance of such activity on political identity and mobilization. As Raganathan states:

> The nature and reach of technology has sparked utopian projections of the Net, especially in the political sphere. However, technology by itself is not effective. Certain social and political conditions need to be in place if the technology of the Internet is to be exploited to its fullest potential in the political sphere, especially in the creation of national identity.[70]

When I initiated this research project as a dissertation topic, my goal was to investigate whether or not access to the unregulated and limitless media space and new one-to-one and one-to-many webs of communication enabled by the Internet are resulting in increased nationalism and/or strong(er) national identity among minorities with access to the Web. While I did not find that Internet use necessarily increased nationalism or buttressed national identity, I did find that the Internet's impact on national minorities is not neutral. The following chapters, which cover these and other manifestation of Web-based nationalist projects, are intended to provide an incipient investigation of such activities and their impact on the future of minorities around the world.

Notes

1. I define globalization as the connectivity and interdependency which results from commercial, cultural, economic, and political interaction between states and non-state actors driven by sustained linkages of goods, people, communications, and transport networks.

2. The flipside of this world order transformation was, of course, new economic challenges stimulated by the shift towards a worldwide neoliberal economic system and the difficulty of sustaining local quiddity against the onslaught of global creolized culture in all its insidious forms.

3. I borrow this concept from Richard Langhorne's 2001 book *The Coming of Globalization: Its Evolution and Contemporary Consequences*.

4. For more on the Soviet Union's complicated relationship with globalization, see the chapter "Who Lost Russia" in Joseph E. Stiglitz, *Globalization and Its Discontents* (New York: W.W. Norton & Co., 2002).

5. As media historian Eric Louw points out, "The US's global hegemony, envisioned by the Atlantic Charter, could not be fully realized until Soviet power unraveled in the 1980s"; see Eric P. Louw, *The Media and Political Process* (London: Sage, 2005), 135.

6. During July 1944, 730 delegates from all 44 Allied nations gathered at the Mount Washington Hotel in Bretton Woods, New Hampshire for the United Nations Monetary and Financial Conference. The post-World War II economic system took its name from the location of this conference.

7. Richard Caplan defines shared sovereignty as "engagement of external actors in some but not all of the domestic authority structures of the target state for a limited period of time and on a consensual basis"; see Richard Caplan, "From Collapsing States to Neo-Trusteeship: The Limits to Solving the Problem of 'Precarious Statehood' in the 21st Century," *Third World Quarterly* 28, no. 2 (March 2007): 231-244.

8. William H. Mott, *Globalization: People, Perspectives, and Progress* (Westport: Greenwood, 2004), 51.

9. Gladys D. Ganley, *Unglued Empire: The Soviet Experience with Communications Technologies* (Westport: Ablex Publishing, 1996).

10. Interestingly, as the Soviet Bloc saw its surveillance regime undermined by the advances in ICT, Western governments—particularly the United States—began expanding their own capacities to monitor citizens at home and abroad; see Vincent Mosco, "Communication and Information Technology for War and Peace," in Colleen Roach, *Communication and Culture in War and Peace*. Newbury Park: Sage, 1993.

11. See Hedley Bull, *The Anarchical Society: A Study of Order in World Politics* (London: Macmillan Press, 1977); Valery A. Tishkov, "Forget the Nation: Post-Nationalist Understanding of Nationalism," *Ethnic and Racial Studies* 23, no. 4 (November/December 2000): 625-650; Jürgen Habermas, *The Postnational Constellation: Political Essays* (Cambridge: MIT Press, 2001); and Sheila L. Croucher, *Globalization and Belonging: The Politics of Identity in a Changing World* (Lanham, MD: Rowman & Littlefield Publishers, Inc., 2004).

12. Joshua A. Fishman, "The New Linguistic Order," *Foreign Policy* 113 (Winter 1998-99): 26-40.

13. Aihwa Ong, *Flexible Citizenship: The Cultural Logistics of Transnationality* (Durham: Duke University Press, 1999).

14. Samuel P. Huntington, "Clash of Civilizations," *Foreign Affairs* 72, no. 3 (Summer 1993): 22-49.

15. See for instance, the essays in Rey Koslowski, *International Migration and the Globalization of Domestic Politics* (London and New York: Routledge, 2005).

16. Benjamin R. Barber, "Jihad vs. McWorld," *Atlantic Monthly* 269 (March 1992): 53-65.

17. Bull, *The Anarchical Society*, 258.

18. Olivier Roy, *Globalized Islam: The Search for the New Ummah* (New York: Columbia University Press, 2004).

19. Rey Koslowski, *International Migration and the Globalization of Domestic Politics* (London and New York: Routledge, 2005), 1.

20. Barber, "Jihad vs. McWorld."

21. Zbigniew Brzezinski, *The Choice: Global Domination or Global Leadership* (New York: Basic Books, 2004), 42.

22. Jerry Z. Muller, "Us and Them," *Foreign Affairs* 87, no. 2 (March/April 2008): 18-35.

23. Robert A. Saunders, "Buying into Brand Borat: Kazakhstan's Cautious Embrace of Its Unwanted 'Son,'" *Slavic Review* 67, no. 1 (Spring 2008): 63-80.

24. See Terry Martin, *The Affirmative Action Empire: Nations and Nationalism in the Soviet Union, 1923-1939* (Ithaca and London: Cornell University Press, 2001).

25. Surprisingly, the Russian Federation—the successor state to the Soviet Union—avoided the fate of the Yugoslav Federation with the exception of the two Chechen conflicts (1994-1996 and 1999-2009). Arguably, this was the result of President Boris Yeltsin's realpolitik embrace of asymmetrical federalism, which granted almost total sovereignty to many of the country's ethnic republics such as Tatarstan, Yakutia (Sakha), and Kalmykia.

26. Tim Heleniak, "Ethnic Unmixing and Forced Migration in the Transition States," *Beyond Transition* 10, No. 4 (August 1999), http://www.worldbank.org/html/prddr/trans/julaug99/contents.htm (12 October 2004).

27. Ole Wæver, "Europe since 1945: Crisis to Renewal," in Kevin Wilson and W. J. van der Dussen, *What is Europe? The History of the Idea of Europe* (New York: Routledge, 1995), 198.

28. Stefan Wolff and Marc Weller, "Self-Determination and Autonomy: A Conceptual Introduction," in Marc Weller and Stefan Wolff, *Autonomy, Self-governance and Conflict Resolution* (London: Routledge, 2005), 2.

29. Susana Borras-Alomar, Thomas Christiansen and Andres Rodriguez-Pose, "Towards a 'Europe of the Regions'? Visions and Reality from a Critical Perspective," *Regional & Federal Studies* 4, no. 2 (Summer 1994): 1-27. Formal institutions associated with the "Europe of Regions" include Assembly of European Regions (AER) and the EU's Committee of the Regions (CoR).

30. Gerard Delanty, "Northern Ireland in a Europe of Regions," *Political Quarterly* 67, no. 2 (April-June 1996): 127-134.

31. Bull, *The Anarchical Society*, 254-256.

32. Jean-Germain Gros, "Towards a Taxonomy of Failed States in the New World Order: Decaying Somalia, Liberia, Rwanda and Haiti," *Third World Quarterly* 17, no. 3 (September 1996): 455-471.

33. Until 2004, Ajaria—a region on the country's southern Black Sea coast—also functioned outside of Tbilisi's control. Populated by Muslim Georgians known as Ajars, the region functioned outside the scope of the central government and enjoyed strong support from the Kremlin which maintained a military base in the capital Batumi. However, upon his election to the presidency, Mikheil Saakashvili forced the issue and restored central control over Ajaria.

34. Only the Republic of Georgia and the Taliban regime in Afghanistan extended recognition.

35. See Robert A. Saunders, "A Conjurer's Game: Vladimir Putin and the Politics of Presidential Prestidigitation," in George Kassimeris, *Playing Politics with Terrorism: A User's Guide* (London: Hurst & Company, 2007), pp. 220-249.

36. Jeffrey Goldberg, "After Iraq," *Atlantic Monthly* 301, no. 1 (January/February 2008): 68-79.

37. Robert D. Kaplan, "The Coming Anarchy," *Atlantic Monthly* 273, no. 2 (February 1994): 44-77.

38. Michael Santianni, "The Movement for a Free Tibet: Cyberspace and the Ambivalence of Cultural Translation," in Karim H. Karim, *The Media of Diaspora* (London and New York: Routledge, 2004), pp. 189-202.

39. Joshua Kurlantzick, "The Unsettled West," *Foreign Affairs* 83, no. 4 (July/August 2004): 136-143.

40. Samuel P. Huntington, *The Clash of Civilizations and the Remaking of World Order* (New York: Simon and Schuster, 1997).

41. David Brown, "From Peripheral Communities to Ethnic Nations: Separatism in Southeast Asia," *Pacific Affairs* 61, no. 1 (Spring 1988): 51-77

42. E. San Juan, Jr., "Ethnic Identity and Popular Sovereignty," *Ethnicities* 6, no.3 (September 2006): 391-422.

43. In his comprehensive study *An Ethnic History of Europe since 1945: Nations, States and Minorities*, Panikos Panayi categorizes European minorities (including those in the USSR/Russian Federation) into the following three categories: dispersed peoples, localized minorities, and post-World War II immigrants and refugees. While this is a viable schema, I have found the need to further subdivide Panayi's categories given the increasingly complicated nature of minority national identity after 1989.

44. In such cases, the various "islands" of the nation are divided by internationally-recognized borders, even when these peoples possess cultural and conceptual contiguity.

45. Inbom Choi, "Korean Diaspora in the Making: its Current Status and Impact on the Korean Economy," in C. Fred Bergsten and Inbom Choi, *The Korean Diaspora in the World Economy* (Washington: Peterson Institute, 2003), pp. 9-27.

46. It should be noted, however, that in rare cases (Syria under the Alawite al-Assad dynasty, Iraq under the Arab Sunnis, South Africa under apartheid, etc.), ethnic minorities have actually maintained control of the state apparatus (see Chua 2002).

47. Jeffrey Layne Blevins, "Counterhegemonic Media: Can Cyberspace Resist Corporate Colonialism?" in Bosah Ebo, *Cyberimperialism? Global Relations in the New Electronic Frontier* (Westport, CT: Praeger, 2001), pp. 139-152.

48. Mark Poster, "National Identities and Communications Technologies," *Information Society* 15, no. 4 (October-December 1999): 235-240.

49. See Lorna Roth, *Something in the Air: The Story of First Peoples Television Broadcasting Canada* (Montreal: McGill-Queen's University Press, 2005).

50. Manuel Castells, *The Internet Galaxy* (Oxford: Oxford University Press, 2001).

51. See Maja Mikula, "Virtual Landscapes of Memory," *Information, Communication & Society* 6, no. 2 (June 2003): 169–186 and Paul Cooke, "Surfing for Eastern Difference: *Ostalgie*, Identity, and Cyberspace," *Seminar—A Journal of Germanic Studies* 40, no. 3 (September 2004): 207-220.

52. Albert Gabrial, "3,000 Years of History, Yet the Internet is Our Only Home," *Cultural Survival*, 10 June 2001, http://www.atour.com/government/docs/20010610a.html (22 October 2004).

53. For representative examples of each see, see http://www.geocities.com/Athens/4280/eng_index.html, http://www.euronet.nl/users/sota/krimtatar.html, and http://www.agalgz.org/, respectively.

54. Fishman, "The New Linguistic Order," 32.

55. Rohan Jayasekera, "Waiting for the Kingdom: Nations in Cyberspace are No Substitute for the Real Thing," *Index on Censorship* 29, no. 3 (May/June 2000): 140-145.

56. See Mark Abley, *Spoken Here: Travels among Threatened Languages* (Boston and New York: Houghton Mifflin, 2003).

57. Judy M. Iseke-Barnes, "Aboriginal and Indigenous People's Resistance, the Internet, and Education," *Race, Ethnicity and Education* 5, no. 2 (Summer 2002): 171-198.

58. The distribution of Latin American immigrants in the United States is a clear example of this new trend. Latino communities in the US, while remaining the largest in those states which are contiguous with land and sea routes (Texas, California, Florida, and New York), are flourishing in the Carolinas, the Plains states, and other non-traditional settlement areas for foreign migrants.

59. Face-to-face contact, however, is still a hurdle that the Internet is incapable of solving, but the dynamics of modern information and communications technologies certainly enable smaller communities to establish themselves outside the tradition entrepôts favored by immigrants (e.g., New York, London, Paris, etc.).

60. Abril Trigo, "Cybernation (Or, *La Patria Cibernetica*)," *Journal of Latin American Cultural Studies* 12, no. 1 (March 2003): 95-117.

61. Paul Ricoeur, *Memory, History, Forgetting*, trans. Kathleen Blamey and David Pellauer (Chicago: University of Chicago Press, 2004), xvi.

62. Michael Dahan and Gabriel Sheffer, "Ethnic Groups and Distance Shrinking Technologies," *Nationalism & Ethnic Politics* 7, no. 1 (Spring 2001): 85-107.

63. Dahan and Sheffer, "Ethnic Groups and Distance Shrinking Technologies," 90.

64. Jim Falk, "The Meaning of the Web," *Information Society* 14, no. 1 (November 1998): 285-293

65. Maya Ranganathan, "Potential of the Net to Construct and Convey Ethnic and National Identities: Comparison of the Use in the Sri Lankan Tamil and Kashmiri Situations," *Asian Ethnicity* 4, no. 2 (June 2003): 265-279

66. Thomas Hylland Eriksen, "Nationalism and the Internet," *Nations & Nationalism* 13, no. 1 (January 2007): 1-17.

67. Michael Marien, "New Communications Technology: A Survey of Impacts and Issues," *Telecommunications Policy* 20, no. 5 (June 1996): 375-387.

68. George Bugliarello, "Telecommunications, Politics, Economics, and National Sovereignty: A New Game," *Technology in Society* 18, no. 4 (December 1996): 403-418.

69. Maya Ranganathan, "Nurturing the Nation on the Net: The Case of Tamil Eelam," *Nationalism and Ethnic Politics* 8, no. 2 (Summer 2002): 51-66.

70. Ranganathan, "Potential of the Net to Construct and Convey Ethnic and National Identities," 265.

Part II
Homo-Cybericus—Genus and Species

Chapter 4
Electronic Irredentists: Albanians Seeking Unity in Digital Space and Virtual Places

Merriam-Webster defines irredentism as "the principles, policy, or practice of a party or of persons that seek to incorporate within their national boundary territory of which their nation has been deprived or of which the population is ethnically closely related to that of their nation."[1] The term derives from the Italian word *irredento* ('unredeemed'), a rallying cry from the mid-1800s when Piemontese, Romans, and Genoese struggled to create a unified state out of the various Italian-speaking polities that stretched from the Alps to the Straights of Sicily. In the nineteenth century, such national redemptions certainly relied on "blood and iron" to reach fruition, but they were equally dependent on the effective use of media by political elites to attract a critical mass of supporters.[2] Various mass media from newspapers to motion pictures to radio and television have been used to promote such national projects. However, in each case, the ability to disseminate propaganda faced the threat of interception by state actors. The original irredentists, the Italians, had to avoid the Habsburg secret police and armed Pontifical Volunteers alike in order to provide supporters with printed materials supporting the Risorgimento. Latter-day irredentist projects—from the Irish's campaign to unite the Emerald Island to Chinese efforts to reclaim Taiwan—have all had to grapple with the difficulties of penetrating the well-policed airwaves of their neighboring states. Yet with the end of the twentieth century, the emergence of cyberspace made reaching out to sympathetic forces somewhat more plausible. This revolutionary communications platform is now being employed in irredentist projects from Western Europe to Southeast Asia.

The Albanians—a nation whose language and cultural identity have been consistently suppressed by waves of conquerors (Romans, Byzantines, Ottomans, Serbs, etc.)—make an especially interesting case study for understanding the impact of new media on national identity in the postmodern era. This chapter examines the use of the Internet as a tool for achieving irredentist goals, specifically, the linking together of Albanians in Albania proper, in the irredenta, and in diaspora. Although this "redemption" is occurring in virtual rather than geopolitical space, it is my contention that the use of the Internet is promoting conceptual contiguity among the Albanians who have long been riven by international borders. My research demonstrates that

95

cyberspace is promoting linguistic and cultural homogeneity among Albanians across time and space. In order to provide a historical backdrop for this phenomenon, I begin with a discussion of the peculiar nature of national identity in the Balkans, and the impact of post-Ottoman state-building projects on the Albanian nation. I then proceed to a discussion of the Internet as a mechanism for enabling diasporic identity across large spaces, political boundaries, and generations. Subsequently, I discuss the role of the Kosovo War as a catalyst for the creation of a robust and multi-continental pan-Albanian cyberspace. I then turn to the advances made in crafting a shared culture and homogenizing the Albanian language since 1999. I end the chapter with some reflections on the Internet's impact on the political conditions of the Albanian people, specifically on its role in ameliorating the historical lack of national contiguity through a new virtual propinquity.

Millets into Nations: Ottoman "Cultural Pluralism" Gives Way to the Procrustean Nation-State

In Southeastern Europe, the problem of reconciling the state and the nation has proved especially acute. Prior to the nineteenth century, the Balkans' ethno-religious heterogeneity was accommodated through the Ottoman Empire's *millet* system, which allowed Orthodox Slavs, Ladino-speaking Jews, Turkish Muslims and dozens of other ethnies to live side-by-side in relative peace. According to Balkan specialist Jean-Arnault Dérens, "Millets were intermediary organizational groups to which non-Turks owed primary loyalties: the head of a millet then owed his loyalty to the Ottoman state."[3] This imperial structure allowed mediated forms of authority, with the religious leader functioning as the preceptor for the empire, as well as the shepherd of the flock. Historian George W. Gawrych terms this system an early modern form of "cultural pluralism."[4] As the domains of the Ottoman Empire shrunk, new nation-states sprouted up across the Balkan Peninsula, and with them came marooned nationalities.

> The appearance of national minorities was a direct consequence of the drive to create nation states: where the political legitimacy of the state is not founded on ethnic/national criteria, the concept of national minority is meaningless. And areas within the new state frontiers could not possibly coincide exactly with the territories of the new nations, which were mostly ideological constructs. The inevitable result was the creation of transborder minorities.[5]

Though the homogeneity of Western European countries is often overstated, the internal ethnic diversities of the French, British, and Spanish populations are minimal when compared to that of the Balkans states, where an area the size of Maryland can have contain as many as thirty different nationalities, including such groups as the Armenians, Sephardic Jews, Rusyn, Pomaks, Circassians, Goranac, Torbesi, Szeklers, Vlachs, and Jevgs.

The Albanians, as a majority Muslim population (though containing sizeable Orthodox and Catholic groups), were faced with an especially difficult quandary as Ottoman power waned in the Balkans. According to noted Balkan historian Maria Todorova, "The position of acquiring autonomy without breaking away from the empire was dominant among the Albanians, who not only became its strongest champions but staunchly supported it to the end."[6] Writing in 1878, the Albanian reformer Sami Frashëri (also known as Şemsettin Sami) articulated the extent of Albanian nationalist goals: a "special homeland" (*vatan-i hususi*) for the Albanian people within the "general homeland" (*vatan-i umumi*) of the Ottoman Empire.[7] This orientation was rooted both in *realpolitik* and idealism, including "the fear of encroachments of the newly formed neighboring nation-states" and "a political affinity based on religion and the special status Albanians had acquired in the empire."[8] Ethnographer Stark Draper concurs stating, "[T]here was little reason for the [Albanian] Muslims to identify on national bases; they were the favored people of the Empire with many of their best and brightest serving in the Ottoman administration."[9] As the nineteenth century waned, the territorial appetites of the Greeks, Serbs, and Bulgarians—all whom were pursuing "greater" versions of their recently-independent rump states—grew dependent on the inclusion of the lands inhabited by the stateless peoples of the Balkans, i.e., the Albanians and—to a lesser extent—the Macedonian Slavs. As Muslims who lacked a powerful European patron, most Albanians naturally sought to preserve the status quo as long as possible (though it would be misleading to imply that all Albanians happily submitted to the Ottoman yoke). In doing so, the Albanians, at least for a time, became the paragon of Ottomanism.[10] From the Turkish *Osmanlılık*, Ottomanism promoted a convoluted brand of imperial patriotism that allowed for—in theory at least—cultural pluralism and equal treatment of all groups (Muslims and non-Muslims alike) before the law.

In explaining the failure of the Albanians to rally in support of the nascent nationalist movement initiated by the League of Prizren in 1878,[11] historian Misha Glenny identifies the absence of the institutional precursors for national mobilization: "They had no school system; they were without a properly codified language; communications among them were appalling; and they were divided not just by religion, but by class and regional tradition."[12] In comparison to their neighbors (Slavs and Greeks alike), the Albanians program for national development was severely stunted.[13] It was only the Young Turks' failed policies of Ottomanization and Islamicization after 1908—seen as predatory by many Albanians—that permanently turned the nation's elites against Istanbul.[14] Fortunately for the Albanian nation-makers, British diplomacy, Austria-Hungary's grand scheme for the Balkans, and Italy's craving for an informal colony on the eastern shores of the Adriatic serendipitously coincided in such a way as to procure an independent Albania in 1913, under the leadership of its reluctant German-born monarch Wilhelm of Wied. However, the young state collapsed within weeks of the outbreak of the Great War. Washington unpredictably intervened on behalf of Albania in the post-war negotiations, safeguarding the country against its neighbors' territorial ambitions.

As an independent state, Albania is uncharacteristically lacking in minorities when compared to its Balkan neighbors.[15] While there are small communities of Greeks, Aromanians, and Roma living in Albania, the population is overwhelmingly (98 percent) ethnic Albanian; these statistics, however, are highly controversial. Recently, the American Hellenic Institute denounced the U.S. State Department's publication of what it referred to as "inaccurate and misleading data" that Albania's Greek community accounts for only 1.17 percent of the overall population, a number which differs significantly from Greek NGO estimates of 8-12 percent.[16] Regardless of the heterogeneity of the Albanian state's population, the Albanian nation's contiguity suffers greatly from the border-making of the last 150 years. While many Albanians will quickly express their nation's good fortune in obtaining any sort of country out of the chaos of the Balkan Wars (1912-1913), the Albanian state has always failed to include large portions of the Albanian nation. As such, the Albanian nation represents a near-textbook model for irredentist politics, a fact not lost its Greek and Slavic neighbors who themselves are no strangers to the allure of irredentism. Out of total population eight million, less than half of all Albanians in live in Albania. Today, nearly 2 million Albanians live in Serbia and Montenegro: roughly 1.7 million in Kosovo, 67,000 in Serbia proper, and 31,000 in Montenegro. Another 500,000 Albanians reside in Macedonia. And while the numbers of indigenous Albanians in Greece is highly disputed, the figure is at least in the tens of thousands, and may be much higher.

Besides the archipelago Albanians—those who reside in states neighboring Albania proper—there are also the diasporic Albanian populations of Europe, Asia, North America, and elsewhere.[17] According to one estimate, "By the present day, approximately 25 percent of [Albania's] total population, or over 35 percent of the labor force, has emigrated";[18] this figure does not include the significant number of Kosovar and Macedonian Albanians who fled the strife of Yugoslavia's decade-long collapse. There are some 600,000 Albanian migrants in Greece today; and Italy has over 230,000 ethnic Albanians, most of whom are recent immigrants, but also included in this figure are the roughly 80,000 members of the long-settled Arbëreshë community.[19] The remaining million-strong emigrant community principally resides in Scandinavia, Switzerland, Germany, and other Western European countries.

In addition to the recent emigrants, there are older diasporic communities around the world. There are upwards of 5 million ethnic Albanians in the Turkish Republic;[20] however, the vast majority of this population is assimilated and no longer possesses fluency in the language, though a vibrant Albanian community maintains its distinct identity in Istanbul to this day. Egypt also lays claim to some 18,000 Albanians, supposedly lingering remnants of Mohammad Ali's army.[21] Sizeable second- and third-generation ethnic communities reside in the U.S. and Canada as well, though some members of these communities are being assimilated into their host societies.

The Kosovo Conflict on the Web: Catalyst and Catharsis for a Challenged Nation

Taking the above figures into account, one can easily argue that there are today more Albanian-speakers outside of Albania than inside it. Thus, the spread of the Internet was a welcome event for the dispersed Albanian nation. This is especially true regarding those Albanians living in wealthy European and North American countries where accessing ICT is rather easy and affordable. The Albanian enthusiasm for the Internet stems primarily from its potential to increase communication between members of all Albanian communities, especially those separated by interstate borders. However, Internet use remained rather tepid in the 1990s, due in large part to economic hurdles associated with Internet adoption. It was the catalyst of the Kosovo War that launched a critical mass representing the Albanian nation into cyberspace. "Albanians in Kosovo, lacking access to the traditionally most important electronic media and operating in a climate of Serbian police repression before the summer of 1999, relied on the Internet to build links and maintain contacts."[22] The events surrounding the Yugoslav government's increasingly repressive treatment of Albanians in Kosovo during the 1990s served as lightning rod for national identity, and simultaneously promoted increasing levels of political activity in cyberspace.[23] While not all Albanians view the same sites nor do they all communicate regularly with large numbers of co-nationals, Internet-enabled Albanian elites have constructed a significant pan-Albanian movement in cyberspace, one which had important implications for Albanian national identity.

Much of this activity revolved around creating a single ethno-political "space" for the Albanian people, a phenomenon which enemies of the Albanian cause increasingly characterized as "irredentism," itself a highly politicized term in the heterogeneous Balkans. Belgrade consistently framed the Kosovo crisis as a direct result of Tirana's non-existent attempts to create a "Greater Albania" by redeeming the irredenta in Montenegro, Kosovo, western Macedonian, and even Greece. The proliferation of Albanian Web sites, typically authored by diasporic or former Yugoslav Albanians, featuring maps showing such an enlarged state only fueled this fire. Such polemics (both on- and off-line) have left their imprint on an international community fearful of permitting any border changes, which they worry will inflame further irredentas, more ethnic cleansing, and additional wars in Southeastern Europe.

The beginning of a full-scale war in 1999, the federally-imposed information blackout in Kosovo, and Belgrade's accompanying disinformation campaign provided many Albanians around the globe with a reason to log on to the Internet for the first time. Uploaded images of dead Kosovar Albanians, orphaned children, and mosques in rubble peppered the Internet providing fuel for nationalist rhetoric.[24] Information-starved Albanians in diaspora, as well as minority Albanians in the former Yugoslav republic of Macedonia turned to the Internet to learn about the events going on inside Kosovo. Certain factions with the national liberation movement also began to use the Web for political organization and/or cyber-attacks on high profile symbols of Yugoslavia/Serbia. According to diaspora scholar Joshua Kaldor-Robinson:

> The conflicts within Yugoslavia were one of the first times when diasporas made use of new media, both as consumers and as producers…This ability to act both as consumers and as producers was of particular importance as it meant that two-way information flows between the homeland and members of the diaspora became achievable in a manner that was virtually impossible to regulate or censor. These information flows served to radicalize some sections of the various diasporas and at the same time allowed members of the diaspora to provide support to specific, and often extreme nationalist, groups within the homeland, in particular the [insurgent Kosovo Liberation Army].[25]

A number of major sites emerged as tool for information distribution in the Albanian language including Kosovo News Agency (http://Kosovopress.com) and Kosovo Information Center (http://www.Kosovo.com).[26] According to media specialist Łukasz Szurmiński, these local news sites provided a "priceless source of information for analysis allowing insight to given event from different and often new points of view."[27] Though these sites tended to be plagued with overt propaganda, they provided Albanians and other interested parties with "useful documents and articles that

[were] not easily found elsewhere."[28] Kosovopress, the media organ of the Kosovo Liberation Army, broadcast news via the Internet throughout the war, even when most other Albanian-language media outlets in Kosovo were shut down. Though the Serbian authorities and various Internet-enabled elites acting in support of Yugoslavia eventually launched an information counter-offensive in an attempt to demonize the Albanian netizens, "the Albanian side was the first to perceive the advantages of this modern medium and opened its own websites, with the most active being that of the Kosovo Information Centre, controlled by Albanian leader Ibrahim Rugova."[29]

English-language sites like the Kosovo Crisis Center (http://www.alb-net.com/index.htm) not only served to provide information to the Albanian community in the US, UK, Australia, and Canada, but also helped shape the discourse, perception, and policy positions of Western governments and their publics. Calvert Jones' research on the Kosovo Crisis Center Web site demonstrates how the site's authors attempted to globalize the ethno-political issues in Kosovo by framing Serbia's new anti-Albanian education policies as "apartheid," an apartheid which (according to the site) was alive and well in the "heart of Europe."[30] Jones argues that sites like the Kosovo Crisis Center were especially effective for two reasons: 1) NATO countries encouraged their citizenry to track developments in Kosovo online; and 2) Western media outlets frequently pointed their readers to local, pro-Albanian sites.[31]

The Kosovo War has been widely referred to as the first "Internet war."[32] According to Thomas Keenan, Director of the Human Rights Project, "it deserves the name only because the medium became a battlefield and information a weapon, for almost all of the combatants."[33] William Elison, a scholar of online rebel movements, points out that even in the middle of a bloody conflict, the site Kosovo Crisis Center Web sought elevate the debate about Kosovo's status by providing links to academic texts on the antiquity of Albanian presence in the Balkans, maps of the region, and the text of Rambouillet Interim Agreement (Elison 2000: 129).[34] Today, the site still hosts these documents along with such dated texts as "The Most Recent Serbian Blueprint for Extermination of Albanians from Kosovo" (1997), "Memorandum on Kosovo and the Albanian Question in Former Yugoslavia" (1991), and a variety of stale articles from the *New York Times* about Serb atrocities in the province.

Perhaps the most salient use of the Web for political coordination was the establishment of a Web address for the provisional government of Kosovo (http://www.Kosovo.org) in the midst of the conflict. As Elison states:

> Although the net government is a virtual government, it still has some of the symbols of an official government—the declaration of intent, the double eagle, and a roster of leaders. It relies on the Rambouillet Conference of February 23, 1999, as a kind of founding document. It lacks some of the apparatus found on official government sites, such as ministries. Still it is a concept and has an existence in cyberspace, if not in fact. Here the idea precedes the reality and, the Albanians hope, may shape it. [35]

At roughly the same time, a similar Web site, the "Republic of Kosovo," also staked out a claim of sovereignty at http://www.Kosovo-state.com. Though not the first polity to declare and attempt to perpetuate their independence in cyberspace, the

Albanian Kosovars seem to be set to achieve the most successful realization of such cyberspatial claims of sovereignty thus far.[36]

Besides the establishment of a virtual government, ethnic Albanians turned to other Internet-based activities to promote their cause—most notably, informational warfare and political organization. Information warfare is defined as "the offensive and defensive use of information and information systems to deny, exploit, corrupt, or destroy, an adversary's information, information-based processes, information systems, and computer-based networks while protecting one's own. Such actions are designed to achieve advantages over military or business adversaries."[37] Just as the media coverage of the Kosovo War came to be defined, at least in part, by the Internet, so did the methods of conflict.

The most common form of informational warfare was the defacement of enemy sites—a practice which both sides employed. According to the *Los Angeles Times*, the Kosovo conflict "turn[ed] cyberspace into an ethereal war zone where the battle for the hearts and minds [was] waged through the use of electronic images, online discussion group postings, and hacking attacks."[38] As early as 1998, cyber-attacks emerged as part of the Kosovo crisis when Serbian hackers altered the Kosovo Liberation Army's (*Ushtria Çlirimtare e Kosovës*) Web site. In sympathy with the fellow victims of Greater Serbian nationalism, Croatian hackers blocked access to the National Library of Serbia for several days. The Serbian response was to disrupt the activities of the premiere Croatian news agent *Vjesnik*.[39]

Such attacks were most often conducted far from the battlefield—from Belgrade (and, purportedly, also from St. Petersburg and Moscow) in the case of the Serbs and often from Western Europe in the case of the Albanians. According to political scientist Florian Bieber, "Albanian hackers who sympathized with the KLA replaced the content of private Serbian sites with messages supporting the KLA and vilifying Serbs. In a climate of mutual recrimination and no dialogue, the Internet provided another stage to proclaim the hatred of the other nation."[40] Albanian hactivists also used email bombs and other Web-based tools to disrupt and distort the Yugoslavian government's Web sites and digital resources. According to a representative of Network Solutions, the Internet's original domain name registrar, Albanian hackers damaged almost 2,000 Web addresses during the conflict.[41] High profile Albanian hacks include:

- An attack on the Yugoslav Government's Web site which caused both the Albanian flag to appear and the national anthem to play[42]
- The Serbian Ministry site being plastered with the title "Serbian Ministry of Lies"[43]
- An attack on Serbian Orthodox Church's Eparchy of Raska and Prizren in which the hackers deleted the Eparchy's archive, and posted the inscription: "Kosovo shall be independent from Serbia"[44]
- A coalition of European and Albanian hackers known as the Kosovo Hackers Group (http://come.to/k-h-g) replaced at least five Serb Web sites with black and red "Free Kosovo" banners[45]
- Attacks on the French KFOR (NATO Kosovo Force) Web site (http://www.nato.int/kfor/kfor/nations/france.htm) in response to France's perceived efforts to maintain the dependent status of Kosovo within Serbia/Montenegro[46]

The Serbian Web-based psychological operations (PSYOP) response to Albanian cyberspatial activities tended to be quite sophisticated. KLA-FOR Online (http://www.kfor-online.com/) was an example of a Web site that was a spoof of the official KFOR and NATO Web sites. It depicted the United Nations' Special Representative of the Secretary General and the NATO Secretary General as Nazis.[47] "The layout and colors are similar, as is the subject matter. But the twin site advertises what it calls KLA-FOR, referring to the ethnic Albanian Kosovo Liberation Army. The website that flashes up celebrates the diminishing numbers of Serbs in Kosovo and applauds KLA commanders in mockery of KFOR's impartiality."[48]

Slobodan Milošević's regime, after initially ignoring the Internet, eventually made cyber-warfare a vital part of propaganda, as well as military operations under the direction of the notorious Australian army reservist and Serb paramilitary veteran "Captain" Dragan Vasiljković.[49] "During the Kosovo conflict, Belgrade hackers were credited with conducting such attacks against NATO servers. They bombarded NATO's web server with 'ping' commands, which test whether a server is running and connected to the Internet. The effect of the attacks was to cause line saturation of the targeted servers."[50] Neutral observers in Belgrade during the Kosovo War reported the existence of government offices being filled with young technophiles attempting to develop viruses and other malignant tools for disrupting the operations of anti-Serb groups in neighboring countries and farther abroad.

In the realm of political organization, the Kosovo Liberation Army and other Kosovar paramilitary and political entities also made modest use of the Web to achieve certain organizational outcomes. As Denning states:

> During the Kosovo conflict, the Kosovo Task Force used the Internet to distribute action plans to Muslims and supporters of Kosovo. A March 1999 Action Alert, for example, asked people to organize rallies in solidarity with Kosovo at local federal buildings and city halls on April 3 at 11 a.m.; organize public funeral prayers; make and encourage others to make daily calls or send email to the White House asking for Kosovo independence, sustained air strikes until there was total Serb withdrawal from Kosovo, and arming of ethnic Albanians in Kosovo; and make and encourage others to make calls to their representatives and senators.[51]

The Internet also became an almost indispensable tool for dealing with the fallout of the conflict. According to one observer, "A Macedonian group has created an ambitious Web site for the thousands of Albanian families searching for missing relatives."[52] The article suggests that the Web directory is especially helpful for members of the widespread Albanian diaspora who are seeking to aid their relatives who may have been displaced by the ethnic cleansing efforts of the Serbs and the subsequent bombing of the region by NATO forces. Professor Gary Selnow, Executive Director of World Internet Resources for Education and Development, made a more personal comment on the issue in his 2000 speech to the U.S. State Department:

> I wish you could have seen the 15-year-old Kosovar girl who asked if I could help her find a cousin who had fled before the war. The two best friends hadn't heard from each other in nearly two years. A Web search turned up a possibility in London, and the teenager e-mailed a message, hoping this note-in-a-cyber-bottle would find the girl she sought. The next day, she logged onto her Hotmail account and screeched at the sight of the "You Have Mail" message from her cousin. Before I left, she asked me to take her picture with my digital camera. Then she e-

mailed it to London...What do you think this e-mail episode said to these kids about a free exchange of information and about an open society?[53]

The Internet has also become a major part of the diasporic humanitarian aid process in aftermath of the Kosovo and Macedonian crises.[54] Surprisingly, given the tone of the nationalist rhetoric of Balkan cyberspace, the Internet also served to heal some of the wounds of the Kosovo War. In 2005, Albanian Kosovar journalists from KosovoLive (Prishtina) and Serbian reporters at Beta (Belgrade) moved towards journalistic rapprochement in hopes that their respective audiences will follow suit. Their Web site, the Albanian-Serb Information Forum, provided the first direct news and information exchange channels between Kosovo and Serbia. It continues to provide comparatively unbiased reports from Kosovo in the Albanian, Serbian, and English languages, in addition to surveys and opinion polls which are intended to promote national reconciliation.

While the conflict in Kosovo effectively ended with the Serbian withdrawal, the issues confronting Albanians in other parts of the former Yugoslavia have continued. Predictably, hacking and other forms of Web-based political action have not abated.

During the war in Macedonia in 2001 between [the National Liberation Army of Macedonia] rebels and Macedonian armed forces, cyberspace was also the only dependable source of information. The most popular Web site that had everyday news from the war zone in Macedonia was www.liriakombtare.com. This website was also active in collecting humanitarian help to the villagers whose houses were bombed by the Macedonian paramilitary forces. Macedonian government condemned this Web site as an Albanian nationalistic site on their major TV station *MRTV*.[55]

The site was subsequently hacked and posted with nationalist symbols of the Macedonian government. The Albanians did not sit idly by. In 2002, self-declared Albanian cyber-terrorists defaced the home page of respected Macedonian economic analyst Sam Vaknin in a three-day cyber-attack. According to Deliso, "When one opens the page (www.geocities.com/vaksam), the following greeting appears: 'this page has been hackde (sic) by metal team.' Above this is a graphic of the double-headed eagle Albanian flag (adopted by the NLA), with the phrase 'proud to be Albanian.' Further text in Albanian reads: 'f*ck all Macedonian mothers and everyone who works with Macedonia.'"[56]

In early 2004, a "phantom Web site" posted a threat of possible attacks by the hitherto unknown National Army of Montenegro (*Ushtria Kombëtare e Malit të Zi*) to "oppose what it calls discrimination against ethnic Albanians" in the republic.[57] "Ethnic Albanian leaders in Montenegro have dismissed the message, pointing to curious spelling errors in an Albanian language text supposedly written by Albanians."[58] Despite this denial of legitimacy, the Web site's demands for a international debate on the status of Albanians in those lands which are historically Albanian—potentially involving parts of Serbia, Macedonia, and even Greece—has resonance in Albanian on- and offline discourse. Farther south, the so-called "Albanian Security Clan" targeted the sites of various institutions in Greece (including Greek Telcom and the Ministry of Interior) recently in response to the perceived ill treatment of Albanians in the country.[59]

After the various regional conflicts subsided, cyberspace emerged as an important field for promoting Kosovo's independence both before and after the formal declaration of international sovereignty on 17 February 2008 at 15:49 CET. Western newspapers such as the *Independent* saw record numbers of anti-Albanian and anti-Serbian on their Web sites in the wake of prominent articles about the impending declaration of independence by Kosovo's parliament and blogs such as *Serbianna* took up the legality of the declaration as a cause célèbre. The Web site "Who Recognized Kosovo" (http://www.kosovothanksyou.com/) appeared around the time of independence to track those countries that extended recognition to the new country, along with the full text of these declarations of recognition. More importantly, various organizations of the Kosovo government established their presences in cyberspace, including the offices of the president and prime minister. However, as of writing, the Internet Assigned Numbers Authority (IANA), the organization that oversees the global allocation of IP addresses, has not issued a ccTDL (Country Code Top Domain Level) for Kosovo, thus forcing the offices of the President and the Prime Minister to use .net TDLs for their respective Web sites. Such restraints on the cyberspatial sovereignty of the new nation-state are especially irksome to many Albanian Kosovors given the existence of a .cat ccTDL for Catalonia—a constituent part of Spain—and the growing popularity of the .yu ccTDL which, ironically, symbolizes a country that no longer exists: Yugoslavia.

The Albanian Cyber-Community: Reifying the Nation in the Age of Globalization

Historically, the Albanian nation's relationship with mass media leaves much to be desired. Unlike the Christian millets under Turkish suzerainty, the Albanians were consistently denied access to education in the mother tongue, thus leaving the vast majority of the population illiterate until the advent of an independent state in 1913. Certainly, an educated elite existed, but their linguistic medium of thought and practice tended to be Ottoman Turkish (*Osmanlı Türkçesi*) rather than the language of their peasant brethren.[60] When Albanian printed materials made their way into the Ottoman-administered Balkans, they typically originated in diasporic communities in Boston, Paris, Bucharest, Sophia, Cairo, Istanbul, and various parts of Italy.[61]

During the early twentieth century, two world wars and a stormy interwar period plagued by the weakness of an Albanian state beset with internal and external threats stunted the drive towards universal literacy and the development of robust media products. After 1945, however, the communist government instituted the necessary infrastructure for the solidification of a cogent national identity. According to Stark Draper, "They established a comprehensive state schooling system; normalized the disparate local and non-written cultures of the country into a single high culture; isolated the Albanians from other peoples; and, succeeded in standardizing the Albanian language."[62] However Enver Hoxha's Stalinist regime (1944-1985) kept a tight lid on the development of media, allowing only the prosaic voice of the communist party to be heard. During the decades of totalitarian rule, few had access to any form of external media, especially after Tirana eschewed Chinese patronage and plunged the country into autarky in the late 1970s. The only window to the outside world was through surreptitious reception of Italian television broadcasts, a luxury limited to those Albanians living on the coastal plane.[63]

The media environment was somewhat preferable in neighboring Yugoslavia, at least after the Second World War.[64] State subsidization Albanian identity in the late 1960s, the new openness of "market socialism" which allowed inbound tourism and occupational sojourning in Western Europe, and Tito's rapprochement with Tirana all benefited Albanian cultural development and media production in Kosovo (Pavlowitch 1988: 83-84).[65] Educational opportunities and media outlets in the Albanian language were, however, sharply curtailed after the death of the Socialist Federal Republic of Yugoslavia's founder in 1980. Unfortunately, Albanians living in Greece could expect little media freedom in their native language and were the victims of a steady Hellenization campaign (for Orthodox) and expulsion (for Muslims) from the early twentieth century onwards.[66]

As such, the end of one-party rule and concurrent spread of new media technologies is a welcome occurrence for many Albanians who wish to see wide and rapid change in the ways in which their countrymen access information and organize themselves politically, specifically in such way as to support pan-Albanian projects. Unfortunately, Internet adoption in Albania was slow in coming due to a mixture of economical, social, and cultural reasons. While the country's incipient marketization and liberalized media laws after the 1997 revolt promoted some forward movement, Albania had yet to fully embrace informatization by the end the decade. Albanian cyberspace—like Eritrean, Bangladeshi, and certain other national cyberspaces—is crafted in large part by the diaspora rather than those residing in the ethnic homeland. As Albanian journalist Alfred Nune states:

> The major function of the Internet is providing access to knowledge. The fact that the Internet registers an unlimited quantity of information makes this medium the biggest archive of knowledge in digital form. A great number of Internet page "producers" add in their homepage information on national history and culture; an ever-increasing number of photos and documents will allow future generations to access and transmit this knowledge by the click of a mouse. We are not referring to the mere 45 sites originating in Albania. The Albanian virtual space contains 120 times more information, coming not only from Kosovo, Montenegro and Macedonia but also from the five continents Albanians have immigrated to.[67]

Despite Nune's sanguine assessment, the painful fact is that Albania has a scant 75,000 Internet users (2.5 percent of the population) according the September 2005 report by the International Telecommunication Union. While this is up sharply from 2002, it still puts Albania at the bottom of the European countries in terms of Internet usage.

According to NationMaster.com, Albania ranks 134th out of 150 countries in Internet users per capita; this puts the country just three spots ahead of Bhutan, which only legalized the Internet and television in 1999. Contrast those numbers with Internet penetration rates in the principal receiving countries for Albanian emigrants: Sweden (75 percent); Denmark (70 percent); the United States (68 percent); Norway (68 percent); Australia (68 percent); Switzerland (65 percent); Canada (64 percent); United Kingdom (63 percent); Germany and Austria (57 percent); Italy (49 percent); France (42 percent); and Greece (40 percent).[68] The page views of the Macedonian-oriented Web site National Freedom (http://www.liriakombtare.com) provides some

insight into the distribution of Albanian Internet users. The daily average of visitors
to the site is 1480; 21.2 percent of viewers are in the United States, 18.6 percent from
Switzerland, 11.8 percent from Germany, 6.4 percent from Macedonia and the re-
mainder from Sweden, Norway, Austria, Canada, Denmark, etc.[69]

Reflecting the lopsided distribution of Internet access among members of the
nation, Internet forums tend to be decidedly diasporic in nature.

> Over 90% of the participants in discussions are young students under 25 years of
> age, mainly residing in EU countries like Italy, Greece, Austria, Germany, Swit-
> zerland and France, and especially in the USA and Canada. The first Albanian In-
> ternet pioneers came from these countries. Like their compatriots who 80 years
> ago started publishing the first newspapers in immigration, they became the pio-
> neers of the Albanian mass-media, building up the first web pages and creating the
> first discussion forums in this new medium.[70]

While diasporic Albanians are vastly overrepresented in cyberspace, this does not
mean that "homeland" issues are ignored. According to Nune, Albanians in diaspora
have launched locally-oriented Web sites intended to provide cyberspatial representation for their home villages, thus providing especially evocative examples of the
local-global nature of Albanian identity.[71] The real driver of Albanian cyberspace
may be the European and North American diaspora, but there are also positive signs
in the Balkans. Paradoxically, the repressive nature of the Milošević regime can arguably be seen as promoting Internet adoption in Kosovo since the freedoms afforded Internet users and Web-based journalists sharply contrasted with the dismal
situation in traditional media environments.[72] And as soon as the bombs stopped falling on Kosovo, Prishtina clamored back onto the information superhighway with a
fury.

A *CNN* report asserts, "E-mail is not a luxury in addition to the regular mail. For
many people in the new Kosovo, it is the only mail. 'Everyone has friends and relatives in Europe and in America. It's the cheapest way to stay in touch,' [Internet
café-operator Luan] Oruqi said. 'It's a way to break the walls between Kosovo and
rest of the world.'"[73] The dispatch goes on to discuss Radio21, a popular independent
station in Prishtina, which began broadcasting over the Web twenty-four hours per
day in the summer of 2000. According to the station's director Afërdita Kelmendi,
"We began on the Web and then moved to the old-style radio airwaves. We were
forced to survive on the Web, and that survival showed us that anything is possible."[74] While Kelmendi hopes to reach some Albanian Kosovars living in the province, her core audience is the diaspora, specifically Albanians with the financial resources to assist the development of her war torn homeland.

It is perhaps not surprising that archipelago Albanians are emerging as technological leaders among the Balkan Albanians. In comparing the Kosovo Albanians to
their "Albanian Albanian" counterparts, international relations scholar Patrick Artisien lauds their "more diversified customs and culture, higher living standards, [and]
greater freedom of movement and religious practices."[75] Despite the trauma of the
late 1990s, the sophistication of the Kosovar and Macedonian Albanians remains in
tact, thus providing a sturdier base from which launch the Albanian nation into the
what American political commentator Robert Kagan calls the "postmodern paradise"
of twenty-first century Europe.[76] In my research, the most telling example of this
trajectory is the Web site Gay Kosovo (http://www.gayKosovo.com/). The mostly

(simplified) Albanian-language postings on the message board are accompanied by small flags symbolizing the authors' countries of residence. The unmistakable two-headed, black eagle on a red background commanded a plurality, but there also flags representing (in order of prevalence) Switzerland, Great Britain, Germany, the United States, Belgium, the Scandinavian countries, and even a few posts from Brazil and Iran. The Kosovars also seem to be much more prone to pan-Albanianism which tends to accentuate their presence in cyberspace. As Radio Free Europe journalist Jolyon Naegele states, "Virtually all Kosovo news-media refer to events in neighboring Albanian-inhabited countries as being — *në vendi* — in the country, as if they were happing in a single country. However, Albania's news media do not share this perception and place such items in the category of occurring — *në rajoni* — in the region, i.e. not in Albania."[77]

Ironically, the war's displacement of many Kosovars promotes their interests in cyberspace vis-à-vis those of their more stable co-nationals in Albania proper. Kathy Sherrell and Jennifer Hyndman's ethnographic study of Kosovo refugees in British Columbia found that Internet use played a seminal role in the lives of these immigrants. One participant in the study stated, "Through internet is everything available. You can search anything you want – radio, TV, theatres, political situation, economy, everything."[78] According to the study, "Weekly internet newspapers and online news agencies that are published in Albanian have allowed the Kosovars to monitor current events. In Vernon, [British Columbia] where the Kosovars we interviewed were not computer literate, the employment counsellor at the local immigrant and refugee-serving agency would print out the weekly online newspaper for them."[79] The near universal appeal of the Internet to Kosovar Albanians (both at home and abroad) is coloring the nature of Albanian-language cyberspace.

Despite their position of dominance in Albanian cyberspace, archipelago Albanians tend to defer to their counterparts in the ethnic homeland when it comes to issues of linguistic purity and cultural norms. As such, there is an important place for the least technologically-savvy segment of the Albanian nation within the pan-Albanian cyberspace project. Former Yugoslav Albanians, like other victims of linguistic oppression such as Scots-speakers in Britain, First Nations in North America, Aborigines in Australia, and Assyrians in the Middle East, are using the communicative tools of the Internet to better than language skills with "citizen-experts" online. In diaspora, the children of Serbo-Croatian-educated Albanians are using the Web to communicate with speakers of "proper Albanian," a phenomenon which, if it continues, will ineluctably harmonize written Albanian and may even have some effect on spoken Albanian, as well. While it is important not to overestimate' the importance of the Internet to the development of the Albanian language, few would contest the assertion that the advent of cyberspace is the most important catalyst to linguistic harmonization since 1972 when Tirana hosted the Congress on the Orthography of the Albanian Language with the participation of delegates from the Yugoslav territories of Kosovo, Macedonia, and Montenegro, as well as Calabria.[80]

Contemporary popular culture plays a major role in linking the Albanian people across time and space; Albanian cyberspace is filled with sites providing music downloads, entertainment news, and sports highlights. Furthermore, Albanian Internet-users are gaining real-time access to wealth of Albanian historical, cultural, and linguistic resources. Anthems, legends, genealogies, histories, photographs, maps, demographic data, manuscripts, and other tangible assets of Albanian national cul-

ture are currently being protected, distributed and accessed in cyberspace. My research suggests that such developments are reinvigorating the irredentist sentiments
the Albanian nation, though in a way which differs markedly from previous efforts to
unite the nation over the past 150 years. The Internet, rather than the nation-state, is
the principal medium for this new form of irredentism, and thus the telos of this new
project is unlikely to resemble the outcomes of nineteenth century irredentist
projects.

The Albanian national identity project in cyberspace—though still superficially
aping the nationalist projects of the last century (obsession with territory, incorporation of all members in a single legal-political community, etc.)—is, in fact, a postnational undertaking. It is a paradigmatic of the "complex, non-territorial, postnational
forms of allegiance" identified and prophesied by Arjun Appadurai in *Modernity at
Large*.[81] If we assume that Benedict Anderson's paradigm of the imagined community will persevere, it is only natural to expect that as transnational and interactive media (Internet, satellite TV, mobile telephony) eclipse statist, broadcast platforms
(print newspapers, over-the-air TV, etc.), nationalism will undoubtedly reflect the
contours of the new delivery format(s). According to Appadurai, "[These] new organizational forms [will be] more diverse, more fluid, more ad hoc, more provisional,
less coherent, less organized, and simply less implicated in the comparative advantages of the nation-state."[82] Paradoxically, while the Albanian national identity is
reifying and harmonizing through the Internet, the ultimate prize of Albanian nationalism—a nation-state encompassing the whole nation—is unlikely to be aided by
Internet activity. The transient and corporatist nature of cyberspace may even undermine long-term commitment of Albanians to the nationalist cause if it continues
to adhere to the late nineteenth century form of irredentism. As Draper cautions, the
only way for Albanian nationalism to become a "successful and constructive force"
is for the Albanian elites to foster "a very open and cosmopolitan ideal that readily
spans state borders."[83]

The events surrounding the Kosovo War directly led to the growth of Albanian
cyberspace, as well as the numbers of Albanians online. The chaos of the war, the
need for information about relatives, friends, and co-nationals, and the disinformation campaign of the Milošević regime created a nexus which loudly demanded Albanian Web literacy. When combined with the nettling problems which have always
plagued media exchanges between all Albanians—a archipelago nation living as
indigenous peoples in four states (Albania, Serbia/Montenegro, Macedonia, and
Greece) and as a significant diasporic community in more than a dozen others (Germany, Switzerland, the U.S., UK, the Scandinavian countries, Turkey, etc.), the need
for Internet-based information, communication, and coordination increased even
more steeply.

Importantly, Albanian journalist Fatmir Ibraimi points out that the Internet does
raise one issue of division among the Albanians: religion. Certain Albanians in North
America (and occasionally Europe) tend to use the Internet to vigorously promote
Islam amongst their countrymen, an undertaking which is looked upon unfavorably
by other communities in Albanian cyberspace.[84] My research among the Albanian
Muslim community of Staten Island, NY suggests that certain segments of the Alba-
nian-American community are embracing a staid, de-localized, and universalist form
of Sunni Islam in diaspora—a belief system which many of their atheist, agnostic,
secularist, Christian, Bektashi, and even Sunni co-nationals might find unpalatable

when impelled to embrace it by fellow netizens. However, this phenomenon is play-ing out in the Albanian homeland as well where there is a strong push by Saudi and other Arab Muslim outreach organizations to encourage Albanians to abandon their localist traditions to adopt "traditional" forms of Islam.[85]

The use of instant messaging, email, chat rooms, and other communicative devices across national borders is subtly unifying (if not homogenizing) the Albanian nation in other ways. While the difference is in degree and not type from the effects of those late nineteenth century contraband newspapers smuggled in from Boston, Cairo, Par-is, and Istanbul, one should not underestimate the power of this new medium to ac-complish what has long eluded the Albanian nation: conceptual contiguity. Through mass-mediated communication over the Internet, the dispersed Albanian peoples have been able to (re)create the bonds of community without regard for propinquity. The Albanians I spoke with in my research frequently affirmed that the Internet al-lows the nation to come together for the first time in history, albeit in virtual rather than "real" space. For the Albanians (and other challenged nations), cyberspace is evolving into a decentralized nodal area which links the nation—even across borders and oceans. I argue that sustained Internet activity has thus created a new ecumene that enables many of the communicative, cultural, and socio-economic exchanges which, in the previous 150 years, could only have existed within the structure of a nation-state.

Arjun Appadurai links electronic mass mediation to the creation of "invisible colleges" which educate, inculcate, and disseminate ideas, orientations, and modes of practice among ethnic groups separated by time and space.[86] For Albanians in dias-pora (and increasingly in their ethnic homelands), the Internet is indeed beginning to function as a "school" of sorts for the nation—providing cultural, linguistic, socio-economic, and political tutelage. The phenomenon is not trivial, and as Appadurai suggests, may come to deeply impact the political life of mass mediated communities like the Albanians. "The transformation of everyday subjectivities through electronic mediation and the work of the imagination is not only a cultural fact. It is deeply connected to politics, through the new ways in which the individual attachments, interests, and aspirations increasingly crosscut those of the nation-state."[87] While the on-going negotiation of Albanian identity via the World Wide Web and the emer-gence of conceptual contiguity amongst all Albanians have not yet resulted in a "real-world" realization of irredentist goals, it is clear that the migration into cyber-space has provided at least a virtual redemption for the Albanian nation.

Notes

1. See "Irredentism," *Webster's Third New International Dictionary, Unabridged*. Mer-riam-Webster, 2002, http://unabridged.merriam-webster.com.

2. In Italy's irredentist project, the core group of elites included Giuseppe Mazzini, Giuseppe Garibaldi, Count Cavour, and Victor Emmanuel II; however, the term irredentism itself gained popular usage for its association with the *Associazione pro Italia irredenta*, a nationalist society founded in 1877 by Matteo Imbriani; see Laura Murray, "Examining Irre-dentism: Irredentism and International Politics (Review)," *Journal of International Affairs* 45, no. 2 (Winter 1992): 648-652.

3. Jean-Arnault Dérens, "Forgotten Peoples of the Balkans," *Le Monde diplomatique* (English edition), 2003, http://mondediplo.com/2003/08/04Derens (25 August 2005).

4. George W. Gawrych, "Tolerant Dimensions of Cultural Pluralism in the Ottoman Empire: The Albanian Community, 1800-1912," *International Journal of Middle East Studies* 15, no. 4 (November 1983): 519-536.

5. Dérens, "Forgotten Peoples of the Balkans."

6. Maria Todorova, *Imagining the Balkans* (Oxford: Oxford University Press, 1997), 167.

7. Gawrych, "Tolerant Dimensions of Cultural Pluralism," 524.

8. Todorova, *Imagining the Balkans*, 167.

9. Stark Draper, "The Conceptualization of an Albanian Nation," *Ethnic & Racial Studies* 20, no. 1 (January 1997): 123-144.

10. Gawrych, "Tolerant Dimensions of Cultural Pluralism."

11. The league's primary purpose was to defend the Albanian lands from annexation by Slavic states.

12. Misha Glenny, *The Balkans: Nationalism, War and the Great Powers, 1804-1999* (New York: Viking, 2000), 154.

13. It was not until 1900 that the linguist Sami Bey compiled a proper grammar. He had created a formal orthography for the Albanian language some four years prior; see Gawrych, "Tolerant Dimensions of Cultural Pluralism."

14. Stevan K. Pavlowitch, *The Improbable Survivor: Yugoslavia and Its Problems, 1918-1988* (Columbus: Ohio State University Press, 1988), 80.

15. Serbia, Montenegro, Croatia, Bulgaria, Romania, Macedonia, and Bosnia all have minority (or non-titular) populations which range from 11-60 percent of the overall population. Of the Balkan countries, only Greece claims to have a homogenous ethnic population; however, this assertion is weakened by the undeniable existence of substantial Slavic communities in the northwest, Aromanian (Vlach) populations in the central part of the country, as well as Turkish, Albanian, Romani, and other minorities.

16. "Greek Minority in Albania," Unrepresented Nation and Peoples Organization (UNPO) Web site, 9 August 2004, http://www.unpo.org/news_detail.php?arg=23&par=1060 (21 January 2006).

17. As the Albanian poet Aleksandër Dardeli eloquently laments, "There is a country. The country is so small you need your grandfather's magnifying glass to find it on the map. Soon the scratched magnifying glass won't help you much. The country gets smaller and smaller with each passing day as its people flee to other countries"; Aleksandër Dardeli, "An Albanian in America," Cool_Albanian Web site (originally published in *Potomac Review*, Winter 1998-99), http://groups.yahoo.com/group/COOL_ALBANIAN/message/25 (12 November 2005).

18. Barjaba Kosta, "Albania: Looking Beyond Borders," Migration Policy Institute Web site (August 2004), http://www.migrationinformation.org/Profiles/display.cfm?id=239 (21 January 2006).

19. The Arbëreshë are descendents of 15th and 16th century Christian Albanian émigrés who fled the expansion of the Ottomans and found refuge in continental Italy and Sicily (then under Aragonese rule).

20. This is a highly disputed and ultimately unverifiable figure because of the Turkish Republic's historical rejection of the existence of national minorities within its borders.

21. Born to Albanian parents in Kavala in what is today northeastern Greece, Kavalalı Mehmet Ali Paşa is often referred to the "father of modern Egypt." His mostly Albanian army was sent to North Africa in 1799 to battle Napoleon's forces. He later established himself as pasha under Ottoman suzerainty and led a rapid modernization and industrialization campaign.

22. Florian Bieber, "Cyberwar or Sideshow? The Internet and the Balkan Wars," *Current History* 99, no. 635 (March 2000): 124-129.

23. The process had begun somewhat early; in the early 1980s, "Belgrade's abrogation of Prishtina's cultural exchanges with Tirana and the subsequent replacement of school and uni-

versity textbooks imported from Albania with Albanian translations of Serbo-Croat texts," effectively isolating "Kosovo culturally and ideologically from Albania"; see Patrick F. R. Artisien, "A Note on Kosovo and the Future of Yugoslav-Albanian Relations: A Balkan Perspective," *Soviet Studies* 36, no. 2 (April 1984): 267-276. However, in 1989, a Serbian-wide referendum severely curtailed the autonomy of the Autonomous Province of Kosovo (as well as Vojvodina). From that point forward, Slobodan Milošević used the real and perceived injustices done to the Serbian minority in the region as a rallying cry for Serbian nationalism, the reduction of the linguistic and cultural rights of Albanians, and settlement policies which increased the number of Serbs in the region.

24. "Inside the First 'Internet War,'" *Wired* 7, no. 1 (January 1999), http://www.wired.com/wired/archive/7.01/mustread.html?pg=15 (12 November 2005).

25. Joshua Kaldor-Robinson, "The Virtual and the Imaginary: The Role of Diasphoric New Media in the Construction of a National Identity during the Break-up of Yugoslavia," *Oxford Development Studies* 30, no. 2 (June 2002): 177-187.

26. The last site was publicly targeted for destruction by the Serbian hacker group Crna Ruka ('Black Hand') in the lead-up to the war; according to one representative of the group, "We shall continue with our effort to remove Albanian lies from the Internet and we plan to remove a NATO web site. We shall first attack the www.Kosovo.com site, which we shall abolish as early as tonight"; see "Serbian Hackers Declare Internet War on Kosovo Albanian Web Sites," *BBC Monitoring European – Political* (text of report by the Belgrade-based independent Radio B92), 22 October 1998. Kosovo News Agency, the main press outlet for the Kosovo Liberation Army, reported it had been attacked in late April 1999 stating, "We inform the Albanian and foreign opinion that the most visited Albanian Internet site Kosovopress [www.Kosovopress.com] has been attacked before two days and is still blocked for a great part of world opinion" (BBC 1999).

27. Łukasz Szurmiński, "The Kosovo Conflict in the Internet," Asociacioni Kosovar i Studentëve të Shkencave Politike Web site, 2003, http://www.asshp.org/downloads/Publications%20Eng/The%20Kosovo%20conflict%20in%20the%20Internet.pdf (11 November 2005).

28. William Elison, "Netwar: Studying Rebels on the Internet," *Social Studies* 91, no. 3 (May/June 2000): 127-131.

29. Dubravko Kolendic, "Serb-Albanian War Rages over the Internet Too," *Deutsche Presse-Agentur*, 1 August 1998.

30. Calvert Jones, "Online Impression Management: Case Studies of Activist Web Sites and Their Credibility Enhancing Tactics During the Kosovo War." Paper prepared for presentation at the conference "Safety and Security in a Networked World." Oxford Internet Institute (OII), Oxford University, UK, 8-10 September 2005.

31. Jones, "Online Impression Management."

32. See Elison, "Netwar: Studying Rebels on the Internet"; Dorothy E. Denning, "Activism, Hacktivism, and Cyberterrorism: The Internet as a Tool for Influencing Foreign Policy," John Arquilla and David Ronfeldt, *Networks and Netwars: The Future of Terror, Crime, and Militancy* (Santa Monica, CA: RAND Corporation, 2000); and Thomas Keenan, "Looking Like Flames and Falling Like Stars: Kosovo, 'The First Internet War,'" *Social Identities* 7, no. 4 (December 2001): 539-550.

33. Keenan, "Looking Like Flames and Falling Like Stars," 543.

34. Elison, "Netwar: Studying Rebels on the Internet"; maps are a central totem to be projected and preserved in Albanian cyberspace (as well as other Balkan cyberspaces). However, such mapping often proves controversial.

35. Elison, "Netwar: Studying Rebels on the Internet," 130.

36. See, for instance, the Web sites of Freedonia (http://www.freedonia.org/), the Dominion of Melchizedek (http://www.melchizedek.com/), the Kingdom of Talossa (http://www.kingdomoftalossa.net/), and Sealand (http://www.sealandgov.org/).

37. Ivan Goldberg, "Information Warfare," Institute for the Advance Study of Information Warfare (IASIW) web site, 2001, http://www.psycom.net/iwar.1.html. (11 November 2005).

38. Cited in Denning, "Activism, Hacktivism, and Cyberterrorism," 240.

39. Mirjana Drakulic and Ratimir Drakulic, "Balkan Hackers War in Cyberspace." Paper presented at the Fourteenth BILETA Conference: "Cyberspace 1999: Crime, Criminal Justice and the Internet," College of Ripon & York St. John, York, England, 29 March 1999.

40. Bieber, "Cyberwar or Sideshow?" 128.

41. Cited in Alfred Nune, "Internet and Albania: A Paradoxical Ambivalence?" in Orlin Spassov and Christo Todorov, New Media in Southeast Europe (Sofia: Southeast European Media Centre, 2003), http://soemz.euv-frankfurt-o.de/media-see/newmedia/newmedia.htm.

42. Jessie Grimond, "Pristina - War Erupts in Balkan Cyberspace But NATO Is As Quiet As a Mouse," Independent, 2 May 2001.

43. Grimond, "Pristina."

44. "Media Analysis 20 December," United Nation Mission in Kosovo (UNMIK), Division of Public Information, Media Monitoring, UNMIK Web site, 2004, http://www.unmikonline.org/press/2004/mon/dec/lmm201204.pdf (12 November 2005).

45. Denning, "Activism, Hacktivism, and Cyberterrorism," 273.

46. "Kosovo Albanian Group Urges Attack on French Peacekeepers Web Site," Serbianna web site, 2005, http://www.serbianna.com/news/2005/02128.html (1 November 2005).

47. Larry K. Wentz, Lessons from Kosovo: KFOR Experience (Washington, DC: Department of Defense, 2002), 508.

48. Grimond, "Pristina."

49. Michael Satchell, "Captain Dragan's Serbian Cybercorps," U.S. News & World Report 126, 18 (10 May 1999): 42.

50. Denning, "Activism, Hacktivism, and Cyberterrorism," 268.

51. Denning, "Activism, Hacktivism, and Cyberterrorism," 257.

52. Michael J. Jordan, "New Refugee Aid Worker: Cell Phone," Christian Science Monitor 91, no. 104 (26 April 1999): 7.

53. Gary Selnow, "The Internet: The Soul of Democracy," Vital Speeches of the Day 67, no. 2 (November 2000): 58-60.

54. Fatmir Fanda Ibraimi, "Albanian Cyberspace," Lajmet.com web site, 2006, http://www.lajmet.com/cutenews//show_news.php?subaction=showfull&id=113769 7213&archive=&template=tit-klasik (22 January 2006).

55. Ibraimi, "Albanian Cyberspace."

56. Christopher Deliso, "Albanian Hackers Deface Macedonian Website," Antiwar web site, 18 January 2002, http://www.antiwar.com/orig/deliso19.html (12 November 2005).

57. Aida Ramusovic, "Playing With Ethnic Regionalism," Transitions, 22 January 2004.

58. Ramusovic, "Playing With Ethnic Regionalism."

59. "Albanian Press: Albanian Hackers Attacked Sites of Greek Institutions," FOCUS News Agency, 17 February 2005.

60. Some literati worked in the other vernacular languages of the Balkans, e.g., Bishop Fan Noli, Albania's foreign minister in the early interwar period, who attended Greek schools in his native Thrace and later in Athens before departing for Egypt and then America.

61. The major pre-independence newspapers originating in diaspora included Kombi ('The Nation'), Dielli ('The Sun'), Liria ('Liberty'), Drita ('The Light'), Meşveret ('Consultation'), Shpresa e Shqypnisë ('Albania's Hope'), and Arnavut ('The Albanian'); see Barbara Jelavich, History of the Balkans: Twentieth Century, Volume II (Cambridge: Cambridge University Press, 1991).

62. Draper, "The Conceptualization of an Albanian Nation," 131.

63. Jolyon Naegele, "A People Scattered," New Presence: The Prague Journal of Central European Affairs 7, no. 3 (Autumn 2005): 32-33

64. The government of interwar Yugoslavia actually tried to cleanse all much of the Albanian population from Kosovo and Macedonia by encouraging immigration to Turkey or Albania; those who stayed were instructed only in Serbo-Croatian and were often displaced by "land-hungry Orthodox Serbian peasants from the barren mountain regions" who poured in; see Pavlowitch, *The Improbable Survivor*, 81.

65. Pavlowitch, *The Improbable Survivor*, 84.

66. Doug Muir, "When Chams Attack," A Fistful of Euros (AFOE) web site, 14 November 2005, http://fistfulofeuros.net/archives/002081.php (18 November 2005).

67. Nune, "Internet and Albania."

68. "Internet Usage Stats and Population," Internet World Stats web site, http://www.internetworldstats.com/ (15 November 2005).

69. Ibraimi, "Albanian Cyberspace."

70. Nune, "Internet and Albania."

71. Nune, "Internet and Albania."

72. Julian Sher, "Ethnic Albanians Use Web in Fight against Serb Control," *Globe and Mail*, 12 October 2000.

73. Julian Sher, "Using the Web to Reconnect and Rebuild in Kosovo," CNN Interactive, 24 August 2000, http://www.journalismnet.com/articles/kosovo.htm (12 December 2005).

74. Quoted in Sher, "Ethnic Albanians Use Web."

75. Artisien, "A Note on Kosovo," 274.

76. Robert Kagan, *Paradise and Power: America and Europe in the New World Order* (Conshohocken, PA: Atlantic Books, 2004).

77. Naegele, "A People Scattered," 32.

78. Kathy Sherrell and Jennifer Hyndman, "Global Minds, Local Bodies: Kosovar Transnational Connections beyond British Columbia," *Refuge* 23, no. 1 (2006): 16-26.

79. Sherrell and Hyndman, "Global Minds, Local Bodies," 20.

80. The conference established a unified literary language which was solidified in the ensuing decade by the publication of several reference texts including *The Orthography of the Albanian Language* (1973) and *The Dictionary of Current Albanian* (1980).

81. Arjun Appadurai, *Modernity at Large* (Minneapolis: University of Minnesota Press, 1996), 166.

82. Appadurai, *Modernity at Large*, 168.

83. Draper, "The Conceptualization of an Albanian Nation," 129.

84. Ibraimi, "Albanian Cyberspace," 2006.

85. Isa Blumi, "Albania," in Kathryn M. Coughlin. *Muslim Cultures Today* (Westport: Greenwood Publishing, 2006).

86. Appadurai, *Modernity at Large*, 8.

87. Appadurai, *Modernity at Large*, 10.

Chapter 5
Post-Imperial Digerati:
Near Abroad Russians Transcending Local
Barriers via Global Technologies

It is likely that future generations of historians will remember the twentieth century as the period that brought an end to empire. The century began with Spain losing the Philippines and its last remaining territories in the New World to the upstart, anti-imperialist America. Two decades later, the Ottoman, Hohenzollern, Romanov, and Habsburg empires all collapsed under the stress of the Great War, birthing more than a dozen new states in Central Europe and the Near East. The British, French, Belgian, Portuguese, and Dutch maritime empires crumbled in the wake of Second World War, producing scores of new states across Africa and Asia. Near the end of the century, the Soviet Empire disintegrated, launching fifteen new countries into existence and creating a "third wave" of newly independent states from Moldova to Kyrgyzstan.[1]

As the scholars of decolonization have demonstrated, independence from imperial rule does not wipe away its legacy overnight. Certain elements of imperial rule continue to persist long after the demise of formal political control. Jamaicans continue to drive on the left-hand side of the road, beignets are still served in Laos, and Asian-inflected Portuguese still echoes in many ports of the Indian basin. Perhaps no single element of the post-colonial condition is as politicized as the continuing presence of descendents of a country's former imperial conquerors.[2] In much of the Western Hemisphere, the historical legacy of independence struggles led by the Anglo-Saxons in North America and the creoles (Sp. 'criollo' and Port. 'crioulo') in Latin America has effectively delinked any association between ethnicity and resurgent imperialism.[3] In Africa, Europe, and Asia, this is not the case. From Eastern Europe to southern Africa to Southeast Asia, human capital functioned as a key element of the colonization process. As a consequence, the descendents of settlers, guest workers, bureaucrats, and soldiers still bear a heavy historical burden for both the real and perceived crimes of their ancestors.

In this chapter, I explore the impact of the Internet on identity formation and maintenance among those ethnic minorities who descend from (or once-comprised) the ruling elites of now defunct empires. I do this via a case study of near abroad Russians, a group which, according to Russian Foreign Ministry estimates, consists of some 30 million people worldwide, making Russians outside of the Russian Federation one of the world largest minorities.[4] Herein, I investigate the role of cyberspace in building commercial and communication networks which in turn provide economic and occupational opportunities for the minorities in question. Furthermore, I analyze the role of the Internet in enabling cultural initiatives, providing constant contact with the ethnic homeland, and allowing access to media in the mother tongue. The chapter also explores the trauma associated with the loss of hegemony, and how cyberspace functions as a psychotropic mechanism for coping with such loss as well as maintaining contact with the larger "Russian world" (*russkii mir*). My research suggests that there a wide variety of responses on the part of post-imperial digerati to their situations but in most cases, those individuals who have chosen to remain "abroad" see the Internet as a way to bridge their ancestral cultures, a complex historical legacy, and the challenge of daily life as minority associated with past imperial rule.[5]

Near Abroad Russians: The Creation of an Instant Diaspora

In 1991, the Union of Soviet Socialist Republics dissolved leaving approximately 25 million ethnic Russians outside the borders of the newly-formed Russian Federation. Incontestably, this community represented an ill-prepared diaspora. Nearly three-quarters of all Russians living in the non-Russian republics considered the USSR to be their homeland as late as December 1990.[6] Within a year, this "homeland" had disappeared from the map, and these marooned Russians were forced to grapple with their newly bestowed status as "national minorities," a politically loaded term from the Soviet era which continues be rejected by most Russians in the Newly Independent States (NIS).[7] Some of these new countries, such as Estonia, Latvia, and Lithuania, were simply reconstituted nation-states that had been deprived of independence earlier in the twentieth century. Other such as Belarus, Kyrgyzstan, and Moldova were novel state formations, lacking strong historical legacies as independent countries. The Russian Federation—the legal and spiritual successor to the USSR—remained the world's largest state; however, it was now "distanced" from its historical periphery by international borders, foreign currencies, and a political reordering involving American and European military and economic alliances. Trapped between these Newly Independent States and the Russian rump state was a fledgling minority: the Russians of the "near abroad."

When the forebears of this new diaspora made the decision to immigrate to what would become the independent states of Central Asia, Transcaucasia, and the Baltics, they had little or no idea that they would one day part of a marginalized "immigrant" community;[8] those who settled in Belarus, Ukraine, and northern Kazakhstan—regions with little to no legal difference from Russia proper for much of the past 250 years—were even less cognizant of ever having transversed any sort of political border.[9] Others, however, specifically fled Russia for religious reasons, especially the Old Believer families who had been resident in the territory of modern-day Baltic States for centuries, easily predating the emergence of Latvian and Estonian national consciousness in their current forms.[10]

While Russians in the new abroad are often described as a diaspora, they share little in common with either historic diasporas (Jews, Armenians, and Greeks) or more recently constituted immigrant communities (e.g., British South Asians, American Filipinos, and German Turks). "The situation of this new Diaspora is paradoxical: its representatives whilst not physically leaving their place of living, had their country taken away from them as a consequence of earlier colonization processes and the break-down of the Soviet Empire."[11] When they or their ancestors were relocated or made the decision to reside in the periphery, there was neither requirement nor preparation for the privations of migrancy. As Nicholas Breyfogle has pointed out, the Romanov and Bolshevik regimes both enabled a form of Russian universalism which made it rather easy for Russians to settle anywhere in the empire without concerning themselves with adapting to adverse social conditions.[12] According to geographer Sergei Matjunin:

> The majority of the members of 'Russian-speaking minorities' are the descendants of ordinary 'soldiers' of the Communist Party: people with no roots, tradition or faith. Most of them are Russians. They still look down on the members of the indigenous populations, and call them their 'younger brothers'. The USSR was their homeland. It guaranteed safety and the status of the privileged. When it suddenly broke down 25 million of the Soviet Russians found themselves in extremely adverse conditions. Instead of being the rulers, they became national minority. Their superiority turned into the subordination to the legal rule of the despised 'younger brothers'. And so they had to choose whether to learn the native language and conform to the new circumstances, or leave for Russia.[13]

Prior to the dissolution, the development of tight ethnic ghettos, civic society, cultural resources, and language protection schemes were unnecessary due to the state's support of "Russianness" in nearly all quarters. This, of course, was a mixed blessing. While such a milieu required little of the Russians under the *ancien régime*, it failed to prepare them for the immigrant experience. Such conditions also set them up as scapegoats after independence when they would come to be variously labeled "aliens," "occupiers," "immigrants," and "foreigners."

Under the Soviet system, ethnic Russians had enjoyed rather high levels of mobility. The ubiquity of the Russian language and governmental preferences for demographic dispersal of the Russian population throughout the peripheral republics encouraged Russians (as well as Russophone Slavs) to settle in the peripheral republics. While Belarus and Ukraine had long possessed sizable ethnic Russian (*russkie*) populations, Soviet-era industrialization buttressed the numbers of Russians living in these areas. By late 1991, there were few places in Eurasia which lacked a sizable Russian population, and in some states the Russians accounted for upwards of a third of the population (Latvia, Estonia, Ukraine, and Kazakhstan). In the wake of the USSR's dramatic denouement, these Russians and ethnically-mixed Russophones— many of whom were quite comfortable with their de-ethnicized "Soviet" identity a few years earlier—were forced to come to grips with their status as national minorities in their states of residence. While ethnic diversity was enshrined in certain post-Soviet republics (Kazakhstan and Kyrgyzstan, in particular), other states pursued policies which doggedly promoted the indigenization of the public sector and even made private life difficult for many non-titulars. This was especially true of the Russians, who came to be viewed as unwanted vestiges of past imperial subjugation.[14]

These Russians, who had previously occupied a role of *primi inter pares* in the imperial periphery, were instantly reduced to second-class citizens, denied citizenship, and, in some cases, faced the possibility of expulsion from increasingly hostile states. Recognizing their precarious position, millions of Russians immigrated to the Russian Federation during the 1990s. They were able to do this by exercising their right under Russia's newly-minted nationality law, which entitled those with a strong emotional attachment to the Russian or Soviet state to "return" to their ancestral homeland and assume Russian citizenship. Today, the number of near abroad Russians has dropped to 19 million signifying an exodus of approximately six million to the Russian Federation or third countries.[15] Those who chose to stay quickly adapted to their new surroundings and have increasingly assumed the mantle of diaspora as best they could under such challenging circumstances. Part of this adaptation has been a rapid migration into cyberspace, at least among those which can afford access to Internet. Ethnic Russians in the near abroad tend to be well-educated, urban, and mobile. As such, significant portions of the population are regular users of the Internet. While Internet penetration to the home is modest in the former Soviet Union when compared to Western Europe, North America, and certain Pacific Rim countries, Web use is a part of daily life in the cities of the near abroad. As I will explore later, this mental migration into cyberspace functions as a salve for the daily challenges faced as a post-imperial minority in the nationalizing state of the near abroad.

While Russians in the Russian Federation regularly employ the Internet for nation-building, transborder jingoism, and even xenophobic attacks on national minorities within Russia, Internet-enabled Russians in the new abroad are developing transnational economic and social networks across Europe and North America. They are also using cyberspace to develop their 'European' credentials, and distinguish themselves from their 'Russian Russian' co-nationals. I argue that sustained Internet use actually has had a de-politicizing and de-nationalizing effect on minority Russians, with diasporic Russian netizens professing less allegiance to either the USSR or the Russian Federation than their non-Internet using counterparts. Increasingly, these Russians are placing themselves in a global rather than a national or ethnic context. Paradoxically, this is occurring while their "brethren" in the Russian Federation are using the Web to build a more cohesive (and in some cases, xenophobic) Russian nation.

Ethno-Politics in Post-Soviet Space

The collapse of the USSR in 1991 launched a host of new (and resurrected many old) identities onto the world stage. During the Stalinist era, the politicization of national identity had long been "officially discouraged" by Moscow, while the cultural aspects of ethnic identity were tolerated.[16] The Soviet Union, which assumed much of the multinational Russian state in 1922, oscillated on its policy toward national groups for a brief period, but ultimately chose to institutionalize national distinction within the state while encouraging linguistic and cultural Russification.[17] Professor of Eastern European studies Pål Kolstø refers to this policy as one of simultaneously and contradictory encouragement and retardation of national identity.[18] This decision has had resounding repercussions in the post-Soviet era as the legacy of Moscow's nationality policy bears unintended fruit in the form of "projects of redemption" for erstwhile suppressed titular majorities in their newly independent states. As Soviet premier Mikhail Gorbachev's triad of reforms (*uskoreniie* 'acceleration,' *perestroika* 'restructuring,' and *glasnost* 'transparency') began to alter Soviet society, national-ism and the politics of national identity grew in popularity, soon dominating much of the public consciousness. In this environment, politically-ambitious elites deftly made use of the national question to maintain and increase their power in the waning years of the Soviet Union. When the USSR disintegrated, these nationalist elites of-ten found themselves at the apex of new state structures. In this environment, the long-enduring façade of the Soviet nation (*sovetskii narod*) cracked to reveal a caco-phony of competing nationhoods and irredentist movements, many of which were contradictory. It soon became apparent that Soviet nationality policy had both created national competition where none had ever existed, and failed to mitigate his-torical, deep-seated ethnic conflicts, thus creating a volatile mixture.

Perhaps unsurprisingly, Russians were the earliest and most enthusiastic adop-ters of the idea of a Soviet nation, and thus saw themselves not as immigrants, colo-nizers or invaders, but mobile Soviet citizens regardless of the republics in which they lived. As sociologist David Laitin argues:

> Russians outside the RFSFR [Russian Soviet Federated Socialist Republic] were protected from coming to terms with their "minority" status...Russians in other re-publics beyond the RSFSR would no longer be called 'minorities' as they had been during the *korenizatsiia* ['indigenization'] period when they were classified as nonti-tulars....But for Russians in the non-RSFSR republics, minority status was unneces-sary; they were a plurality in the Soviet Union. These Russians...were the quintes-sential new Soviet men and women.[19]

As such, the 25 million Russians who found themselves outside the borders of the newly independent Russian Federation in late 1991 faced a particularly challenging crisis of identity.

Most of the Soviet Union's successor states have tended to work assiduously to deconstruct the firmaments of Russianization since independence. This aggressive promotion of their respective titular nationalities' rights has often impacted minori-ties quite negatively (especially the Russian minority). This situation has been most acute in Latvia and Estonia, primarily due to the strength and depth of historical memory associated with the loss of independence in the 1940s. The USSR's illegiti-mate annexation of the Baltic States during World War II—an event which was ac-companied by the deportation of local elites and subsequent settlement policies fa-voring Slavs—continues to serve as the guiding élan of Baltic nationality policy. Fear of language extinction, demographic dilution, and revanchist Russian policies conducted through an imagined "fifth column" of ethnic Russians has promoted an environment of mistrust and nationalist vitriol even as the Baltic States' realize greater levels of democratic pluralism and economic prosperity.

In those areas which failed to gain interwar independence from Moscow, the reactions to ethnic Russians after independence have been less problematic, though not without controversy. In the Central Asian republics where Russians represent a sizeable minority (i.e., Kazakhstan and Kyrgyzstan), they have been woven into the multi-ethnic fabric of the new societies, though only after having been on the losing end of state-supported affirmative actions schemes which elevated the status of the titulars in the government, professional fields, and education. In Turkmenistan, Rus-

sians were actually allowed to maintain dual citizenship with the Russian Federation
for the much of the past fifteen years. Recently, however, this perk was revoked by
the country's late dictator, Saparmurat Niyazov, causing many Russians to hastily
sell their assets and flee over the border. Today, the situation of Russians in this gas-
rich nation is generally poor though the same can be said of most of their Turkmen
counterparts. Uzbekistan, a country where Russians represent a modest percentage of
the overall population, has seen a good deal of out-migration due to economic rather
than ethnic issues, although Uzbekification is rather robust. In Tajikistan, most Russians who had the means fled the country during the Tajik Civil War (1992-1997)
between the Moscow-backed government and Islamist rebels. Only a tiny, and pre-
dominately elderly, minority still remains. In the Caucasus, which like Tajikistan has
seen Russian flight due to economic instability and political strife, the rather small
Russian minority has tended to benefit or suffer as part of a larger geopolitical schema. In Georgian and Azerbaijan, they are at best tolerated, whereas in Armenia—a
stalwart ally of the Russian Federation—they are treated with benign disregard.

The position of the Russians in the Western Republics (Ukraine, Belarus, and
Moldova) is an especially sensitive and complicated issue. In Moldova, a Slavic separatist movement precipitated a civil war in the early 1990s. While hostilities ended
some years ago, the country is still riven by ethnic problems. Transnistria, a self-
declared republic populated principally by Russians and Ukrainians, sits along the
eastern shore of the Dniester River, while the ethnic Romania population remains
concentrated in the western part of Moldova. The political orientation of the large
Russian population in Ukraine became a major electoral issue in the lead up to the
2004 presidential elections which sparked the Orange Revolution. Many—though
not all—Russians supported the pro-Russian candidate and outgoing President Leo-
nid Kuchma's heir-designate, Viktor Yanukovich. Once it was clear that the pro-
European challenger Viktor Yushchenko was going to force a rerun of the disputed
election, the country's ethnic Russians (who are mostly concentrated in the east of
Ukraine) began pushing for a sweeping devolution of power to the regions. Hoping
to gain similar levels of self-government as their Crimean counterparts (60 percent of
who are ethnic Russian and 95 percent Russian-speaking), a significant portion of
near abroad Russians signaled for the first time that they were willing to assume the
mantle of a political rather than just a cultural bloc. The rather underwhelming afte-
reffects of the Orange Revolution have, however, taken the steam out popular support for such proposals. The fluidity of national identity in Ukraine might also explain the rather limited allure of ethno-nationalism in the country. According to
Ukrainian census data from 2001, roughly 3 million ethnic Russians "converted" to
Ukrainian over the previous decade, a phenomenon which reflected the power shift
from Moscow to Kiev.[20]

Perhaps due to the comparatively gossamer boundaries between Belarusian and
Russian identity, the Russians in the Belarus have come to serve the political ends of
the current leadership in Minsk. In the wake of the 2005 presidential elections, President Alexander Lukashenka's government issued statements which suggested that
Western-style democratic traditions for not right for the common nation of Orthodox
Slavs, and that European and American policymakers should keep out of Russian,
Ukrainian, and Belarusian politics. However, despite the seemingly preferential
stance of Minsk towards Russianness, some ethnic Russians in the republic complain
of a stringent regime of forced Belarusianization similar to that employed in the na-

tionalizing states of the Baltics.[21] According to Andrey Dynko, editor in chief of the Minsk-based Belarusian-language weekly *Nasha Niva*, "The number of Russians in Belarus shrank by more than one-fourth in the decade between the last two censuses. This assimilation is advancing even at a quicker pace than that in Ukraine. While in Ukraine it provokes various protests of the Russian minority, in Belarus it is proceeding unnoticeably and everybody seems to take it for granted."[22]

Ethno-politics in Russia have similarly undergone a major transformation in the wake the country's independence from the USSR, though many of the current trends were well underway prior to 1991. As mentioned earlier, of all the Soviet nationalities, the Russians tended to most readily embrace the mantle of Sovietness. However as the USSR began to tear at the seams, Russians living inside of Russia were forced to reexamine the nature of their national identity. According to Russian specialist Vera Tolz, the reification of post-Soviet Russian identity has manifested in several ways:

- Racially-defined Russianness granted solely through *ius sanguinis* ('law of blood')
- Linguistically-defined Russianness, primarily determined by membership in the community of Russophones (*russkoiazychnie*)
- *Primi inter pares* within the larger "Eastern Slav" nation alongside Ukrainians and Belarusians
- Civic Russianness constituted through loyalty to the Russian Federation
- Union identity based on the Russians seminal role in building a multi-ethnic 'nationality' among those people living inside the borders of the former USSR[23]

We can add "negative identity" to this mix; according to sociologist Lev Gudkov, Russians define their national identity in opposition to "Western" values of individualism, pragmatism, and rationality.[24] Professor of religious studies Alexander Agadjanian suggests that this incongruous medley results from the rather "looser ethnic make-up" of Russians throughout history, and the ever-present status of the Russian-dominated state which mitigated the demand for acutely defining Russian national identity.[25] Regardless, new media landscapes have emerged as key battlegrounds for intellectual entrepreneurs to mobilize the masses towards one or more of these identity trajectories as will be explored shortly.

Informatizatsiia Delayed, Not Deferred

During the first half of the Cold War, technological advancement dovetailed nicely with the socialist world's grand stratagem. During the heady days of Sputnik, the world trembled and marveled at the sound of Soviet rockets. It seemed the more that the USSR advanced in technological terms, the better it was able to manage its economy and gain influence abroad. The lead in the space race synergistically contributed to the Soviet Union's nation-building efforts as well. In the 1960s, Moscow deployed its Orbita satellite television network (followed by the direct-to-home Ekran satellite system in 1976) to deliver television to its domestic market guaranteeing that almost every Soviet citizen—from the Baltic to the Pacific—would have access to state broadcasts of news, information, and entertainment. The USSR thus became the first country to deploy ubiquitous television programming via space-based technology trumping even the United States. Despite leading the space race for a decade or more, the USSR failed to support the development and application of advanced technology in the latter half of the Cold War. This decision was directly related to the security and stability concerns of Moscow, as well as an obsession for favoring heavy over light industries.[26]

The introduction of computers, personal telephones, and fax machines into the workforce which accompanied post-industrialism initiated an ideological quandary for totalitarian countries like the USSR. Should they embrace these new technologies and risk opening up their systems to external influence and the free flow of information? Or would it be better to keep the effects of globalization and interdependence at bay? Japan, the United States, Germany and other Western European countries rapidly transitioned from a focus on heavy industry towards becoming "information societies." Conversely, the USSR and its socialist allies refused to remake themselves into "knowledge economies" and embrace the benefits of high technology. Consequently, these economies began to lag behind their capitalist counterparts in the late 1970s.

Mikhail Gorbachev, the Soviet head-of-state from 1985 until its demise in 1991, belatedly attempted to make the USSR an information society. Recognizing the crippling effects of the information technology lock-out of his predecessors, Gorbachev included ICT in his plans for uskorenie of economic development within the Soviet Union.

> Moscow's twelfth five-year plan of 1985 envisaged 1.3 million PCs [personal computers] in Soviet schoolrooms by 1995. But the Americans already had three million in 1985 and, in any case, the main Soviet PC, the Agat, was an inferior version of the outdated Apple II. Mikhail Gorbachev...was keenly sensitive to these problems. *Informatizatsiya* (crudely, informationization) became the buzzword of his [Gorbachev's] new era. His American counterpart, Secretary of State George Shultz, played on this concern periodically giving him minatory tutorials about how the rest of the world was moving from "the industrial age to the information age." At the same time, the communications revolution in phones and faxes, TV and radio, made it even harder to insulate Soviet-bloc citizens from evidence of failure of their regimes and of the lifestyles in the West.[27]

Despite half-hearted attempts to continue repressive policies of technology and information management, KGB surveillance, and ideological control, the virus of opposition spread through Soviet society aided by the radical new technologies of the 1980s (as well as *socially new* technologies like private phones).[28] Information about the West, Stalin's crimes, and the weakness of the Soviet economy spread quickly just as the Kremlin had long feared it would. The emergence of comparatively free information spaces across the USSR and formerly communist Eastern Europe significantly aided the development of a long-retarded civil society and made meaningful coordination with diaspora communities and anti-communist organizations a reality. This change in communicative and informational structures became an important catalyst for the collapse of the Soviet hegemony in the late 1980s and the USSR itself in 1991.

Despite a delayed start, Russians have joined the information revolution with zeal. Wireless telephony and Internet access via mobile phones has been especially rapid. This is in some part due to the retarded state of Soviet Russia's landline telephony network which was chronically neglected by the state.[29] Plans for a city-wide WiFi network were recently announced for the Russian capital, a move which sharply increase the number of Russian Web users by providing access to nearly 4 million households in the capital. Today, there are more than 25 million people in the Russian Federation that regularly access the Internet.[30] This represents 22 percent of the adult population and a 500 percent increase since 2003. Recently, the number of Russian Internet domains reached 500,000 with .ru now being the second-fastest growing domain on the net after China's;[31] furthermore, e-commerce in Russia reached $4.47 billion in 2005.[32] These numbers reflect a strong increase in the penetration of the Web into the Russian domestic market, as well as among sites for and by Russians in the new abroad.

Russian cyberspace even has its own name: RuNet. RuNet refers to all Russian-language sites as well as though hosted in the Russian Federation,[33] and may also be seen as encompassing all Russian language communication flows in cyberspace.[34] Russian cyberspace started out as an environment which was dominated by members of the "old diaspora" of Russians in Western Europe and North America, however this is now changing. Dmitry Shishkin, a senior producer at BBCRussian.com, states, "It used to be true for any Russian site that approximately 40 percent of the audience would be from inside Russia and 60 percent from abroad...In the last five or so years we noticed a growing domestic audience, particularly in Russia itself and among Russian speakers in the other ex-Soviet states."[35] Today, while traffic originating in the United States Germany, and Israel collectively account for just over 10 percent of RuNet activity, nearly all other RuNet users reside in the former Soviet Union.[36] With the shifting nature of its users and the increasing Russification of the Internet experience including wider use of Cyrillics in cyberspace and the increasing dominance of Russian portals such as Yandex and Rambler over Yahoo! And MSN, "[t]he Internet is no longer a Western import but is seen as something genuinely Russian."[37]

In the near abroad, Russians also have acute stimuli for utilizing the Internet for news and information. At the most basic level, the Internet functions as a viable platform for receiving news in their own language, as well as a communications tool for connecting with friends and family in other parts of post-Soviet space. It also serves as a mechanism for circumventing the stifling media censorship of the post-Soviet "managed democracies."[38] Lack of press freedom has driven many Russians into cyberspace for their news. In fact, the Muslim republics of the former Soviet Union all scored abysmally on Freedom House's 2009 report on press freedom. In this group, Kyrgyzstan ranked the highest at 158 out of 195 countries surveyed. The Central Asian republic of Turkmenistan tied for second-to-last place with Burma; only North Korea scored lower. The non-Muslim republics of Belarus (188), Moldova (148), Armenia, (151), and Ukraine (115) did not fare particularly well either (only the Ukraine score in the "Partly Free" category).[39] However, greater freedom of information does not solely account for embracing the Internet as an alternative medium.

Since independence, the Newly Independent States of Eurasia have all, to varying degrees, reduced the role of the Russian language in print, radio, and television media. Whereas its was once the standard that all media were dominated by the Russian language, today the titular languages reign supreme in most of the former Soviet republics (although in certain areas such as eastern Ukraine and northern Kazakhstan, Russian remains the dominant idiom in traditional mass media). Such cir-

124   Chapter 5

cumscription mirrors similar efforts to promote the titular languages in the political,
scientific, and educational milieus. For Russians and Russophones living in the new
abroad, the war of attrition on the Russian language has been viewed as a political—
rather than cultural—move intended to artificially promote the interests of the titular
majority at their expense.

Latvia is a case in point. Today, Latvia is a paragon of the "nationalizing
state."[40] Despite the drowsy start to the nationalist project, Latvia has indeed embraced what has been labeled "sleeping beauty nationalism," i.e., an overly aggressive form of nationalism which suddenly becomes enabled when imperial subjugation ends.[41] Latvian elites have gone to great pains to extirpate Russian, Soviet, and
other "foreign" elements associated with external rule from the new Latvia, while
simultaneously rushing headfirst in European Union accession and encouraging
German, British, Finnish, and Swedish investment in the country and cultural exchange with the 'West'. Even though Latvia ranks as one of the freest media environments in the world (tied with Taiwan at 23rd place and ahead of Spain in 2009),[42]
Russians and Russophones complain of limited access to print and broadcast media
resources in their own language and press biases against them and the issues which
they believe are important. The increasing domination of media by the respective
titular languages in the NIS is forcing many Russians into cyberspace in search of
relevant and intelligible media products. As Maya Ranganathan states, "Logically,
the Internet as a medium of communication assumes importance when there is a total
denial of access to the organization by the mainstream media."[43] On the Internet,
there is no problem in getting access to information and entertainment exclusively in
ones native language, especially as Russian is the tenth most used language in cyberspace. There is also the question of bias in locally-produced media as well. Many
near abroad cyber-Russians claim that media in their states of residence tend to ignore events in Russia and other parts of post-Soviet space in favor of reporting on
"meaningless" local events. Furthermore, when state media covers international
affairs, such reports are only focus on Europe and America.[44] Russophone Web surfers thus seek out news from Russian-language sources in order to fill vacuum they
felt has grown since 1991.

One of my respondents pined away for the "old days" (read Soviet period) when
she would go to the cinema and the movies would all be in Russian or at least with
Russian subtitles. On the Internet, she asserts, there is no problem in getting access to
all the information and entertainment she wants in her native language. The added
benefit of the Internet immediacy and time-saving nature makes it her number one
choice for information and communication. Another respondent lamented Latvian-
language media's obsession with current events in Western Europe and the U.S. at
the expense of coverage of important issues in post-Soviet space, especially in
neighboring Russia and Belarus, as well as Ukraine and Central Asia. For him, Internet-based sources in Russian do not suffer from the belief that the world ends at Latvia's eastern border. The Latvian-speaking Russians with whom I spoke lacked a
spiritual connection to Russian-language media; instead their preference for Russian
media was almost always enunciated as the only practical option. Russian-language
Internet sites and sites originating in the Russian Federation were often preferable
simply due to the fact they conveyed more international information and had a wider
scope.

Perhaps the most interesting finding in my research among Latvian Russians re-volved around perceptions of reality beyond the borders of the state. Any discussion of "life in Russia" produced sharp contrasts between cyber-Russians and non-Internet users. Non-Internet users tended to romanticize the situation for the "average Russian" in the Russian Federation and drew distinct contrasts between the ways that the Latvian government treats its own Russians. Many even talked about higher sala-ries and lower costs for services in Russia (even in Moscow!). Latvian cyber-Russians, however, tended to have a view of Russia which was firmly rooted in reali-ty. Their constant communication with friends, relatives, and business contacts in the Russian Federation provided more accurate insight into the travails the average Rus-sian faced on a daily basis. Communications scholars Asu Aksoy and Kevin Robins' article on Turkish Cypriot communities in Britain and their relationship with Turkish satellite television is helpful in contextualizing this phenomenon. In "Banal Transna-tionalism," Aksoy and Robins argue that Turkish TV helps dispel many of the ideal and timeless images promoted in the diaspora by representing Turkey as "banal and everyday."[45] Similarly, cyber-Russians seem to be less likely to romanticize life in Russia through the optic of Soviet nostalgia.

This finding is especially interesting since both groups tend to travel to Russia regularly, however, Internet users tend to be better informed about the breadth and width of social, economic, and political conditions in the "ethnic homeland." My study also revealed that cyberspatial interactions tended to promote perceptions of distinction and difference between "Baltic Russians" (a group which a majority of my respondents made reference to without prompts) and their "Russian Russian" counterparts. In their discussions of their co-fatherlanders, cyber-Russians tended to eschew any fundamental sameness with the Russians of Russia—a community with whom they felt they shared little in the way of collective action, disposition, etc. This lack of solidarity seemed to be reinforced rather diminished by the Internet.

The *Samizdat* World of National Minorities

With its precipitous growth in the 1990s, cyberspace began to enable a *samizdat world* where anyone with access to an Internet-enabled device and a modicum of knowledge about Web design could impact public and private opinion on almost any issue without the interference of government censorship, editorial review boards, or any other information regulating entity. I use the term "samizdat" for two reasons. The first is to draw attention to the self-published nature of much of the content available via the Internet. The second is to draw a connection between cyberspatial national identity production and the distribution of information about national minor-ities in the Soviet Union in the 1970s and 1980s. There are significant parallels be-tween current self-published information about national identity on the Web and the underground media of the Soviet era. In fact, allusions to the Internet as samizdat are not new.

Sergei Kovalev, a prominent Soviet dissident, has called samizdat the "Internet-for-the-poor." Samizdat emerged in the 1950s and was simultaneously a mechan-ism for reproduction of and an institution for dissemination of unavailable texts. By reproducing in a typewritten form never published texts and texts that were out

of print due to ideological reasons, samizdat activists overcame the shortage of literature created by the state monopoly on publishing.[46]

Perhaps more important than the "self-made" character of the Internet is the choice it
gives its users in the consumption of media. Netizens can pick the time they want to
download information, the source of the content, and even the language of distribution. Certain authors have described cyberspace as a "fourth place," that is, a virtual
complement to the "third places" such as the German Biergarten, the French café,
and the Chinese teahouse.[47] Zixue Tai, in his description of the role the Internet plays
in civil society, describes cyberspace as an "imperfect Habermasian public sphere"
for the twenty-first century.[48] The deterritorialized nature of the platform allows
communication and media consumption without regard for geographic location, assuming the user has access to the Web. Taken together, the attributes of this new
mass media have radically altered the consumption and production of information by
national minorities, diasporas, and stateless nations.

Despite its potential for production and maintenance of national identity, the Internet is a double-edged sword for national identity projects. As British journalist
Rohan Jayasekera states, "All in all, the effect is schizophrenic; Web users celebrate
the Internet's ability to transcend national borders, but fall over themselves to place
themselves in corners of cyberspace with national identities."[49] Cyber-Russians frequently noted that the more time they spend on the Internet, the more they think of
themselves as "global citizens" even as they spend time, effort, and money connecting to their national brethren. In conducting interviews with cyber-Russians in Latvia
and the Republic of Kazakhstan, it has become clear that nationalist aspirations
quickly take a back seat to personal desires in cyberspace among this particular coterie. Russians are seeking to break out of a claustrophobic environment imposed on
them by political systems over which they seem to have little control. Orienting
themselves towards a self-serving and often callous Russian establishment achieves
little, but choosing to embrace the greater Russian community across Europe, Eurasia, North America, and even Australia is a viable methodology for personal advancement and identity maintenance. This is where new media become central.

The lack of attraction to nationalist paths among new abroad Russians can only
partially be explained by the dazzling totems of globalism which decorates cyberspace. It also stems from unique characteristics of the Russian nation and the Soviet
past. Perhaps most important is the well-documented weakness of Russian national
identity.[50] While the Russians have never lacked for identity anchors—civilizational
messianism colored both the tsarist and Soviet social constructs of Russianness—
many scholars suggest that Russianness manifests in a way that differs greatly from
the modernist national identities of other European nations. Russian national identity
is diluted by its historical syntheses with and/or derivation from religious identity
(Eastern Orthodoxy), the Russophone population, pan-Slavism, and, of course, Soviet universalism.[51] Of these, the latter paradoxically predisposed new abroad Russians toward globalism—that is, an outlook which is worldwide in scope and one
which placer a higher premium on worldwide issues than on national issues.

Among my respondents, there was a constant refrain that globalization offered
tech-savvy, English-speaking people mobility in both real and occupational terms.
Using language strangely reminiscent of Ferdinand Tönnies' theories on *Gemeinschaft* and *Gesellschaft*,[52] these cyber-Russians argued that knowledge and skills

allowed them to break out of the ethnic shackles which bind their less fortunate comrades. Just as the Soviet system created a vast space where a single language, culture, and ethos dominated, so has globalization. In this new world order, English has replaced Russian as the lingua franca; a creolized global mélange[53] has displaced Pushkin and Chekhov as the cultural standard. Likewise, a tantalizing nexus of neoliberalism, consumerism, and individualism has replaced Marxism-Leninism as the guiding force for human development (such an orientation sets cyber-Russians in the new abroad in firm opposition to those Russian Russians professing a form of Gudkov's previously referenced negative identity). While the capitalist and individualistic nature of this new weltanschauung probably has Lenin and Stalin spinning in their graves, new abroad Russians point out that under both world orders one need not be constrained by putatively immutable ethnic, regional, or national traits. As long as an individual's behavior is consistent with that prevailing philosophy's prescriptions, success is attainable for nearly anyone.

Cyber-Russians in the near abroad tend to have weaker attachments to the USSR, Russia, the Russian nation, and their country of residence than their non-Internet enabled brethren. They did, however, demonstrate a profound willingness to engage with what they construe to be the global community. They tended to articulate this predilection in terms of promoting their personal opportunities as members of an "unjustly" persecuted minority in their counties of birth. By shifting towards a non national (non-ethnic) paradigm, these cyber-Russians were better able to leverage their skills and talents. In effect, cyber-Russians—though still linked to the local—are transcending national boundaries by embracing the global market place—a powerful imaginary girded by the medium of cyberspace. Thomas Hylland Eriksen has observed: "As theorists of nationalism have shown, there is no contradiction between individualism and the growth of abstract communities; on the contrary, they are directly interrelated. The nation is a collective of individuals and a collective individual."[54] The Russophone Netizens of the near abroad personify this fundamental principle.

Weakening Nationalism One Click at a Time

Internet-enabled Russians in the near abroad are not generally committed to colonizing cyberspace in the name of the nation. Instead, they are employing the Web to enhance their personal, professional, and economic opportunities across global space. Cyberspace has become a powerful mechanism for upward mobility; it also serves as a way for marooned Russians to embrace a new, deterritorialized European identity. Despite the pervading notion that Web use among national minorities tends to strengthen national identity, my research on near abroad Russians does not find that increased Internet use strengthens national identity for Russian qua Russians. In effect, sustained Internet activity acts as a dampener on nationalism among near abroad Russians despite myriad opportunities for nationalist mythmaking and political mobilization in cyberspace. Furthermore, my findings contradict the prevalent notion that diasporic Russians in the former Soviet Republics might follow the path of ethnic Germans in the newly independent countries of Eastern Europe in the interwar period. Rather than becoming fifth columns promoting the interests of a revanchist rump state, the vast majority of cyber-Russians, i.e., Web-enabled ethnic

Russians, in the near abroad are instead employing the Internet build transnational personal and commercial networks across Europe and Eurasia and to develop their English skills for employment and educational opportunities in Western Europe and elsewhere.

While Russian cyberspace is generally nationalistic (sometimes rabidly so), I found that the vast majority of this sort of discourse emanates from within the borders of the Russian Federation. That is not to say that diasporic Russians refrain from jingoist rhetoric on Web. My research uncovered quixotic attempts to re-Russify lost territories such as Moldova, Tajikistan, Ukraine, and elsewhere. However, empirical research collected among Internet-enabled Russian populations in Kazakhstan, Latvia, and Estonia as well as through interviews conducted in cyberspace suggests that the Internet is less a landscape for nationalist agitation than for personal advancement.[55] Importantly, the Internet is serving to denationalize ethnic Russians in the near abroad despite its potential utility for other, more ethno-nationalist undertakings. In fact, I found that cyberspatial activities between near abroad Russians and Russia mirrored Web use among recent immigrant groups in the United States in that it served as tool for keeping in touch with friends and family and did not have a decidedly political bent whatsoever. The large difference from immigrant communities in the U.S. was the way that near abroad Russians used the Internet for personal advancement such as developing commercial networks, improving English skills, and preparing for work or study in Western Europe.

The shock of the collapse of the USSR, the often painful demands of living as an "immigrant" in one's birth country, and the concurrent psychic traumas of globalization have created a powerful nexus which have deeply impacted younger near abroad Russians. The Russians I polled have turned to cyberspace to help them make sense of their place in world. Through such actions, Web-savvy Russian elites are increasingly acting as agents of globalization within their own communities. Such patterns are paradoxical when compared against the extant literature on cyberspace's impact on national identity which has hitherto suggested that the Internet strengthens minority identity by enabling ethnic entrepreneurs to create virtual ghettos that are—as paradoxical as it may seem—global in nature. As stated earlier, the Web has been a godsend to the small, powerless nations who now have access to a mass medium that endows their communities with the ability to replicate the functionality of TV, radio, and the newspaper on a single platform. While the Russians in the near abroad certainly have the capacity to do likewise, they have instead opted to use cyberspace to develop transnational networks (often with non-Russians), to learn a third language (English), and to develop their attributes as "global citizens," and in doing so are becoming what I have referred to elsewhere as denationalized digerati.[56]

The Internet is acting as a dampening agent for both emergent Russian nationalism and Soviet nostalgia, and instead tends to promote notions of difference rather than sameness across the Russian ethnic space. This is despite the fact that Russian cyberspace now teems with an impressive array of nationalist sites which are readily accessible to anyone with fluency and Internet access.[57] It is important to note that near abroad Russians were, to a great extent, shielded from the evolution of post-Soviet Russian identity production after 1991. Boris Yeltsin's era (1991-1999) of national identity projects were a lukewarm affair within the Russian Federation itself and therefore could be expected to have even less impact on diasporic Russians who were typically beyond Moscow's immediate reach. Cyber-Russians—influenced by the corporatist, non-territorial structure of the Internet—are slowly but steadily eschewing nationalist mythmaking and instead opting for personal economic and social advancement outside the confines of the "nation." In effect, the Internet is the glue which binds together a number of elements of globalization effectively promoting the emergence of postnational identities among near abroad Russians.

Curiously, non-Internet enabled Russians in the near abroad show a comparatively high tendency to associate themselves with the Russian nation, the Russian Federation, the Putin administration, and the USSR.[58] While I do not suggest a causal relationship between lack of Internet access and increased nationalism, I do suggest that the socio-economic factors that limit Web use may also serve to economically and socially marginalize minorities Russians within their states of residence, further cementing their identity as Russians *qua* Russians vis-à-vis the titular majority. The results thus lend support to existing studies of Russian minorities in the near abroad which suggest moderate to strong levels of attachment to multiple "homelands" in both the past (the Soviet Union) and the present (Russia and the country of residence).[59]

Cyber-Russians, however, tend to have weaker attachments to the USSR, Russia, the Russian nation, and their country of residence. In effect, Russian Internet users are less bound to places and things than their non-Internet using counterparts in the near abroad. Instead, "global" pulls on identity are displacing nationalist attachments of all stripes. Furthermore, it appears that Web-based communication and media consumption have led to a fracturing of Russian identities, rather than a harmonization of what it is to be Russian. Internet-enabled Russians see themselves as set apart from the greater Russian community with whom they feel to share little in the way of the key components of "identity": collective action, disposition, etc.[60] This lack of solidarity seemed to be reinforced rather diminished by the Internet. Thus, residual and reborn Russian nationalism among near abroad Russians is rather rare among the digerati of the near abroad. The Internet has so far failed to become a major breeding ground for agents of Russian nationalism among the diaspora, precisely because those individuals who tend to be attracted to such messages are less likely to be regular Internet users.

I believe this to be the case for two reasons. Firstly, Internet-enabled Russians tend to have a more realistic view of life in the Russian Federation than their non-Internet enabled counterparts. This distinction is directly connected to nationalist tendencies among the near abroad Russians. Those Russians who feel life is better in contemporary Russia operate under the wrong-headed assumption that little has changed there since the collapse of the USSR and that Russians are happy with conditions in the new Russia. Most cyber-Russians have a rather negative view of life in the Russian Federation and one which is steeped in reality rather than fantasy.

Constant communication over the Internet with friends and family residing in the country is central to this perception. Cyber-Russians seem to have a better grip on the challenges faced by Russian Federation Russians in their everyday lives and eschew any fundamental sameness with the Russians of Russia. Internet usage, mobility, and economics all play a key role in this identity rupture. This is especially true among cyber-Russians in Latvia and Estonia who have enthusiastically adopted the mantle of Baltic Russians. However, it is also palpable among Central Asian cyber-Russians who maintain contact with Russians who had immigrated to the Russian Federation only to face economic hardship as well as the ironies of "ethnic" prejudice and maltreatment based on their status as "immigrants" in their ethnic homeland.

Secondly, the Internet offers users a new realm of experiences and possibilities, especially for marginalized groups like the near abroad Russians. Cyber-Russians are using the Web for well-laid plans for working and/or studying abroad. Internet connections with Russians in the "far abroad" (Germany, UK, U.S., etc.) serve to provide powerful imaginaries of escape and success. In effect, the Internet functions as tool for both imagining and realizing the pathways of intrepid emigrant Russians who have gone before them. Conversely, cyber-Russians who are committed to staying put often point to the Internet as a reason why they were sanguine about their future in their country of residence. The Internet functions as an indispensable tool for improving English language proficiency and learning more about the "outside world." It also enables new skills and facilitates new economic opportunities unknown in Soviet times. As a private, deterritorialized medium it is also beyond state control and thus desirable for marginalized groups. Despite being a national minority, near abroad cyber-Russians feel that Internet expertise allows them a better chance at future economic success than that possessed by their English-challenged, non-netizen counterparts (both ethnic titulars and Russians) whose attractiveness to multinational corporations is quite limited.

In effect, the Internet is to some extent globalizing the Russian minority in the near abroad by providing a international, meritocracy-based alterative to their ethnically-determined societies. American sociologist Saskia Sassen identifies the emergence of "communities of practice" that create increasingly relevant networks of communication, solidarity, and collaboration which she deems "micro-instances of partial and incipient denationalization."[61] Cyber-Russians of the near abroad are exemplars of this phenomenon. For cyber-Russians, the relationships and activities which are promoted in cyberspace are not necessarily conducive to nationalism or national pursuits per se, but instead build on familial ties, personal comradeship, and business opportunities. Many respondents pointed out that the Web does not make anyone more Russian, it just allows you to realize your wants and desires and thus it represents an evolutionary rather than revolutionary medium. It is thus evident that the Internet plays an important part in shaping communication practices, perceptions of spatial connections, and information consumption. However, cyberspace does not seem to play a meaningful or even marginal role in strengthening national identity among the Russians of the near abroad.

While reduced access to ethnic media in nationalizing states seems to encourage greater Internet use among the minority Russians, regular use of the Internet seems to act as a dampener on nationalist sentiment among the near abroad Russians. Notwithstanding, the effect of the Internet on the Russian minorities in the near abroad is not neutral. Increased Internet use is having an impact on societal relations by stimulating Russians to seek global rather than national paths to personal development. Cyber-Russians are satisfying their ambitions outside of national frameworks which are in many ways determined by the titular majorities in the states in which they reside.

The unending barrage of cosmopolitan and consumerist values which the elites among the new abroad Russians have had to contend with has further weakened their national identity of Russians *qua* Russians, especially those shielded from the half-hearted efforts of the Russian Federation to (re)create a old/new national identity for

Russians. The collapse of the USSR and its mythos had a crippling effect on Russian identity. Those sources of renewed identity since 1991 have mostly been state-centric (with the exception of the Vladimir Zhirinovsky's revanchist ethno-nationalism) and have thus left many the new abroad Russians cold (as well as many Russians within the Russian Federation). Russia's subsequent diminution of power in Eurasia must also be viewed as a contributing factor in the lukewarm nature of Russian national identity in the virtual new abroad. Though the Russian Federation has often intervened on the behalf of its "co-fatherlanders" in the Newly Independent States, the general perception among the new abroad Russians is that such actions are unhelpful, often worsening their situation. Russia's failure to make the Commonwealth of Independent States into a viable entity, the weakening of Russia's sports program, Russia's fiscal crises of the 1990s, the expansion of the United States into Russia's sphere of influence (the Baltics, Ukraine, Georgia, and parts of Central Asia), and the disastrous war in Chechnya all serve as crucial reminders of Russia's status downgrade on the world stage.

Conversely, the European Union's incorporation of countries with a significant Russian population (Latvia and Estonia) and vibrant relationships with neighboring and nearby countries (Ukraine, in particular) offers a competing identity anchor for new abroad Russians. Many Russians in the Baltics are readily embracing new trans- or pan-European approaches to identity which are underpinned by physical and occupational mobility, "European values," and Continental cultural harmonization. Even in Central Asia, there is talk among the Russian community of pan-Eurasian identity connected to new economic spaces enabled by globalization, education, and communication. The Internet and other media are playing prominent roles in these new identity trajectories.

All this is leading to a form of "banal globalism" where the global is "a back-cloth to the world of exceptional co-presence."[62] For those minority Russians who regularly use the Internet, the allure of "Russianness" is diluted in the deterritorialized, consumer-oriented mediascapes of cyberspace. Likewise, the constrictive (and even restrictive) structures imposed on them by their titular counterparts can be circumvented through engagement with the "world community." According to sociologists Bronislaw Szerszynski and John Urry, globalized mass media consumption (as opposed to previous forms of mass media which were state-centric) promote new world views which are based on cosmopolitanism, a predisposition which "involves the search for, and delight in, the contrasts between societies rather than a longing for superiority or for uniformity."[63] Such a worldview is built on mobility, consumption, curiosity, risk-taking, reflexive mapping of the self, interpretive semiotic skills, and openness.[64] All these characteristics can be applied to the cyber-Russians who constituted my case studies in Latvia, Estonia, and Kazakhstan.

Notes

1. Elsewhere, the socialist federations of Yugoslavia and Czechoslovakia began their respective dissolutions, producing a host of additional European states by the end of the millennium.
2. This was most dramatically underscored by the choice given to Algeria's Pieds-Noirs in early 1960s: "*la valise ou le cercueil*" ('the suitcase or the coffin').

3. Although it should be stated that leftist uplift movements have tended to employ anti-white messaging as part of their campaigns to gain popular support amongst the overwhelmingly indigenous populations of Andean countries or the African and mixed race populations of the Caribbean basin.

4. The term near abroad (*blizhnee zarubezh'e*) or, less often, new abroad, is commonly used by Russians both in and outside of the Russian Federation to refer to those states which formerly comprised the Union of Socialist Soviet Republics (excepting Russia itself). The term, however, is controversial for many living in the Newly Independent States as it is seen to connote that these areas remain with the exclusive realm of Russian influence.

5. Digerati, a portmanteau of digital and literati, describes opinion leaders in cyberspace who promote the internet and other information and communications technologies as transformational elements within their societies. The term was purportedly coined in the early 1990s in the USENET. It gained widespread usage in 1996 with the publication of John Brockman's *Digerati: Encounters with Cyber-Elite*.

6. Emil Payin, "The Disintegration of the Empire and the Fate of the 'Imperial Minority,'" in Vladimir Shlapentokh, Munir Sendich, and Emil Payin, *The New Russian Diaspora: Russian Minorities in the Former Soviet Republics* (Armonk, NY: M. E. Sharpe, 1994), pp. 21-36.

7. Most Russians living in the near abroad are visibly uncomfortable with the mantle of "national minority." Nearly all respondents eschewed the term when asked if it applied to them personally. The legacy of the Soviet Union shapes the discourse surrounding the term and to some, groups with an ethnic homeland whether it is the Russian Federation, the Republic of Kazakhstan, or Latvia cannot be classified as a national minority because they have someplace to "go home to."

8. Laura E. Kauppila, "The Baltic Puzzle: Russia's Policy towards Estonia and Latvia, 1992-1997." Pro Gradu Thesis in Political History, Department of Social Science History, University of Helsinki, 1999.

9. That is prior to the establishment of USSR in 1922; however, Kazakhstan was an administrative unit within Russia until 1936 when it gained SSR status.

10. The Old Believers are a schismatic sect which broke the Russian Orthodox Church in the mid-17th century. In order to avoid persecution, many Old Believers fled to the periphery of tsarist Russia including Latvia, Estonia, and Alaska. For more information, see Irina Paert, *Old Believers: Religious Dissent and Gender in Russia, 1760-1850* (Manchester: Manchester University Press, 2003).

11. Henrike Schmidt, Katy Teubener, and Nils Zurawski, "Virtual (Re)Unification?: Diasporic Cultures on the Russian Internet," in Henrike Schmidt, Katy Teubener, and Natalja Konradov, *Control + Shift: Public and Private Uses of the Russian Internet* (Norderstedt: Books on Demand, 2006), 124.

12. See Nicholas B. Breyfogle, Abby Schrader, and Willard Sunderland, *Peopling the Russian Periphery: Borderland Colonization in Eurasian History* (Abingdon, UK: Taylor & Francis, 2007).

13. Sergei Matjunin, "Bonded by the Past, Culture and Language," *A Minority Different from Others,* EuroDialog Web site, 1998, http://www.znak.com.pl/eurodialog/ed/aktualny/index.html.en (3 May 2006).

14. Titular majority refers to the nominal majority nationality in a given republic, thus the Russians were the titular majority in the Russian SFSR, the Estonians in the Estonian SSR and so on. With the exception of the Kazakh SSR, titular majorities also formed demographic majorities as well.

15. The conditions that greeted such re-migrants in Russia, however, were often unpleasant and many have since left, often returning to their republics of origin.

16. L. M. Drobizheva, "Etnicheskaia identichnost': Sovetskoie nasledie i sovremennie podkhody" [Ethnic Identity: The Soviet Heritage and Contemporary Approaches], *Demoscope Weekly* (3 March 2003).

17. Such a paradoxical approach derives from an uncomfortable synthesis of Leninist and Stalinist responses the nationality question. While Vladimir Lenin promoted a Bolshevik variant of Wilsonian self-determination for the various nations which comprised Soviet Russia, Joseph Stalin preferred a system of *divide et impera* combined with a heavy dose of Russification to assure the loyalty of the Soviet Union's constituent nationalities.

18. Pål Kolstø, "Territorialising Diasporas: The Case of the Russians in the Former Soviet Republics," *Millennium: Journal of International Studies* 28, no. 3 (December 1999): 607-631.

19. David Laitin, *Identity in Formation: Russian-Speaking Populations in the Near Abroad* (Ithaca: Cornell University Press, 1998), 69.

20. Oleg Varfolomeyev, "Notes from Kiev: Where Have All the Russians Gone?" *Transitions,* 10 February 2003.

21. Paul Goble, "Where 'Putin' is 'Putsin': Russian Nationalist Discontent in Belarus," *Radio Free Europe/Radio Liberty Newsline,* 31 August 2004.

22. Jan Maksymiuk, "Dynko: Soviet Nationalism as Lukashenka's Strategy of Survival," *Radio Free Europe/Radio Liberty Newsline,* 10 December 2003.

23. Vera Tolz, "Forging the Nation: National Identity and Nation Building in Post-Communist Russia," *Europe-Asia Studies* 50, no. 6 (September 1998): 993-1022.

24. Lev D. Gudkov, *Negativnaya Identichnost* [Negative Identity] (Moscow: Novoe Literaturnoe Obozrenie, 2004).

25. Alexander Agadjanian, "Revising Pandora's Gifts: Religious and National Identity in the Post-Soviet Societal Fabric," *Europe-Asia Studies* 53, no. 3 (May 2001): 473-488.

26. Terhi Rantanen, "The Old and the New: Communications Technology and Globalization in Russia," *New Media & Society* 3, no. 1 (March 2001): 85-105.

27. David Reynolds, *One World Divisible: A Global History since 1945* (New York: W.W. Norton & Co., 2000), 519.

28. See Rantanen, "The Old and the New."

29. Rantanen, "The Old and the New."

30. See "Survey Shows 25 Mln Russians Used Internet At Least Weekly Jan-Mar," *Prime-TASS News,* 19 April 2006.

31. See "Number of Russian Internet domains hits 500,000," *RIA Novosti,* 7 April 2006.

32. See ""Russian E-Commerce Totals $4.47 Bln for 2005," *Novecon,* 31 March 2006.

33. Anna Bowles, "RuNet A Cyberian Adventure," *Russian Life* 48, no. 2 (April/May 2005): 41-47.

34. Schmidt, Teubener, and Zurawski, "Virtual (Re)Unification?" 125.

35. Patrick Jackson, "News Fuels Russian Internet Boom," *BBC News Online,* 10 April 2006.

36. Schmidt, Teubener, and Zurawski, "Virtual (Re)Unification?" 125-26.

37. Henrike Schmidt and Katy Teubener, "'Our RuNet'?: Cultural Identity and Media Usage," in Henrike Schmidt, Katy Teubener, and Natalja Konradov, *Control + Shift: Public and Private Uses of the Russian Internet* (Norderstedt: Books on Demand, 2006), 17.

38. Managed democracy can be best described as "a political system in which emphasis is placed on political stability, elections are held but results are more or less foreordained, and serious political challenges to executive power are either absent or muted"; Stephen K. Wegren and Andrew Konitzer, "Prospects for Managed Democracy in Russia," *Europe-Asia Studies* 59, no. 6 (September 2007): 1025-1047.

39. See the Freedom of the Press 2009 Survey at http://www.freedomhouse.org/.

40. See Rogers Brubaker, *Nationalism Reframed: Nationhood and the National Question in the New Europe* (Cambridge: Cambridge University Press., 1996), 5-6.

41. Ronald Grigor Suny, *The Revenge of the Past: Nationalism, Revolution, and the Collapse of the Soviet Union* (Stanford: Stanford University Press, 1993), 3.

42. See *Freedom of the Press 2009* (Washington, D.C.: Freedom House, 2009).

43. Maya Ranganathan, "Potential of the Net to Construct and Convey Ethnic and National Identities: Comparison of the Use in the Sri Lankan Tamil and Kashmiri Situations," *Asian Ethnicity* 4, no. 2 (June 2003): 265-279

44. This phenomenon was much more prominent in the Baltic States than in Kazakhstan which maintains much closer relations with the Russian Federation.

45. Asu Aksoy and Kevin Robins, "Banal Transnationalism: The Difference the Television Makes," in Karim H. Karim, *The Media of Diaspora* (London: Routledge, 2003), 97.

46. Serguei A. Oushakine, "The Terrifying Mimicry of Samizdat," *Public Culture* 13, no. 2 (Spring 2001): 191-214.

47. Zixue Tai, *The Internet in China: Cyberspace and Civil Society* (New York; London: Routledge, 2006), 162-71.

48. Tai, *The Internet in China*, 183.

49. Rohan Jayasekera, "Waiting for the Kingdom: Nations in Cyberspace are No Substitute for the Real Thing," *Index on Censorship* 29, no. 3 (May/June 2000): 140-145.

50. See, particularly, Astrid S. Tuminez, *Russian Nationalism since 1956: Ideology and the Making of Foreign Policy* (Lanham: Rowman & Littlefield, 2000); David Brandenberger, *National Bolshevism: Stalinist Mass Culture and the Formation of Modern Russian National Identity, 1931-1956* (Cambridge: Harvard University Press, 2002); Taras Kuzio, "Russian National Identity and Foreign Policy Toward the 'Near Abroad," *Prism* 8, no. 4 (30 April 2002); and Peter J. S. Duncan, "Contemporary Russian Identity between East and West," *Historical Journal* 48, no. 1 (March 2005): 277-294.

51. See, for example, Tuminez, *Russian Nationalism since 1956*; Payin, "The Disintegration of the Empire"; and Tolz, "Forging the Nation."

52. Ferdinand Tönnies, *Community and Society*, English ed. (Mineola, NY: Dover Publications Inc., 2002 [1887]).

53. See Jan Nederveen Pieterse, *Globalization & Culture: A Global Mélange* (Lanham, MD: Rowman & Littlefield, 2003).

54. Thomas Hylland Eriksen, "Nationalism and the Internet," *Nations & Nationalism* 13, no. 1 (January 2007): 1-17.

55. I should note that Russian identity transformation in the Slavic republics of Transnistria, Belarus, and Ukraine has been less pronounced due to preservation of many aspects of the Soviet system. Additionally, there has been a less pejorative approach to nationalization of the state in the post-1991 time frame (at least in the Russophone and ethnically-Russian dominant parts of these countries). Anecdotal evidence suggests that my findings are not completely applicable to these Russian populations.

56. Robert A. Saunders, "Denationalized Digerati in the Virtual Near Abroad: The Paradoxical Impact of the Internet on National Identity among Minority Russians," *Global Media and Communication* 2, no. 1 (April 2006): 43-69

57. See, for instance, Polyuha 2005 for a discussion of Russian Internet users and their attempts to reintegrate the Ukrainian nation into the fold of the "eternal Ukrainian-Russian brotherhood."

58. My research also focused on Russians who did not use the Web in order to provide a control group to compare with the cyber-Russians.

59. See, for instance, Vladimir Shlapentokh, Munir Sendich, and Emil Payin, *The New Russian Diaspora: Russian Minorities in the Former Soviet Republics* (Armonk, NY: M. E. Sharpe, 1994); Pål Kolstø, "The New Russian Diaspora – An Identity of Its Own?" *Ethnic and Racial Studies* 19, no. 3 (July 1996): 609-39; Jeff Chinn and Robert J. Kaiser, *Russians as the New Minority: Ethnicity and Nationalism in Soviet Successor States* (Boulder: Westview Press, Inc., 1996); and Louk Hagendoorn, Hub Linssen, and Sergei Tumanov, *Intergroup Relations in States of the Former Soviet Union: The Perception of Russians* (Hove, UK: Psychology Press Ltd., 2001).

60. Rogers Brubaker and Frederick Cooper, "Beyond 'Identity,'" *Theory and Society* 29, no. 1 (February 2000): 1-47

61. Saskia Sassen, "Globalization or Denationalization?" *Review of International Political Economy* 10, no. 1 (February 2003): 1-22

62. Bronislaw Szerszynski and John Urry, "Visuality, Mobility and the Cosmopolitan: Inhabiting the World from Afar," *British Journal of Sociology* 57, no. 1 (March 2006): 113-131.

63. Szerszynski and Urry, "Visuality, Mobility and the Cosmopolitan," 468.

64. Szerszynski and Urry, "Visuality, Mobility and the Cosmopolitan," 470.

Chapter 6
Cybernetic Vanguard: The Roma's Use of the Web to Protect a Minority under Siege

The focus of this chapter is on those advocates of tiny nations who seek to preserve their identity in the face of crushing acculturation in their states of residence. In each of these cases, there exists a zealous coterie of young ideologues who have committed significant time and resources to "rebirthing" their ancestral tongues and unique cultures in cyberspace. I refer to these "new forces" of linguistic national-ism as a cybernetic vanguard, making reference to quasi-militant nature of their respective missions. This chapter hinges on the dyadic nature of the Internet as a mechanism for homogenization through the promotion of "global languages" like English, Spanish, Chinese, and Russian, while simultaneously creating conditions where miniscule linguistic communities can contest their creeping marginalization due to acculturation and globalization.

I use the concept of "structural violence" to explain the challenges that small nations face in the contemporary world.[1] Though subtle in its manifestations, struc-tural violence functions as suffocating force on small nations, slowly sapping their voices and power vis-à-vis the dominant ethnic population. The progenitor of the concept, Johan Galtung expanded on the notion of structural violence with his 1990 essay "Cultural Violence" in which he states: "Cultural violence makes direct and structural violence look, even feel, right—or at least not wrong.... The culture preaches, teaches, admonishes, eggs on, and dulls us into seeing exploitation and/or repression as normal and natural, or into not seeing them (particularly not exploita-tion) at all."[2] Through the combined effects of *penetration* (infiltration of the minor-ity by elements of the majority), *segmentation* (cordoning minorities within society with the intention of preventing political action), *marginalization* (forcing minority voices to the edge of the larger society), and *fragmentation* (division of the weaker community into smaller and competitive subunits), political elites representing the majority population have virtually guaranteed the extinction of the majority of the world's languages (and by extension, cultures).[3] However, the emergence of the Internet and its accompanying media-production capacity has altered this historical trajectory.

For isolates and small subaltern nations, cyberspace is an exciting new realm where members of small and often ignored nations can meet and exchange information about culture, history, and politics. The minimum requirements for launching a nation into cyberspace are modest. A single advocate for the nation, e.g., a college student with an interest in their nation's history and political situation, merely needs to gain access to the Web on regular or semi-regular basis. In today's world of user-friendly Web services, even a novice can upload a comprehensive site in a matter of hours. Countless Web sites exist on Yahoo's Geocities, Facebook, and other free Web hosting services that expound the values, mores, and attributes of tiny nations from the Amazon to the Caucasus to Oceania.

The Internet's capacity for the resurrection of dead or maintenance of moribund languages has been especially welcome by members of such nations. "Many smaller languages, even those with far fewer than one million speakers, have benefited from state-sponsored or voluntary preservation movements. On the most informal level, communities in Alaska and the American northwest have formed Internet discussion groups in an attempt to pass on Native American languages to younger generations."[4] Cornish, Manx, and other languages that are only a generation or two in the grave have seen new interest from Web-based advocates, including Web-based broadcasting of content in these languages. Scots, the Germanic language prevalent in the Scottish lowlands until the seventeenth century, has benefited from the emergence of instant messaging which provides new learners with a private domain to practice their skills without the fear of humiliation that comes with learning a new language—especially one, which in the case of Scots, was driven out of existence because it was seen as "socially inferior" (a classic case of Galtung's "cultural violence"). Even in face of almost certain annihilation, the existence of the Web stimulates action. This is evidence by seemingly quixotic national identity-building projects online where committed individuals have attempted to revive Ainu, Manx, and other dead or moribund languages in cyberspace (with the ultimate goal of re-launching these tongues into real space after an "incubation" period).[5]

While few analysts expect the Web to keep these endangered languages from falling out of daily use, there is optimism that they will be permanently preserved in cyberspace, thus differentiating the dead languages of today and tomorrow from those countless tongues lost forever in the past. Furthermore, it can be argued that the necessary acts of community-building associated with such linguistic projects endows the groups in question with helpful tools for achieving social justice and may enhance a group's potential for cultural survival.[6] Roughly a third of the world's 6,000 languages have 1,000 or fewer speakers left and many of the younger generation are failing to learn these languages from the parents and grandparents. It is expected that upwards of 80 percent of the world's languages will be dead or moribund by the end of the current century. Much of the blame can be laid at the feet of imperialism which promoted the use of conqueror's language as lingua francas across diverse linguistic spaces (e.g., Spanish in Central and South America, English in North America and Australia, etc.). State languages, either official or de facto, have also been a factor with Hindi, Bahasa (Indonesian), and Russian eclipsing the languages of ethnic minorities. Today, global capitalism keeps the pressure on small languages as the young tend to spend more time on studying English (or another commercial language such as Mandarin or Swahili) than on maintaining their ancestral language. Despite the pessimistic prediction of linguists, a bold new coterie of Internet-enabled elites begun prospecting in cyberspace, hoping to preserve and even expand their mother tongues' geographies. Even those communities who are technologically-challenged have made headway. In this chapter, I explore the digital realm of the Roma, one of Europe's most oppressed minorities.

This essay aims to understand better the role of the Internet as a mechanism for achieving political, cultural, and social advancement of "non-territorial" minorities in the current European context. I do this through a case study of the Roma—characterized by some as the "most European nation"[7]—and Romani cyberspace. The Roma people represent an interesting test case for several reasons. First, the Roma are a geographically dispersed population living in every country in Europe.[8] Second, the Romani language is divided by dialectical differences which have often hindered (though not prevented) communication and coordination among dispersed Roma communities. Lastly, the Roma exemplify minority status, easily meeting the four requirements for being defined as a national or ethnic minority, as they are not a numerical minority in every state in which they reside, do not dominate politically in any state or region, differ ethnically and linguistically from the majority populations of the states in which they reside, and they express feelings of intra-group solidarity in preserving their culture, traditions, and language.

While the Roma provide a compelling case for study of national minorities in the twenty-first century, there are several key differences from other indigenous groups which are worth noting. As mentioned above, the Roma did not consider themselves a "nation" as such until the 1970s. The exonymic use of the "Roma," in fact, obfuscates myriad internal divisions within a community divided by geography, clan loyalties, and dialects.[9] Furthermore, the taboos of *marimé/mochadi* prohibiting non-commercial interaction with non-Roma have precluded many necessary activities for advancing the national project within local, state, and international frameworks. "Traditional" Roma communities, which were historically characterized by extended familial units and encampments, made the formation and maintenance of the institutional structures required for advancing nationalist projects exceptionally difficult.

Due to institutional structures embedded in late-nineteenth century European society, Roma did not enjoy the opportunity develop a learned elite akin to those which emerged among sedentary peasantries of Central Europe (Slovaks, Romanians, Slovenes, etc.). Nor did they prove easily "assimilable" into the majority populations of their respective nation-states after independence from the Ottoman, Habsburg, and Romanov Empires (despite the intermittent efforts of European governments to do so). Furthermore, the Roma have tended to view the "nation" as a alien concept and, as such, inapplicable and undesirable to their particular situation. These factors have had a significant dampening effect on the development of political consciousness—a necessary component for transforming an *ethnie* (an ethnic community that does not necessarily possess a political identity) into a nation.[10] Lastly, and probably most importantly, Roma lack historical associations with a specific territory (excepting the Roma's medieval Indian origins), thus removing one of the most basic components of the traditional nation-building framework. The latter distinction has been reason enough for many policymakers and scholars of nationalism to exclude the Roma (and, for that matter, the Jews prior to the establishment of the modern state of Israel) from the status of nationhood (in many countries, the Roma were even denied minority status until recently). Though as we will see, such handicaps do not prevent nation-building projects in cyberspace or, for that matter, within the postnational European construct which has created conceptual and juridical space for the notion of "non-territorial minorities."

The Late Bloom: The Growth of Roma Nationalism in the Twentieth Century

The Roma—who began migrating to Europe from the Punjab nearly 1,000 years ago—represent, at once, a diaspora,[11] a racialized "Other,"[12] and a transnational ethnic minority.[13] During nearly a millennium of residence in Europe, the Roma (often referred to as Gypsies) have generated a fantastic array of perceptions, images, and prejudices among the *gadje/gorgio/payo* (non-Roma) with whom they share the continent.[14] While the Romani people have been envied for their perceived freedom, vivre, and adherence to traditions, they have simultaneously been excoriated for their secretiveness, chicanery, poverty, and lack of hygiene. Everywhere Roma are viewed as a (usually undesirable) minority living on the fringes of society as well as modernity. Consequently, they have generally been excluded from the national projects of Germans, Poles, Croats, and so on.

Given the consistent "Othering" of Roma within the structure of European identity, few scholars or politicians have, until recently, spoken in terms of a "Roma nation." The reason for this can be found in the ontological prejudices of European thinkers towards nationhood. Historical (and many modern-day perennialist) definitions of the nation require attachment to a particular territory as a prerequisite for nationhood.[15] The Roma lack both a national territory and historical memories of a primordial homeland, thus depriving them of one of the most basic attributes of nineteenth century nationhood, a deficit which hounds them to this day.[16] However, beginning in the late 1970s, constructivist theories of the nation placed a greater emphasis on perceived, invented, or imagined ties of community (see, for instance, Gellner 1983; Hroch 1985; Anderson 1991; Hobsbawm 1992).[17] Reflecting recent anthropological analyses of globalization's impact on nations and national identity, there has been a marked decrease in the importance placed on territory in conceptualizing nationhood. The increasingly recognized salience of hitherto marginalized identity projects among transnational diasporas, resurgent ethnies, and contrived nations are driving this change.

In the globalized world, dynamic ethnoscapes built on shared sentiment, cultural reproduction, and participation in a communications ecumene often count for more than attachment to a piece of earth—though territory still holds a powerful sway in nationalist discourse. Such developments are especially manifest in Europe where sovereignty sharing has become the norm and the Schengen Accord allows the freedom of movement and labor. Globalization and recent redefinitions of state sovereignty have thus altered the established rules of nation-building. As such, ethnographer Cara Feys' identification of the Roma as a "new" nation—i.e., one reflective of the current (postmodern) era rather than resembling the late-nineteenth century (modern) paradigm—seems a valid one.[18] Elites among the European Roma have recently undertaken efforts to form a "virtual community" to redress the historical problems associated with nation-building efforts that stem from their co-ethnics lack an easily definable territory. However, until recently, the proverbial deck was stacked against the Roma.

Whilst French, Romanians, Magyars, and others scrambled to build political containers that would hold the entirety of their respective nations, the Roma chose not to imitate—much less replicate—these projects of modernity. Weak to non-existent political mobilization, certain Romani praxes (marimé, nomadism, rejection of formal education, etc.), and majoritarian apathy and disdain created a nexus which discouraged any meaningful engagement in the processes necessary for late nineteenth century nation-building. However, significant efforts to unite the Roma and internationalize their plight began in the wake of the systematic Nazi extermination of approximately 500,000 Roma from 1938 to 1945. Nascent Roma nationalism was an outgrowth of the politicization of Romani identity vis-à-vis the Roma Holocaust, sometimes referred to as the *Porajmos* ('Devouring').[19] After the war, the Federal Republic of Germany denied reparations on definitional grounds: Roma were "officially" interned for criminality and other social violations—not their ethnicity which allowed Germany to avoid paying reparations during the latter half of the twentieth century.[20] In response, a number of "national" organizations began to coalesce and pool their power to change this situation.

The founding of the Paris-based *Communauté Mondial Gitane* in 1971 (later called the *Comité International Tsigane*) signaled a shift towards transborder cooperation between Roma communities—though Roma non-governmental organizations continued to operate in a federated manner based on nation-state delimited communities.[21] The organization's inaugural conference produced tangible harmonization among the various platforms of Romani elites. A flag and motto were adopted and the demonstrable connections to India were affirmed (India, in fact, partially funded the congress). Another congress followed in 1978, and when the Third World Romani Congress met in May 1981, "all the components and statements about a shared identity which transcended all national borders were present and the Gypsies had in place the traditional symbols of a united nationhood with the symbolic flag and anthem. The idea of a separate Romani nation was growing and strengthening."[22]

Many of these developments were influenced by Yugoslavian Roma who drew benefits from their country's close relationship with India through the Non-Aligned Movement. By breaking centuries of nomadic tradition and sedentarizing a sizeable portion of the Roma, the socialist states of Czechoslovakia, Bulgaria, Poland, Hungary, and Romania created conditions which produced a nascent elite, which differed in its makeup and orientation from the de-legitimized potentates of the "petty kingdoms" of traditional Roma society. These new power brokers were also pivotal in transnationalizing the Romani movement.

Since the 1990s, Romani activists have increasingly used the European Union and United Nations systems to advance their cause. In fact, the United Nations officially granted the Romani people observer status in 1980. The lifting of the Iron Curtain in the 1980s significantly aided this development by allowing greater communication and coordination between Roma in Eastern, Central, and Western Europe. Within the European framework, the establishment of and the Roma's subsequent recognition as a "non-territorial" minority provided, for the first time, true protections for the Roma which could leverage to influence the governing elites of their states of residence (especially in Eastern Europe where adherence to the EU's *acquis communautaire* quickly emerged as a necessary function of statecraft). In effect, nationhood granted an extra layer of (EU) citizenship rights to the Roma, who are now in a better position to defend themselves.

Over time, there has been a marked shift in the goals of the transnational Romani elites—from territorial acquisition (i.e., establishing an autonomous or independent homeland) to "national liberation" in more recent times.[23] In effect, the Roma are recognizing the realities and possibilities of the postinternational system and attempting to overcome the limitations imposed on them as a non-territorial minority. As Romani activist and president of the International Romani Union (IRU), Emil Ščuka, declared in "We, the Roma Nation:"

> We share the same tradition, the same culture, the same origin, the same language; we are a Nation. We have never looked for creating a Roma State [sic]. And we do not want a State today, when the new society and the new economy are concretely and progressively crossing-over the importance and the adequacy of the State as the way how individuals organize themselves. The will to consubstantiate the concept of a Nation and the one of a State has led and is still leading to tragedies and wars, disasters and massacres.[24]

In contrast to Ščuka's optimistic (though subtly normative) declaration of Romani nationhood, law professor Istvan Pogany cautions, "whether in sociological or anthropological terms, talk of a Gypsy or Roma 'national identity' remains premature. However, in political and legal terms the notion of a Roma 'nation' is undoubtedly a valuable tool for securing enhanced recognition of, and provision for, Europe's Roma peoples."[25] Despite the contested cogency of Romani national identity, Romani cyberspace has emerged as a new environment for the Roma to promote their culture, address grievances, and mobilize collective action across borders.

Knitting Together a "New" Nation in Cyberspace: The Politics of Virtual Romanestan

The advent of cyberspace has increased communication between members of all Romani, Traveller, *Gitano*, and other "Gypsy" communities, especially those separated by interstate borders. As Kurt Mills states, "[A] revolution [is] is taking place with the digitisation of identity, the wedding of selfhood and the electronic age, the redefinition, or, conversely the reification, of communal identity via cyberspace."[26] This process has given rise to a proliferation of virtual communities. According to social management specialists Mihaela Keleman and Warren Smith, "'virtual community' is constructed (like any other 'community') through individuals' (temporal and partial) engagement in the production and the consumption of a sense of sharedness and belonging," however, the possibilities of the Internet expand the day-to-day possibilities and the geographical and temporal scope of such a community.[27] It is both a public and private medium, simultaneously endowing its users with the benefits of secrecy and access to a wide audience across the globe. Not surprisingly, the Roma—no strangers to the use of clandestine, transborder communication networks—have adapted quite well to cyberspace despite certain socio-economic factors which make Internet use impractical or cost-prohibitive.

In the realm of politics, the advent of the Internet is a non-trivial occurrence for the Roma nation—especially since the popularization of the Web has coincided with two important phenomena: 1) the collapse of state-socialism in Eastern Europe; and 2) the acceleration of the pan-European project. These changes have resulted in greater mobility for the peoples of East-Central Europe, the spread of the single market to the region, and the harmonization of juridical norms across most of the European continent.[28] Through new media (and especially the Internet), marginalized national groups such as the Roma can now transcend statist media monopolies embedded in the post-Westphalian state structure. Historian of globalization Sheila Croucher argues that "technology also offers opportunities for stateless nations or ethnic groups to subvert the control of the state or states."[29] By providing a converged media platform, the Internet has emerged as an exceptionally welcome tool for widely-dispersed communities whose access to traditional media is contested, censored, or absent. According to Panikos Panayi, "Political ethnicity becomes possible with the backing of an ethnic media and the stereotypes which it perpetuates...Such groups can also develop a national myth through their media, even though they do not have their own nation states."[30]

In the case of marginalized minorities, there has been a sharp increase in political activities in cyberspace including (but not limited to): agitating for political change; advancing nationalist projects in opposition to their states of residence; and building social and economic networks which transcend international borders.

> While a considerable share of all communications and resources that ethnic groups exchange with other actors inside and outside the states in which they dwell is harmless, the existence of ethnic networks and the various communications that are placed through them also cause or contribute to conflicts involving ethnic groups on the one side, and state agencies on the other. Some of these conflicts have wider regional and global ramifications; they threaten state sovereignty and exacerbate inter-state relations as we know them.[31]

As one of the few articles on the Romani Internet asserts, "The Internet offers Roma a place to connect and provides information about Roma to others."[32] *Patrin,* considered to be one of the premier Romani Studies websites, states: "Today Roma are using the Internet to display pride in culture, language and solidarity with other Roma worldwide. The affordability and immediacy of the Internet provides a voice for the Roma, a voice that attempts to educate the public about a misunderstood and much maligned culture."[33]

For some Roma, this—like the collapse of state-socialism in 1989—is a mixed blessing. The Internet unites Roma across borders and provides a much needed communication platform which is beyond the purview of state and local governments. However, the Web simultaneously banishes much of the traditional secrecy which has long shrouded Roma customs, culture, and the language itself. On the MSN Groups page 'GYPSY – ROMA,' a post from a self-proclaimed Roma begged for help in learning Romani and sought Web-based sources to do so. The rather terse response from a user in Germany read: "no i am [very] sorry to tell you that you cannot learn the roma language over the net,,,only if you live the roma life [with] romas ,,sorry [sic]."[34] This statement is untrue. One can search "Learn Romani" on Google and then easily follow the advertising link to Amazon.com to purchase a copy of Ronald Lee's 2005 text *Learn Romani: Das-duma Rromanes* which "explores the vocabulary and grammar of the Kalderash Roma in Europe, the United States, Canada, and Latin America" in eighteen lessons. Alternatively, anyone with an Internet connection can simply download the Adobe Acrobat versions of *Amen Roman Siklojas* ('We Learn Romani')—an immersion method textbook made available by the Romani Project at the University of Graz. The project's charter reads as follows:

> The ROMANI PROJECT considers itself a contribution to the preservation of culture and identity by codifying and developing teaching methods for the language varieties of the Austrian Roma. Due to the assimilation pressure, Romani...which belongs to the Indo-Aryan branch of the Indo-European languages, is threatened with extinction. Thus, not only from the point of view of the native speakers, codifying is essential in order to reduce the probability of the language being lost and consequently becoming extinct in the future.[35]

However, the MSN Group respondent's undisguised disgust with the notion of Web-based Romani instruction is telling of the fractures within the Romani community over access to hitherto "protected" elements of Romaniness and the incompatibility of the values of some traditionalist Roma with the postmodern praxes of nation-building.

Roma are extremely protective of their language, often called *Romani čhib* or sometimes *Romanes*. Despite its ranking as the second largest minority language in the 27-member European Union with between 3-5 million speakers out of a total population of 8 million Roma.[36] Romani trails Catalan which has some 7.2 million speakers, but leads the Western European regional and minority languages of Galician (2.4M), (minority) German (2.2M), (minority) Hungarian (2.1M), Occitan (2.1M), Sardinian (1.3M), Irish Gaelic (1.2M), Basque (700K), and Welsh (500K).[37] Romani čhib still has an air of mystery for those outside the Roma community. This derives both from the lack of a standardized literary form of the language, as well as a normative orientation among its speakers that Romani čhib is a proprietary medium for Roma and the Roma alone.

As linguist Vardan Voskanian states, "For a people that has evolved neither an old literary tradition nor lasting works of material culture, and [whose] past existence is shrouded in the mist of centuries, the single thing in which its historical roots are sure to reside is its language."[38] It is not surprising then that, in many cases, the Roma—a historically insular people—choose to keep their language to themselves (though Romani is far from a cryptolect). There are also practical benefits to dialectal divergence. As human rights specialist Mary Ellen Tsekos points out, "Roma use various forms of deception and pretense to protect themselves. For one, Romanes, the Roma language, has been effectively kept a non-literary language, in part because knowing a secret language affords the Roma a degree of protection."[39]

Whereas digital nation-builders among Switzerland's Romansch, Poland's Kashubians, Latvia's Livonians, and Internet-enabled speakers of other dying European vernaculars unambiguously promote the spread of their mother tongues in cyberspace as well as their use by others, there is a great deal of trepidation in certain quarters of the Roma community about both phenomena. While some Roma believe that putting their language on the Internet will protect traditions and help future communities explore their cultural heritage, others are fearful of the Roma's most unique attribute being co-opted by non-Roma. Like a majority of the world's languages (though this is not the standard in Europe), Romani is an idiom, that has been passed down for generations without the help of primers, newspapers, or novels. As one of my respondents stated: "The net cannot change the Romani language because our language comes from the family...we all have different languages because we all belong to different families" (male Roma, aged 24).[40] The rapid migration of the language into cyberspace has been off-putting to many of its speakers. However, the Roma—unlike Europe's territorial-bound minorities (Bretons, Crimean Tatars, Rusyn, etc.)—can more easily afford their ambivalence about "webifying" their language since the proportion of Romanes-speakers among Roma is high, regardless of the state of residence. In most states with a sizeable Roma population, fluency ranges between 70-90 percent. Only in Hungary and Czechoslovakia does the rate sink to 50 percent.[41]

Mapping Virtual Romanestan: The Sites and Sounds of the Roma in Cyberspace

While the Web has not yet emerged as a fully-functional platform for learning Romani, the language's presence in cyberspace is on the rise. This is due, in good part, to the efforts of academia, though Romani netizens are making increasing use of these resources.[42] The University of Manchester's Romani Project is an important manifestation of this new trend. Created by Yaron Matras, editor of *Romani Studies*, the website is a "virtual home" for Romani, a language which despite time and geography is still demonstrably-linked to the modern languages of India such as Punjabi, Hindi, Gujarati, and Bengali. According to Matras:

> Romani is the classic minority language. It's never a majority language. There isn't any region that is predominately Romani speaking. As a minority language it's never been protected by any states or any form of government or any kind of institution. And now of course Romani faces the challenge of how to survive in a modern world.[43]

The Romani Project (www.llc.manchester.ac.uk/Research/Projects/romani/index.html) was officially launched in January 2006 as the "first interactive historical and regional database of a European language."[44] The online graphic user interface allows comparison of Romani pronunciation and vocabulary across the European continent. The ultimate goal of the project is to assist in codifying the language and attempt to harmonize spelling of Romani čhib, which if successful, will make the language easier to teach.[45] The Roma are now using their language in Internet-based messaging systems, on websites, and in other forms of new media. The surmountable differences between regional dialects allow for a robust communications ecumene, as issues of orthography are fairly easy to overcome in cyberspace given the accommodation and convergence Romani-speaking netizens have demonstrated thus far.[46] My respondents in Romania found Web-based communication with speakers of different Romani dialects to be possible, though many often found using English—"the language the 'Net" in the words of one—to be a better medium for transnational communication.

A number of non-academic newsgroups, Webrings, and chatrooms also exist; these allow for discussion of topics in English, Romani, Angloromani, or any other language for that matter. Prominent discussion groups include: *Romanestan* (groups.yahoo.com/group/Romanestan); *GYPSY – ROMA* (groups.msn.com/ GYPSYROMA); *Roma in the UK* (groups.msn.com/romaintheuk); *Romano Liloro* (groups.yahoo.com/group/Romano_Liloro); *Amalipen* (http://www.amalipen.net/); and the *Gypsy Message Board* (http://members2.boardhost.com/Romany/). These forums follow in the heels of Romnet, an e-mail discussion group for and about Roma founded by the Roma academic Ian Hancock in 1992. Whereas Romnet was once the only available platform for mass-mediated transborder exchanges, the Internet now teems with information and communication options for the Roma. *Patrin* is perhaps the best resource in English. *Patrin* offers dozens of Internet-accessible papers on the Roma, as well as news, Roma history, and cultural resources such as the national anthem and a glossary of Romani čhib. The site's mission statement reads as follows:

> Governments must be held responsible for their mistreatment of Roma. They must be informed and held liable for the criminality of their actions and inaction. The European Parliament and the United Nations must send notice to governments that continued abuse and persecution of Roma, or any minority, will not be tolerated. Patrin will not solve all these problems. However, it can provide doorways for others to see the realities of unjust Roma persecution around the world by benefit of the Internet. And if Patrin is only a collection of links, we hope these links will open doorways to educate and inform others.[47]

The RomNews Society (http://www.romnews.com/) also emphasizes the exchange of information with the aim of reducing ingrained prejudices towards Roma. The site's authors also seek to promote "a common identity" among the Roma and provide a "support network" for political action. Other influential sources include the Hungarian site Roma Page/*Roma Sajtóközpont* (http://www.romapage.hu/), the Russian site Liloro (http://www.philology.ru/liloro/liloro.htm), and the Roma Press Agency/ *Rómska Tlačová Agentúra* (http://www.rpa.sk/) in Slovakia. In addition to Internet-only offerings, hard-copy publications like the Czech magazines *Romano Vodi* (http://www.romea.cz/) and *Amaro Gendalos* (http://www. amarogendalos.cz/) maintain multimedia websites which deliver content in Czech, Romani, and English. *Rádio Rota* (http://www.radiorota.cz/), a Czech-based radio station, streams audio content on Romani issues. *Radio C*, a Hungarian Roma station, similarly broadcasts in cyberspace from its ultra-sophisticated site at http://www.radioc.hu/.

Various non-governmental organizations (NGOs) by and for Roma have homesteaded in cyberspace as well, including: the Dženo Association (http://www.dzeno.cz/), the Voice of Roma (http://www.voiceofroma.com/), Union Romani (http://www.unionromani.org/), and the Union of Albanian Roma/*Amaro Drom* (http://www.unioniamarodrom.org/). These are complemented by pan-European NGO websites which are typically funded by the EU, the Council of Europe, and other intergovernmental organizations. Sites such as the European Roma Rights Center (http://www.errc.org) are primarily accessed by non-Roma; however, the legal databases and country reports do provide value to Romani activists within the community as do academic resources such as Graz University's ROMBASE, a database presenting "didactically edited information on the socio-cultural and socio-historical situation of the Roma, a European nation without its own state." Several of my respondents, mostly law students at Babeş Bolyai University in Cluj-Napoca, Romania, had already established Web-based communications channels with various NGOs in Brussels and elsewhere with the goal of creating local chapters or accessing funds after Romania's 2007 accession to the Union.

Curiously, the Web has also emerged as a way for Indians to reach out their long-lost co-ethnics (and perhaps for reciprocal bonds to be built by Roma to the rising Asian power). Although a bit quixotic given Roma are not Hindus, the World Hindu Council/*Vishwa Hindu Parishad*¯an ally of India's recently defeated Bharatiya Janata Party (BJP)—has begun to mobilize the greater Indian diaspora including the Roma to create an "anti-imperialist" front.[48] The 4 March 2006 posting of an Indian participant in *Yahoo*'s Romanestan chatroom provides context to this incipient movement: "It will be of [great] benefit to the downtrodden roma communities in europe to get more connected to india as powerful Indians (NRIs) in europe will be more forward [sic] to fight for roma once the homeland is more enlightened."[49] The Roma people's lack of a state sponsor has long been seen as a major political weakness; however, if India and Indians continue on this path towards rebuilding bonds which were severed by geography over a millennium ago, the Roma may find themselves in a rather unfamiliar position—one of influence, albeit interstitial.

The Double-Edged Politics of the Web: How the Internet Helps and Hurts the Roma

In theory, the Internet—like all mass media platforms—is neutral until laden with content; however, once ARPANET established the first connections between geographically distant users, the politics of cyberspace began to evolve. With this evolution, there came winners and losers, haves and have-nots, the popular and the pariahs. Power relations in cyberspace are a shadowy reflection of the realities of the offline world.[50] As such, nation-states do possess some inherent advantages in cyberspace, but we should be careful not to overstate their power. As stated earlier, the globalized world—especially postmodern Europe—is less defined by nation-states than at any time in the past 300 years. New congeries are increasingly siphoning off the influence and authority once commanded by the state. And while "nonformal political actors are rendered invisible in the space of national politics...cyberspace can accommodate a broad range of social struggles and facilitate the emergence of new types of political subjects that do not have to go through the formal political system."[51] This duality is keenly felt in the Roma's experiences with the Internet. The crux on which this issue turns is antiziganism or anti-Gypsyism.

Valeriu Nicolae, Secretary General of European Roma Grassroots Organisation (ERGO), defines anti-Gypsyism as more than "just another type of racial discrimination... anti-Gypsyism [is] a complex code of social behavior used to justify and perpetrate the exclusion and supposed inferiority of Roma."[52] Nicolae concludes that anti-Gypsyism is, in fact, an ideology. "Like any ideology, anti-Gypsyism can adapt as Roma remain targeted, regardless of the changes they make in their social status, living conditions and practices, as long as they admit their ethnic roots."[53] Roma identity is thus a powerful issue on- and offline. Many Roma conceal their ethnic identity for fear of persecution, a phenomenon common among many victims of cultural violence. As academic Ian Hancock recounts:

> Roma care very much about anti-Gypsyism while having to hide their identity. For example, I know a successful businessman who asks for all Romnet—a Romani Internet mailing list-messages to be forwarded to him but is quite unwilling to subscribe to or participate on Romnet himself out of fear that his Romani identity could be revealed.[54]

The anonymity provided by cyberspace allows for communication within and outside of the community which is not subject to the same sorts of transparency that characterized previous information ages. Roma can now use the Internet to report abuses to NGOs, the media, and their ethnic kin in foreign countries.

In the late 1990s, the previously mentioned email list Romnet was mobilized in support of Czech Roma who had streamed into the English port city of Dover seeking refuge from conditions in the Czech Republic, but also looking take advantage of Canadian social benefits upon migration to that country via the UK.[55] These benefits—along with what turned out to be the bogus promise of a warm reception—had been marketed to the Roma community by Czech elites, specifically through a documentary which aired on TV Nova, the first privately-owned station in the Czech Republic and the one with the highest market share in the country. According to historian Rick Fawn, the network's 1997 broadcast of *Na vlastní oči* ('In Your Own Eyes')—a blatantly inaccurate report on several Roma families' successes in Canada—emerged as powerful symbol of the new approach to the country's "Gypsy Problem," i.e., encouragement of Romani emigration to the West.[56]

The Romnet mobilization served as a model for Roma activists and their allies moving forward. In 1999, the mayor of the northern Czech city Ústí nad Labem erected a six-foot concrete wall meant to segregate the city's "white" residents from the Roma. The Matiční street wall further solidified the perception that the Czech Republic wanted its Roma to search for greener pastures. Likewise, the ghettoization of the Roma in Ústí also became a *cause célèbre* for Internet-enabled Roma and their advocates. With each successive outrage, the cyber-connected networks of Romani defenders began to develop faster, more effective, and increasingly global responses to antiziganism. When combined with the economic, social, and political power of transnational non-governmental organizations and, especially EU-mechanisms for the protection of Roma, these virtual networks are now functioning as an "early warning system" for triggering action. While none of my respondents had personally reported acts of antiziganism via the Internet, many had read accounts of bias-crimes in their own home country and about incidents occurring abroad.

In recent years, cyberspace itself has become a site of antiziganism. In 2000, a computer game called *Matiční Street* began to proliferate via the Internet. The game's use of racist statements such as "a dead Roma is a good Roma" provoked a significant backlash.[57] Roma activists in Ústí nad Labem quickly mobilized international condemnation of the game in which players are supposed to shoot at Roma who are trying to dismantle the infamous wall which was torn down on 23 November 1999. Another Internet game called *Gypsy Action* was forced off the Web by

Roma groups in 2005. The Roma Press Center in Budapest reported that the game invited players to ethnically cleanse the country of Gypsies offering a variety of firearms to achieve the total eradication of Roma from Hungary. The country's color turned white if the player wiped out the entire Romani population.[58] Sociologist Les Back states that "Virtual forms of racial violence relate to chilling lived experiences while remaining in the 'other world' of computer simulation. They are politically slippery because they blur the distinction between social reality and fantasy."[59] Regardless, Roma cyber-elites rallied to ensure these games were pulled down.

The organization utility of the Web by neo-Nazis, however, represents a more immediate concern for Roma. With the collapse of the social controls of totalitarianism in Eastern Europe, skinhead movements grew at an alarming rate through the 1990s. In Germany, Poland, the Czech and Slovak Republics, Hungary, and Romania, these groups have frequently targeted Roma. In places like Prague's Karlin district, the violence became somewhat ritualized with skinhead and Roma gangs regularly engaging in street warfare in the 1990s. While many of these were groups were homegrown, neo-Nazis are increasingly using the Web to coordinate across international borders and are becoming more radical in the process. The Internet has played a central role in this evolution by functioning as a distribution platform for Nazi propaganda, white power rock, racist games, etc. As Back states, "The Internet is a technology of globalization, interconnecting permeable human cultures. Yet in the racist Networld, the Internet is used to foster an ethos of racial separation."[60] In cyberspace, populist anti-Roma sentiment and its more ominous fascist doppelganger often weave in and out of one another, once again demonstrating that the advent of cyberspace is a mixed blessing for the Roma.

While not overtly threatening (but perhaps even more insidious), the danger of identity loss through *informatization* is also a concern for Roma. Kluver defines informatization as "the process primarily by which information technologies, such as the world-wide web and other communication technologies, have transformed economic and social relations to such an extent that cultural and economic barriers are minimized."[61] My research conducted among upwardly (and outwardly) mobile Roma at Babeş-Bolyai University in Romania suggests that regular Internet usage—combined with English language fluency and the increasing mobility offered by European integration—are promoting incipient denationalization among many Roma elites. One of my respondents remarked, "I don't use the Internet for anything related to the Roma...I use it to improve my Romanian language skills and to look for jobs abroad" (female Roma, aged 23). Another respondent told me that a whole generation of his relatives is growing up with complete Web fluency and they are interested in expanding their knowledge and taking advantage of the new opportunities which cyberspace affords. "Once we leave Romania, we are Romanian—not Gypsies," he pointed out suggesting that the Internet is making emigration much easier by endowing Roma with the tools necessary to "blend in" to European society, something difficult to do at "home" (male Roma, aged 26).

Escaping the unfortunate stigma associated with being Roma is easily facilitated by the anonymity of cyberspace. The unique structure of the Internet allows Roma to represent themselves as Czech, Romanian, or Hungarian citizens and put forth their credentials alongside those of their non-Roma countrymen without referencing their Roma heritage. As such, individuals are judged not on their origins but

150   Chapter 6

their capabilities. As elites embed themselves in cyberspace, they often feel that
their economic and personal potentials have increased many times over. While there
may be some incentives to mobilize the masses towards national emancipation, it is
much more expedient to emancipate one's self first. Just as urbanization reduced the
culture of collectivity and shrunk the depth and length of social relations, so does
the Internet. Cyberspace promotes *Gesellschaft* ('society') over *Gemeinschaft*
('community'), and, like urban space in an earlier era, leads to widespread atomiza-
tion of society and puts the focus on individualism.[62] Moving forward, such trends
pose serious dangers to the perpetuation of both the Romani language and Roma
identity amongst those economic elites which have traditionally functioned as the
"voice of the nation."

The benefits of the Internet, however, seem to clearly outweigh its dangers.
This is especially true when one considers the coordinative capacities of cyberspace. According to political scientist Ilona Klímová-Alexander, cyberspace has
emerged as a critical tool for linking the Roma together; "Internet and E-mail have
become one of the main mobilization tools for Romani activism."[63] As Maria Metodieva, an eRider with the Roma Information Project,[64] points out, Romani wom-
en—particularly young women—have been especially prominent in this campaign,
despite being triply oppressed: as women, as Roma, and as females in what is a
generally a male-dominated ethnic community. New media and information and
communications technology function both as vehicles for improving conditions for
the entire community and expanding women's role within the community by allowing them to emerge as leaders in cyberspatial environments.

> The emancipation of our community will not occur simply by helping Roma
> women become better daughters, wives, and mothers. We need to enable them to
> become better people who contribute to the betterment of our society. This will
> happen by supporting one another, communicating, collaborating, and sharing
> experiences. IT tools are perfect for enabling this collaboration. Through the
> work of our eRider team and other dedicated activists, the Roma women's
> movement is taking on technology whether our men like it or not.[65]

Another example of how Roma women are using the Web is the "I am a European
Roma" campaign by Amnesty International and Mundi Romani. Released on 6
March 2009, the short video, directed by Csaba Farkas, Katalin Bársony, focused
on the importance of women and the complexity of the Roma identity. Intended to
promote the Decade of Roma Inclusion 2005-2015, a pan-European project to promote social inclusion across the Continent, the video included evocative images of
communal violence against Roma, alongside scenes of happy and healthy Romani
schoolchildren and personal histories of Roma women. The literature accompanying the video evokes an attempt to combat the structural violence inherent in media
depictions of Roma:

> We cannot let the mainstream media lead the crusade to ease our societies' grow-
> ing [economic and social] frustrations by destroying our communities. There is
> worrying evidence that the role of the [mainstream] media acts as a tool for dis-
> seminating racist idea and fuelling anti-Gypsysm and Romaphobia....Problem
> areas include distribution of anonymous, violen, anti-Roma racist messages via
> SMS and the internet, real-time encouragement of television viewers or internet

users to participate in racist exchanges....The "I Am a European Roma Woman" campaign is a direct answer to these phenomena.[66]

The video was widely viewed on YouTube in Hungary, Spain, France, the United States, and other countries.

In addition to its impact on gender relations, the use of new media to counteract the deleterious impact of antiziganism in mainstream European media is especially helpful. Roma journalists—attempting to counter media portrayals of their co-ethnics primarily as criminals or musicians—have made important strides in sensitizing the media to Roma concerns.[67] The new cohort of Roma journalists understands the central role of media in promoting positive images of the Roma in European societies. Many of these reporters cut their teeth in Internet-based news forums before moving on to radio and print media. There is a lot of work to be done, however, since anti-Roma reporting has been growing since the mid-1980s when state media organs began scapegoating Roma for the ills of society as a last-ditch effort to shore up support for flagging communist regimes.[68] Panayi states, "The media represent the first way in which 'public opinion' practices ethnic exclusion because the press, radio and television play a central role in determining the thoughts of the population in a given state."[69] The Roma—due to economic and social marginality, the historical absence of an external sponsor or protecting state, and (sometimes) physical difference—make easy targets for such exclusion.

Historically, European media have been overly enthusiastic in ethnicizing crime, especially in relation to the Roma.[70] "If a Rom is apprehended in connection with an alleged criminal act, society tends to immediately link this with his or her ethnic origin. And the media tend to mention this ethnic origin in their reports. It is indeed a well-known centuries-old cliché that Roma steal."[71] Mass mediated vilification of Roma has been especially disturbing in Romania where media coverage of individual crime often results in collective action taken against Roma communities, usually with the tacit support of the state.[72] Sadly, reporting on anti-Roma crimes has been less prevalent, though this is now beginning to change. Today, Web-linked Roma journalists and activist NGOs comprised of Roma promoting more accurate reporting of violence against Roma.

Using the Web to strengthen civil society is perhaps one of the most visible examples of how the Internet aids European Roma. The global broadcast of the 2002 Łódź Conference of 30 Roma organizations is a case in point. The summit, held at the behest of Finnish President Tarja Halonen, brought together civic associations from Central Europe, Germany, and Scandinavia. But, more importantly, the program was transmitted live on the Internet in the hopes of reaching those without the means to attend.[73] This suggests a new realization that elites among the Roma nation are gaining access to the information they need to improve the lot of their communities. Supported by grants from the EU, individual governments, and private donors, scores of Roma youth are today studying law, public administration, and other professions in the hope that they can start to overcome a historical deficit of formally educated leadership. Furthermore, a number of European governments that previously ignored racism have now begun to acknowledge its presence in their midst, creating some programs to combat discrimination and promising others.[74]

Roma student clubs and other organizations are today working to alleviate the forces of assimilation and produce a new, self-assured generation of Roma intellec-

152   Chapter 6

tuals.[75] This emergent elite is Web-savvy and well-versed in the mechanisms of the "New Europe." NGOs like the Dženo Association (Prague) are increasingly focused on making the bureaucracy in Brussels work for the Roma—such a shift ends the passive relationships Roma elites have tended to cultivate with the non-Roma political structures around them.

While it is clear that a new class of Romani activists is emerging and that cyberspace plays a key role in this process, the political, social, and economic benefits of the Web have yet to materialize for most Roma. While the Internet functions well for distributing information, its utility as a mechanism for political change is unrealized. The Roma, however, are well-served by the emergence of a trans-border communication platform which buttresses the community's increasing utilization of the EU's protection regime for non-territorial minorities. While cyberspace is currently unlikely to facilitate radical reshaping of the geopolitical landscape, it does provide a welcome landscape for information exchange, media production, and transnational coordination for groups like the Roma. By reaffirming and more closely linking pre-existing networks over borders, cyberspace offers tangible benefits to the Roma—a people who have long been marginalized by various European states. Such benefits may prove fleeting however if the emergent Roma elite fail to solidify their position among their constituencies.

My research also suggests other lurking dangers, including the threat posed by informatization which may encourage voluntary abandonment of Roma identity for economic or social advancement. The incipient in-gathering of Roma elites in cyberspace will only produce long-term dividends if they can replicate the Roma's virtual unity in the real world. Regardless, the modest success of the Roma's utilization of cyberspace bodes well for other European non-territorial minorities. Europe has experienced to major waves of migration in the past four decades. The first wave (early 1950s-1973) has produced large communities of second- and third-generation "immigrants"—that is diasporic, non-territorial minorities including Sikhs, Muslims, Kurds, "Africans," etc. During the more recent era of European immigration (late 1980s-present), large-scale, intra-continental migration has resulted in sizable non-territorial populations of Poles, Russians, and Albanians in the EU states. As such, Europe is an increasingly complex ethnoscape comprised of multiple non-territorial minorities living alongside "territorial minorities" (e.g., Bretons, Vlachs, and Sámi) and majority populations (French, Germans, and Russians). Cyberspace offers opportunities and challenges for all these groups as they seek to redefine their relationship to the nation-state in the twenty-first century.

Notes

1. See Johan Galtung and Tord Höivik, "Structural and Direct Violence: A Note on Operationalization," *Journal of Peace Research* 8, no. 1 (1971): 73-76.
2. Johan Galtung, "Cultural Violence," *Journal of Peace Research* 27, no. 3 (August 1990): 291-305.
3. Galtung, "Cultural Violence," 294.
4. Joshua A. Fishman, "The New Linguistic Order," *Foreign Policy* 113 (Winter 1998-99): 26-40.

5. It is helpful to remember the matrix-womb connection discussed in Chapter 2 in this context.

6. My thanks to one of the anonymous referees of my original manuscript for this point.

7. Peter Vermeersch, "Ethnic Minority Identity and Movement Politics: The Case of the Roma in the Czech Republic and Slovakia," *Ethnic and Racial Studies* 26, no. 5 (September 2003): 879-901.

8. Angus Bancroft, *Roma and Gypsy-Travellers in Europe: Modernity, Race, Space and Exclusion* (Aldershat, UK: Ashgate, 2005).

9. Many individuals and groups who self-identify as Roma do not speak Romani, thus lessening their authenticity in the eyes of some Romani-speakers. Furthermore, many individuals who are labeled as "Roma" by non-Roma reject the term itself, instead preferring the label "Gypsy," which is widely recognized as pejorative in its various incarnations (Rom. *ţigan*; Rus. *tsygan*; Hun. *cigány*; Spa. *gitano*, Fr. *tzigan*; etc.).

10. See Anthony Smith, *National Identity* (Reno: University of Nevada Press, 1991), 21-26.

11. Radu P. Ioviţă and Theodore G. Schurr, "Reconstructing the Origins and Migrations of Diasporic Populations: The Case of the European Gypsies," *American Anthropologist* 106, no. 2 (June 2004): 267-281.

12. Gail Kligman, "On the Social Construction of 'Otherness': Identifying 'the Roma' in Post-Socialist Communities," *Review of Sociology* 7, no. 2 (November 2001): 61-78.

13. Vermeersch, "Ethnic Minority Identity and Movement Politics."

14. I use "Roma" to refer to the European ethnic group whose origins lie in Indian Sub-continent and who self-identify as Roma, Sinti, or Gypsies. My definition of Roma does not necessarily include British or Irish Travellers, the Swiss *Jenische*, Norwegian *Omstreifere*, Spanish *Quinquilleros*, and other itinerant groups which are sometimes labeled "Gypsies," but lack the linguistic and purported genetic connections to northern India. For more on the definition of "Gypsies," see David Mayall, *Gypsy Identities 1500-2000: From Egipcyans and Moon-men to the Ethnic Romany* (London and New York: Routledge, 2004).

15. Anthony Smith, perhaps the most well known of the current authors on national identity, makes "a territorial unit, with clear borders, one that is a translocal, but a bounded community...which shapes the character and identity of the people" the first of his five determiners of nationhood; see Anthony Smith, "When is a Nation?" *Geopolitics* 7, no. 2 (Autumn 2002): 5-32.

16. Istvan Pogany, "Accommodating an Emergent National Identity: The Roma of Central and Eastern Europe," *International Journal on Minority and Group Rights* 6, nos. 1-2 (Spring 1999): 149-167.

17. See, for instance, Ernest Gellner, *Nations and Nationalism* (Ithaca: Cornell University Press, 1983); Miroslav Hroch, *Social Preconditions of National Revival in Europe: A Comparative Analysis of the Social Composition of Patriotic Groups among the Smaller European Nations* (Cambridge: Cambridge University Press, 1985); Benedict Anderson, *Imagined Communities: Reflections on the Origin and Spread of Nationalism* (London: Verso, 1991); and Eric J. Hobsbawm, "Introduction: Inventing Traditions," in Eric J. Hobsbawm and Terence Ranger, *The Invention of Tradition* (Cambridge: Cambridge University Press, 1992). Coincidentally, Roma nationalism began to develop at the same time; however, such developments were arguably independent of trends within the academic community.

18. Cara Feys, "Towards a New Paradigm of the Nation: The Case of the Roma," *Journal of Public and International Affairs* 8 (1997), http://www.geocities.com/~Patrin/paradigm.htm (20 March 2006).

19. The term "Porajmos" has been popularized by the Romani academic and activist Ian Hancock (*né* Yanko le Redžosko), currently Director of the Program of Romani Studies and the Romani Archives and Documentation Center at the University of Texas at Austin.

20. In 2000, reparations began after nearly half a century of lobbying.

154   Chapter 6

21. In the interwar period, transnational organizations and "world conferences" had been held, but these strongly reflected the interests of the Romanian Roma population; see Ilona Klímová-Alexander, *The Romani Voice in World Politics: The United Nations and Non-State Actors* (Aldershat, UK: Ashgate, 2005).

22. Mayall, *Gypsy Identities*, 205.

23. Vermeersch, "Ethnic Minority Identity and Movement Politics."

24. Emil Ščuka, "Declaration of a Roma Nation," International Romani Union, 1 January 2001, http://www.hartford-hwp.com/archives/60/132.html (20 April 2006).

25. Pogany, "Accommodating an Emergent National Identity," 158.

26. Kurt Mills, "Cybernations: Identity, Self-determination, Democracy and the 'Internet Effect' in the Emerging Information Order," *Global Society* 16, no. 1 (January 2002): 69-87.

27. Mihaela Keleman and Warren Smith, "Community and Its 'Virtual' Promises: A Critique of Cyberlibertarian Rhetoric," *Information, Communication & Society* 4, no. 3 (October 2001): 370-387.

28. James A. Goldston, "Roma Rights, Roma Wrongs," *Foreign Affairs* 81, no. 2 (March/April 2002): 146-162.

29. Sheila L. Croucher, *Globalization and Belonging: The Politics of Identity in a Changing World* (Lanham, MD: Rowman & Littlefield Publishers, Inc., 2004), 110.

30. Panikos Panayi, *An Ethnic History of Europe since 1945: Nations, States and Minorities* (Harlow: Longman, 2001), 15.

31. Michael Dahan and Gabriel Sheffer, "Ethnic Groups and Distance Shrinking Technologies," *Nationalism & Ethnic Politics* 7, no. 1 (Spring 2001): 85-107.

32. "A Home for Roma," *Foreign Policy* 127 (November 2001): 96.

33. See The Patrin Web Journal: Romani Culture and History at http://www.geocities.com/~Patrin/patrin.htm.

34. Post by Giny1gmxde2, "Re: In Need of Serious help Plz!" MSN Groups "GYPSY – ROMA," 27 December 2004 (26 April 2006).

35. See http://romani.uni-graz.at/romani/teach/amenroman.en.shtml.

36. Yaron Matras, "Romani Today," Voices, BBC website, http://www.bbc.co.uk/voices/multilingual/romani.shtml (May 2006).

37. Romanes also trumps Russian which has some 2 million native speakers in the Baltic states of Estonia, Latvia, and Lithuania; however, certain pressure groups argue that the total number of Russian-speaking EU residents is upwards of 6 million; see Vladimir Socor, "East of the Oder: Introducing the Baltic 'Interfront' Candidates," *Wall Street Journal Europe*, 11 June 2004, A7. This larger estimate must be treated with caution, however, as it would most certainly would include hundreds of thousands of post-Soviet *Volksdeutsche* returnees to Germany, nearly all adult residents of the Baltic States, and all Russian guest workers and economic immigrants in the EU.

38. Vardan Voskanian, "The Iranian Loan-words in Lomavren, the Secret Language of the Armenian Gypsies," *Iran and the Caucasus* 6, nos. 1-2 (Summer 2002): 169-180.

39. Mary Ellen Tsekos, "Minority Rights: The Failure of International Law to Protect the Roma," *Human Rights Brief* 9, no. 3 (Spring 2002): 26-29.

40. In support of this study, I interviewed small *n* sample of Romani netizens in cyberspace over a nine-month period from November 2005 to July 2006. During the same period, I conducted one month of field research among upwardly-mobile, Internet-enabled Roma at Babeş-Bolyai University in Cluj-Napoca, Romania. This research was supported in part by a grant from IREX (International Research & Exchanges Board) with funds provided by the U.S. State Department through the Title VIII Program. None of these organizations is responsible for the views expressed.

41. Peter Bakker and Marcia Rooker, "The Political Status of the Romani Language in Europe," Mercator-Working Papers 3, CIEMEN (Escarré International Centre for Ethnic Minorities and Nations), 2001. PDF available at http://www.ciemen.org/mercator/pdf/wp3-

def-ang.PDF. Spain and the UK are excepted from these statistics as novel varieties of Para-Romani developed in these counties (Cálo and Angloromani, respectively), which have displaced the form of Romani spoken in much of the rest of Europe.

42. By definition, these are literate elites with access to the Internet. Recent research demonstrates that socially- and politically-active netizens wield markedly greater influence over their friends, family, and acquaintances than do non-Internet enabled elites; see Joseph Graf, "Political Influential Online in the 2004 Presidential Campaign." Report published by the Institute for Politics, Democracy & the Internet, The Graduate School of Political Management at George Washington University (Washington, DC), 2004. PDF available at: http://www.ipdi.org/Influentials/
Report.pdf. (see Graf 2004).

43. Quoted in Clark Boyd, "Romani Language Report," PRI's *The World*, 7 March 2006.

44. Joe Plomin, "Linguists Track Romani Dialects across Europe," *Guardian Unlimited*, 25 May 2001.

45. See "Web to Preserve Romani Heritage," *BBC News*, 29 January 2006, http://news.bbc.co.uk/1/hi/england/manchester/4660290.stm (29 March 2006).

46. See Boyd, "Romani Language Report" and Bakker and Rooker, "The Political Status of the Romani Language."

47. See "The Patrin Web Journal: Romani Culture and History" at http://reocities.com/Paris/5121/.

48. Sanjay Chaturvedi, "Diaspora in India's Geopolitical Visions: Linkages, Categories, and Contestations," *Asian Affairs: An American Review* 32, no. 3 (Fall 2005): 141-168.

49. Tapan Shah, "Re: [Romanestan] Re: hello," Romanestan Web board (groups.yahoo.com/group/Romanestan/), 4 March 2004. A non-resident Indian (NRI) is an Indian citizen who has migrated to or was born in another country. For taxation and other official purposes the government of India considers any Indian national away from India for more than 180 days in a year an NRI. There are approximately 25 million NRIs outside of India.

50. Saskia Sassen, "The Impact of the Internet on Sovereignty: Unfounded and Real Worries," in Christoph Engel and Kenneth H. Heller, *Understanding the Impact of Global Networks in Local Social, Political and Cultural Values* (Baden-Baden: Nomos Verlagsgesellschaft, 2000).

51. Saskia Sassen, "Globalization or Denationalization?" *Review of International Political Economy* 10, no. 1 (February 2003): 1-22.

52. Valeriu Nicolae, "Anti-Gypsyism – A Definition," European Roma Information Office website, 2006, http://www.erionet.org/Antigypsyism.html (1 June 2006).

53. Nicolae, "Anti-Gypsyism."

54. Ian Hancock, "The Struggle for the Control of Identity," *Transitions* 4, no. 4 (September 1997): 34-44.

55. "From Open Road to Internet," *The Economist* 346, no 8061 (28 March 1998): 29.

56. Rick Fawn, "Czech Attitudes towards the Roma: 'Expecting More of Havel's Country?'" *Europe-Asia Studies* 53, no. 8 (December 2001): 1193-1219.

57. Nick Carey, "Roma Community Fears Anti-Roma Internet Game," *Radio Prague Enews*, 28 February 2000, http://archiv.radio.cz/news/EN/2000/28.02.html (29 March 2006).

58. "Gypsy Game Forced Off Internet," *New York Times*, 16 February 2005, Sec. A, 8.

59. Les Back, "Aryans Reading Adorno: Cyber-culture and Twenty-first Century Racism," *Ethnic and Racial Studies* 25, no. 4 (July 2002): 628-651.

60. Les Back, "White Fortresses in Cyberspace," *Unesco Courier* 54, no. 1 (January 2001): 44-46.

61. Randy Kluver, "Globalization, Informatization, and Intercultural Communication," *American Communication Journal* 3, no. 3 (June 2000). Available at: http://acjournal.org/ (23 March 2003).

62. Robert A. Saunders, "Denationalized Digerati in the Virtual Near Abroad: The Paradoxical Impact of the Internet on National Identity among Minority Russians," *Global Media and Communication* 2, no. 1 (April 2006): 43-69.

63. Klímová-Alexander, *The Romani Voice in World Politics*, 8.

64. Supported by George Soros's Open Society Institute, eRiders are roving technology consultants who provide technical support and advice to a host of non-governmental organizations supporting Roma communities in Romania, Hungary, and other Central European countries. According to the Roma Information Project web site, "eRiders are 'part trainer, part management consultant, part computer expert.' They provide consulting and assistance with technology strategy development, make repeated visits to the organizations they serve, and provide advice and information by phone and e-mail. They can work locally, or in entire regions. eRiders often 'cross-pollinate' the groups they service, by transmitting insights, tools, and tips as they travel throughout the sector."

65. Maria Metodieva, "No Longer behind the Curve," Tech Soup web site, 2 April 2003. http://www.techsoup.org/learningcenter/consultants/archives/page10297. cfm (4 November 2009).

66. Rómedia Foundation, "I am a European Roma Woman," Roma Decade web site, 6 March 2009, http://www.romadecade.org/ (4 November 2009).

67. Jeffrey R. Cooper, "Diplomacy in the Information Age: Implications for Content and Conduct,"   *iMP: Information   Impacts*   (July   2001),   http://www.cisp.org/ imp/july_2001/07_01cooper.htm (28 March 2003).

68. György Kerényi, "Roma in the Hungarian Media," *Media Studies Journal* 13, no. 3 (Fall 1999): 140-147.

69. Panayi, *An Ethnic History of Europe since 1945*, 216.

70. Zoltan Barany's study of Roma in Macedonia found that the country's comparatively successful integration of its Roma population may correlate with the lack of ethnic identification of criminals in the media which contravenes Macedonian law; see Zoltan Barany, "The Roma in Macedonia: Ethnic Politics and the Marginal Condition in a Balkan State," *Ethnic and Racial Studies* 18, no. 3 (July 1995): 515-531.

71. Karin Waringo, "Europe: Bark Louder, Please," *Transitions*, 28 February 2005.

72. Panayi, *An Ethnic History of Europe since 1945*, 249.

73. Peter S. Green, "Roma Seeking Sense of Unity to Combat Racial Bias," *New York Times*, 10 May 2002, Sec. A, 15.

74. Goldston, "Roma Rights, Roma Wrongs," 148.

75. Cooper, "Diplomacy in the Information Age," 75.

Chapter 7
Virtual Prophets: Ummahists and the Construction of a New Imagined Community

For nearly three centuries, scholars have asked "what is the nation?" While academics continue to quarrel over the origin and antiquity of nations, the debate has produced a rather consistent set of markers for identifying nations. However, the radical restructuring of society associated with globalization and its accompanying economic, political, social, and cultural upheavals has reframed the parameters of what defines national identity. In this final case study, I attempt to further the conceptual evolution of the nation by analyzing the global *ummah*—the worldwide community of Muslim believers—through the lens of national identity. In doing so, I make the case that the ummah should increasingly be treated as a new nation, though one with some perennial qualities.

The larger goal of this chapter is to explore the Internet's usefulness in reviving older and creating new pan-ethnic groups. With the advent of a global, deterritorialized mass medium for communication and the production and consumption of news and entertainment, the old norms of nation-building have been challenged. One of these challenges has come from individuals promoting transnational identity projects which are generally antithetical to the existing status quo based on nation-states. My focus is on the virtual prophets who are attempting to unite pan-ethnic groups to forge new "imagined communities" in cyberspace. The chapter provides an analysis of the cyberspatial activities of cyber-Muslims and their attempts to create transnational solidarity among the ummah (the worldwide Muslim community). The focus in on creating a binding nexus based on adherence to a minimalist set of political, legal, economic, and social tenets (Islamism), a language (Arabic, though English is frequently the primary lingua franca), and information and communication technologies (the Internet, satellite TV, DVDs, mobile telephony, etc.) to form an imagined political community roughly analogous to a nation. The focus is on Muslims living outside the *Dar al-Islam* (Islamic world), specifically those in wealthy, industrialized states in Western Europe. As ethnic and religious minorities, these individuals have employed the Web to construct virtual realities that join them

to their co-religionists across the globe, thus lessening the trauma of minority identity and economic marginalization in their non-Islamic home countries.

While my analysis seeks to answer some of the questions surrounding the
transnational Muslim community, my primary goal herein is to interrogate the very
concept of nationhood in the twenty-first century, an era in which deterritorialized
national projects have become common. I use both historical and current phenomena to address the question of *ummah as nation*. In particular, I focus on the controversy surrounding the Danish newspaper *Jyllands-Posten*'s September 2005 publication of cartoons depicting the Prophet Muhammad as a watershed event,
particularly the ummah's global response to the "Cartoons Affair" and how reactions underscored the development of a robust collective identity among the world's
Muslims, particularly Muslims in Western Europe. My contention is that fallout of
this global imbroglio cannot be adequately explained within the framework of religious fellowship. Instead, I put forth that mobility, the Internet, and the emergence
of a new, deterritorialized elite among transnational Muslims has allowed for the
proliferation of "ummahism," a sentiment which more closely resembles nationalism than religiosity.

In 2003, the *Economist* opined that "Muslims see their religion as a source of
identity and fellow-feeling that is often stronger than nationalism."[1] I contend that
there is no fellow-feeling stronger than nationalism, and that it is important for
scholars to recognize that ummahism bears all the hallmarks of nationalism (in addition to being sanctified by its religious origins). In doing so, I attempt to debunk
eminent scholar of Islamic politics James Piscatori's claim that the ummah "is not a
political concept"[2] by demonstrating the depth and potency of political affiliation
associated with membership in the global ummah. My analysis treats the events
surrounding the recent Cartoons Affair as a tipping point in the reification the ummah as a transnational political community, with the Internet and cyberspace serving as the primary vehicles for this transformation.

The "Nation" and the "Ummah": Historical Debates and Conceptual Ambiguities

After famously pondering "what is a nation?" in 1882, French philosopher Ernest
Renan concluded that it is the perpetual affirmation of a "great solidarity" maintained through a "daily plebiscite."[3] While many scholars adhere to aspects of Renan's conceptual foundation, the "nation" remains a perennial topic of debate
among historians, political scientists, sociologists, and anthropologists. At the root
of the debate over the nation lies the question of whether or not nations are contrived or ahistorical. The primary schools of thought on the nation are as follows: 1)
the nation is perennial (existing in nature without reference to time); 2) the nation is
constructed (crafted from building blocks determined by pre-existing culture); and,
3) the nation *is functional* (a free-form entity that is dependent on rational decisions
based on expected outcomes).

Laying the foundations for the perennialist interpretation, Prussian poet and
critic Johann Gottfried von Herder popularized the notion of a *Volksgeist*, i.e., a
'spirit' unique to each race or people, while Savoyard diplomat de Maistre argued,
"Nations have a general *soul* and a true moral unity which makes them what they

are" ([1884] 2001: 109).[4] Benedict Anderson and Anthony Smith provide key examples of the constructivist school which contends that the nation depends on organic cultural components. As referenced earlier in the text, Anderson defines the nation as an "imagined political community" in which a member of a nation will never know or even see most of his co-nationals no matter how small the nation, yet they feel an interconnectedness or "a deep, horizontal comradeship."[5] Smith conceives of the nation as a human population with a popular culture that seeks equality for all its members in the economic, legal, and political milieus.[6] A paragon of the functionalist school, British historian Eric J. Hobsbawm dismisses the idea that the nation is ahistorical, instead describing the commonalities that make nations as "invented traditions" based on functional outcomes derived from a limited set of shared attributes (language, perceptions of history, etc.) which can and do change over time.[7] Similarly, Czech political theorist Miroslav Hroch argues that different groups 'pick and choose' which attributes suit their national projects—a process which is wholly dependent on political expediency.[8]

One distinguishing characteristic, however, permeates these various literatures: *sentiment.* According to Max Weber, "a nation is a community of sentiment which would adequately manifest itself in a state of its own; hence a nation is a community which normally tends to produce a state of its own."[9] As such, the desire to be one community—despite barriers of language, faith, and/or geography—is the keystone of the nation. During the modern era, nations—once content to be governed by other "cultural communities"—came to believe that they alone should govern themselves. Rapid socio-economic changes in West during the 1800s and the rest of the world in the twentieth century enabled the realization of many of these nationalist projects. Such developments were dependent on the emergence of politically-astute elites who urged the masses into action. In the postmodern era, mass media, mobility, and new forms of mobilization have emerged as powerful tools for the activation and reification of national identity. The glue that binds these projects has been and continues to be common sentiment, i.e., the desire to be a nation. Importantly, territory, which was a vital component of earlier national movements, has lessened in importance in the current era of mass migration, deterritorialized communication platforms, and neo-liberal economic structures. By synthesizing these various strains of thought, it is evident that the concept of nation is built on imagined ties of perennial kinship amongst a group of people who are biologically related or given the status of relatives by ritual. These people believe themselves to share a common history, customs, and values, which can be collectively deemed culture. Such ties are reified through sentiment and reinforced by elites.

Just as the interrogation of the nation has spawned countless treatises, so has the conceptual debate over what constitutes the "ummah." Reflecting the confessional diversity and steady de-politicization of faith in post-Westphalian Europe, Westerners generally tend to regard the Islamic ummah as a religious community analogous to the Jews, Christians, or Hindus;[10] however, the concept's definition within the Muslim world is more complex and historically fluid. The term is used more than sixty times in the Qur'ân, and appears frequently in the *hadith* (the recorded words and deeds of the Prophet Muhammad). The conceptualization of ummah as a religious distinction stems from the early history of Islam when the ummah referred to the emerging Muslim community constituted both by Arabs (divided by tribal loyalties) and non-Arabs. Piscatori explains the early Islamic worldview as such: "Although the *umma* incorporates all the [Muslim] believers, it will eventually become universal and include all mankind."[11] Reflecting these early conceptual ambiguities, there are a number of other translations of ummah including the non-religious concepts of "community," "race," and "brotherhood."

Etymologically speaking, the word is more closely linked to the gloss of 'people', and is thought to be a cognate of the Hebrew *am* and Aramaic *ummetha*. Reflecting such usage, ummah has been historically translated as 'nation,' and is often used in Arabic to denote the Western concept of "nation," e.g., *al-Umam al-Muttahida* (the United Nations). However, according to cultural theorist Ronald A. Judy, "it would be an error to translate *umma* as 'nation,' because the term means 'the collecting of people' as a function of heritage, convention, or faith, or even a way of life."[12] Other scholars disagree; German-Syrian political scientist Bassam Tibi suggests that is wrong to conceptualize the ummah as coterminous with Islam's "righteous believers" ('*al-mu'minun*) since "Islam has always been characterized by complexity and diversity."[13] Politics professor Sayed Khatab argues that the term itself "established a variety of concepts that have been the driving force of Muslims' political, social, economic, intellectual and moral lives....The term *ummah* then is a political term...the term *ummah* signifies a united nation (not nations), that is, the nation of the Islamic creed."[14] International relations scholar Fred Halliday supports this interpretation, arguing that "the very definition of an *umma* as a community of shared values, religious or not, has political implications."[15]

Political Movements and Putting the "Ummah" to Use

European imperialism directly contributed to the conceptual linking of nationalism to the ummah. Jamāl al-Dīn al-Afghānī (1839-1897), an outspoken critic of European encroachment into the lands where Muslims formed the majority, regularly employed the term ummah in its national sense. Al-Afghānī described Islam as religion "which constitutes a nation, a culture or a civilization, forms its basis and foundation, and provides the most secure bond that holds it together."[16] A contemporary of Renan, al-Afghānī admonished Muslims that only through collective action could they overthrow the imperial systems which dominated Egypt, India, and other Muslim countries at the end of the 1800s. "In his usage, *umma* referred to a nation in the modern sense, that of the Muslims being on par with the English, the French, the Germans."[17] More recently, the preeminent Islamist theoretician of the twentieth century, Sayyib Qutb, declared that a Muslim should have no nationality except one's belief,[18] a conceit which is increasingly echoed in Islamist quarters today. A contemporary of Qutb, the renowned scholar and founder of Pakistan's Islamic Party Abul A'la Maududi argued the Muslims should not be wooed by Western-style narrow-minded nationalisms which perpetuated barbarity and pitted Muslim against Muslim. Only through a renewed embrace of the ummah (as an alternative to nation) might Muslims be able to regain their lost universalism and "willingness to defend the Islamic common weal against all attack."[19]   (Despite transnational aspirations, Islamist scholars such as Qutb and Maududi were forced to work within the structure of individual nation-states. However, their twenty-first century counterparts confront a world where international borders are less salient).

Colonial-era pan-Islamist movements pioneered the use of ummah as nation in order to accumulate political capital. In previous centuries, Wahhabism, Deobandism, and Jadidism simultaneously functioned as platforms for anti-imperialist action and community-building. By linking the social, economic, political, and cultural lives of the ummah together, they found ways to resist foreign domination (whether Turkish, British, or Russian). Each movement employed at least some rudimentary form of mass media and elite mobility to gain adherents. Such activities produced ever-larger imagined communities within a communication ecumene or a nodal network of ideas, sentiment, and action.[20] In the wake of imperial decay, pan-Islamist organizations began to confront new enemies. Turkish international relations scholar Muhittin Ataman identifies the paradox of the ummah and post-Westphalian constructions of statehood which seeped into the Muslim world as European imperialism ebbed: "With the emergence of Muslim nation-states, Muslims [were] confused about their identities, whether the primary loyalty belongs to the "*ummah*" or to the nation-state."[21] For Islamist organizations such as the Muslim Brotherhood, the colonial empire was effectively exchanged for the secular state as the constitutive "Other" against which the ummah was defined. Established by Hassan al-Banna in Egypt in 1928, the Society of Muslim Brothers is a globally-oriented Islamist movement which seeks to install an Islamic Caliphate across the Muslim world. With the advent of this and other groups, the hitherto important role of geography in the shaping of Muslim consciousness began a slow process of decline with Islamist projects slowly becoming untethered to their original loci.

Contemporary Islamist movements build on the transborder, political framework established by the Muslim Brotherhood. While Western media often brand these groups as religious fundamentalists, it would be more appropriate to label them political factions. Al Qaeda is a case in point: its platform pays lip service to a return to the purity of the *salafi* (contemporaries of the Prophet), but its actions, organizational structure, and stated aims all have the hallmarks of a nationalist movement. Al Qaeda-inspired jihadis see themselves as perpetuating the struggle against external foes (Western imperialists) and internal oppressors (corrupt elites, apostate leftists, and American lackeys). Likewise, Osama bin Laden employs an adapted version of the Marxist-Leninist vernacular to articulate their aims and draw support from the masses. "[Al Qaeda's] intended audience is not primarily the population of a single country, but the entire *umma*."[22] Preeminent French analyst of Arab affairs Gilles Kepel argues that, after the Afghan War, Al Qaeda was little more than an obscure Arab jihadi group; however, when bin Laden embraced a global struggle in defense of the ummah, the "Base" skyrocketed in popularity and influence.[23] Bin Laden clearly understands the power of the ummah and regularly uses the construct for his own purposes with statements such as: "Our *umma* has known humiliation and contempt for over eighty years. Its sons are killed, its blood is spilled, its holy sites are attacked, and it is not governed according to Allah's command."[24] After bin Laden's successful re-branding of Al Qaedism as a global rather than local force for change, active and passive recruits began to align themselves with the *movement*, not as co-religionists, but as political agents fighting for the imagined community of the ummah. In the wake of bin Laden's September 2001 attacks on New York and Washington, membership in the ummah itself became politicized as media framing of the event consistently promoted notions of a "clash of civilizations" between Islam and the West.

The ummah—as I explore below—is frequently used as an identity anchor by contemporary Muslim elites to build effective coalitions and achieve concrete outcomes, thus easily satisfying the functionalist scholars' requirements for what constitutes a "nation." Based on the examples given above, it is also reasonable to argue that the postulation of ummah as nation also has appeal for both perennial and constructivist scholars of the nation if viewed through the lens of the current postmodern era of globalism.

European Muslims as the Vanguard of Ummahism

Unlike most nations which enjoy ethnic contiguity, the ummah faces severe limits on its intra-community communication and organizational capacity. However, certain elements of the faith have consistently perpetuated an "imagined community." "Islam's transnational character is diffuse but powerful, and it derives its power from the ways in which rituals reproduce, and histories remind Muslims of, the shared duties and practices of Muslims across political boundaries."[25] The annual *hajj* ('pilgrimage') has long served as a mechanism for making the global ummah a reality. Likewise, the obligatory recitation of prayers unites the worldwide community of Muslims in both deed and thought five times per day. Each phenomenon can be easily classified as a paradigmatic example of Benedict Anderson's "mass ceremony," the central force necessary to bind a modern nation (1991: 32-36).[26] In fact, Anderson paraphrases G. W. F. Hegel in describing the daily reading of the newspaper as a substitution for the "lost art" of daily prayer, stating: "It is performed in silent privacy, in the lair of the skull. Yet each communicant is well aware that the ceremony he performs is being replicated simultaneously by thousands (or millions) of others of whose existence he is confident, yet of whose identity he has not the slightest notion."[27] Despite the Andersonian components of nationhood that underwrite the ummah as a national construct, Muslims have historically been more divided than united. Political borders, tribal rivalries, sectarian disputes, geographic barriers, and linguistic diversity have all worked against the realization of the ummah since the ebbing of Arab expansion in the eighth century.

Curiously, the greatest boon to the reification of ummah as nation has stemmed from postcolonial Muslim emigration from the *Dar al-Islam* to Europe. Over time, these Muslims and their descendents have adapted to the conditions of living outside of the Muslim world. For many, part of this adaptation has included strengthening the concept of the ummah. "Muslims living in diaspora—particularly in the West—are of varied and diverse ethnic origins. What links them together, however, is a shared sense of identity within their religion, an idea most clearly located within the concept of the *ummah*."[28] This does not exclusively apply to observant Muslims, but also to "ethnic" or heritage Muslims who feel bound to others of the "Islamic creed" by a shared difference from those non-Muslims who dominate the host society. Such "us-and-them" constructions were on vivid display during the cartoons controversy. Social isolation associated with migrancy has been a major factor in creating a community of common sentiment. Many of the ethnic, regional, and linguistic differences that would have created division in the Muslim homeland are overshadowed by the shared difficulties of living as ethnic *and* religious minorities in Britain, Germany, France, etc. While the migration patterns to each of the countries differed, there is much that united them, e.g., the post-World War II economic boom, the need for laborers to do the jobs Europeans would not do, social and physical segmentation of immigrant populations within European space, institutional discrimination against the descendents of these immigrants, etc. For Muslims (even legacy Muslims), the commonality of faith—even when it is only nominal—proved to be an important factor in determining social bonds. French researcher Olivier Roy, who has popularized the notion of global, de-ethnicized Islam, partially dismisses the ummah as an "abstract universal,"[29] while simultaneously arguing that it is a powerful magnet for minority Muslims in Europe and elsewhere who have lost contact with the pristine cultures of their ancestral nations whether Berber, Turk, or Bengali.[30]

The American immigrant experience provides a conceptual model for understanding this phenomenon. The first generation of African-Americans who arrived in bondage from polities including Benin, Biafra, and Dahomey came from radically different linguistic, cultural, and religious backgrounds. However, their descendents coalesced into a relatively homogenous community in diaspora. Likewise, German immigrants arriving in nineteenth century America increasingly downplayed their confessional, regional, and dialectic differences, ultimately manifesting allegiance to the "German nation." For Muslim immigrants, the diasporic experience is producing analogous outcomes. Bosnian professor of Islamic Studies Enes Karić contends that "Muslims in Europe, particularly those who have the status of *gastarbeiter*, are going through the so-called 'Jewish stage' in Europe, the stage that European Jews once went through in struggling for the institutions in which they could preserve their religious and cultural identity."[31] According to American cultural historian Sander Gilman, "religion for the Jews of pre-Enlightenment Europe, and for much of contemporary Islam, was and is a 'heritage' to be maintained in the secular world of diaspora."[32] Considering current trends, the emergence of a mass political movement akin to Zionism is not out of the question. It is worth remembering that Theodore Herzl's pan-Jewish, nationalist movement was itself a reaction to populist anti-Semitism in *fin-de-siècle* Vienna, a city defined by transience, "multiculturalism," and the proliferation of mass media. These conditions are not dissimilar from the current environment experienced by Muslims in the European Union. At this stage of development, we might call this emergent pan-Muslim project "ummahism," the political doctrine which promotes common cause, shared sentiment, and collective action among all Muslims regardless of location and/or religiosity. Consequently, it is useful to distinguish between pan-Islamist and pan-Muslim at this juncture in order to clarify that ummahism is not constrained by the explicitly faith-based boundaries of the pan-Islamist movements.

Ummahism has found fertile ground in the marginalized Muslim ghettos of European cities. It is fueled by the curious combination of Muslim disenchantment with the minority experience, the ebbing of older forms of political and national identity, and the invigorating freedoms of expression, movement, and religion in postmodern Europe. An EU passport and passable fluency in English provides second- and third-generation Muslims with exceptional opportunities for coordination and cooperation. As such, Europe—an increasingly meaningful geopolitical space—is the hothouse of ummahism. The current ummahist project is girded by perspectival constructs based on the global transmission and consumption of local/national media (mediascapes), transborder flows of capital (financescapes), the mobility of peoples (ethnocapes), the diffusion of technologies (technoscapes), and the spread and cross-pollination of ideologies (ideoscapes).[33] The nexus of information and communications technologies, money, ideas, mobility, and ethnos is incubating a powerful new form of associational allegiance based on the ummah.

The postmodernity of Europe not only frees Muslims from the statist projects of their ethnic homelands, but also limits the requirements of adapting to their host countries (though the Internet is also used by European Muslims as a tool for adapting to the demands of life in the "West"). Many Muslim groups benefit from the structure and freedoms of the European Union which enable organizational systems which are not state-centric and "bypass their own ethnic and national cleavages and to create something closer to what the *ummah* should be."[34] Interestingly, this discourse has been deeply affected by the postmodern European environment which de-emphasizes territory and places a premium on mobility, freedom of expression, and respect for diversity. While Scots, Bulgarians, and Swedes have been rediscovering their common "Europeanness," many ethnic Moroccans, Kurds, and Baloch living next to them have reconnected as members of the transnational Islamic ummah.

Myriad factors are contributing to the construction of an ummah-based community within Europe, not least of which is the complicated status of Muslims in their host societies. Ironically, British and Dutch policies of multiculturalism, France's attempts at assimilation through *laïcité* (fundamentalist secularism), and Germany's segregationist model have all produced surprisingly similar outcomes—variously called a "parallel society,"[35] a "prison of alienation,"[36] and a "virtual ghetto."[37] However one refers to it, European Muslims are perceived to be on one side of an invisible wall and non-Islamic Europeans on the other—a view that was consistently evinced by the Cartoons Affair as well as other recent "Muslim" controversies in Europe such as the Salman Rushdie affair, the French headscarf debate, and lesser flaps over Muslim cultural praxes.[38] Such notions are strongly reinforced by the "seductive idea of political Islam, which preaches a Utopian view of society where all citizens are part of a just and fair 'umma'";[39] although it should be noted that many apolitical Muslims also grapple with the same issues faced by their Islamist counterparts. As a consequence, a meaningful Euro-Muslim sodality has emerged based on cultural, social, political, and other differences from the host society.

> The [European] nation-state is increasingly conceived by second-generation Muslims as operating through an exclusionary process which not only denies them access to citizenship but also fails to acknowledge emerging new identities: on the one hand by persisting in crystallizing Muslims as permanent and essential "others," and on the other by offering them assimilation to the national community through a logic which restricts Muslim politics and identities to a "minority standpoint."[40]

This distinction is constantly reinforced by the press and 'citizen-journalists' both in and outside of Muslim mediascapes. Mainstream European media outlets construct Euro-Muslims as a community of secluded, distrustful, and alien economic underachievers. Muslims, on the other hand, are using communication networks and new media to link themselves together, partly as a response to what they see as prejudice in their host societies, but also as a way to increase their political strength, exchange ideas, and promote unity based on the ummah. Cyberspace is currently the most profound domain for such activities by providing European Muslims with a responsive virtual community that assuages their loneliness and banishes their confusion, while offering a geographic space where some semblance of Islamic unity can be facilitated.

Cyberspace as the Forge of Ummahism

The structure of cyberspace is, by definition, deterritorialized. This has important ramifications for reifying the transnational ummah,[41] especially when set against "the universalist yearning of Muslims who cannot identify with any specific place or nation" such as Britain's "Asians" and France's *beurs*.[42] The Internet is thus allowing Muslims to create a viable imagined community enabling a hitherto impossible embodiment of the global ummah (though one which Muslims dip into an out of at will). This is a paradigmatic example of the use of cyberspace to reclaim public space and build virtual communities online. It should be noted that it is not just Internet users that benefit from such activities; ideas, messages, and news all filter through society via the Net-savvy preceptors of information. Even in societies where Internet penetration remains low, influential netizens are consuming and redistributing information from the Web on daily basis; however, it is becoming clear that activists located near the various nodes of the global communication infrastructure exert greater influence than those on the periphery of the information superhighway. These Internet-enabled elites may differ from the elites of previous eras, but are nonetheless emerging as important political intermediaries. In cyberspace, elites have already initiated a process which is leading to the reification of the ummah, and which—if seen through to fruition—will result in a viable community embodying those national characteristics identified earlier in this chapter.

This reification of the ummah has begun with the establishment of a universally-available communication ecumene which harmonizes thought, provides a global forum for discourse, and enables the coordination of collective action. For transnational Muslims, the Internet has "erased the geographical boundaries...that structured Muslim geopolitics for fourteen centuries."[43] It is important to note that the use of the Internet to create conceptual contiguity among the ummah is an evolution rather than revolution. Since the 1970s, transnational Muslim elites have enjoyed the benefits of new media platforms for identity production, including audiocassettes (Hirschkind 2001),[44] videocassettes,[45] and satellite television.[46] The advent of cyberspace—and more recently, the linkage of ubiquitous mobile phones to the Internet—has vastly expanded this evolving mediascape. Globally-oriented ummahist narratives about "cultural" events such as France's ban on the hijab, George W. Bush's description of the "War on Terror" as a "crusade," and Pope Benedict XVI's remarks on the "evil and inhuman" nature of Islam have all been knitted into the various cyber-Islamic environments where they are further intertwined with international crises involving Muslim populations (e.g., Kashmir, Chechnya, Palestine, etc.).

Today, Internet use is the defining praxis of ummahism through its ability to facilitate information exchange and produce perceived harmonization among dispersed and distinct communities of Muslims living in countries as disparate as Canada, Jordan, and Malaysia. By providing a normative information ecosystem that caters to Muslim netizens, ummahists are able to extend their influence over great distances and diverse populations; according to English scholar of Islam Gary Bunt, "Cyber Islamic Environments are a primary medium for religious, political and ideological guidance."[47] Cyberspace allows active participation with the ummah; the dynamics of such interaction differ greatly the passive relations Muslims have with the religious elite (*ulema*). As forensic psychiatrist and expert on Islamic networks Marc Sageman states, "The Internet stands in for the idea of the *ummah*, the mythologized Muslim community. The Internet makes this ideal community concrete, because one can interact with it."[48] The vibrancy of Internet-based interactions with the ummah has effectively withered the authority of local authority figures, including the ulema.[49] A small number of elites command disproportionate influence in this milieu, which is characterized by the rise of mass audiences, the reduction of barriers to production of information, new spheres of participation, and fluctuating patterns of control.[50] In the words of Middle East expert Peter Mandaville, these new players are becoming dominant forces in *translocal politics,* i.e., "the new forms of politics emerging from the Muslim world's experience with globalization."[51] Rather than trying to dominate a *place* defined by physical territory (e.g., Leeds, Pakistan, or the Middle East), these elites are seeking influence over a *space* conceived around human beings (i.e., the Muslim world including its exclaves in the West), although there are certainly some groups such as Hizb ut-Tahrir (HT) who would like to see the black flag of the caliphate flying over London. HT does, however, demonstrate the efficacy of cyberspace to link together like –minded individuals across time and space. The organization purportedly maintains its worldwide headquarters in London, but is most popular in Central Asia and some Arab states. As a principally mass-mediated, semi-secret organization, HT is now acutely dependent on the Internet to maintain and influence its membership. According to journalist Pablo Escobar, HT's leadership remains "essentially invisible" as they produce and distribute literature in Kyrgyz, Uzbek, Dari, and Russian via a vast "network of underground desktop publishing presses all over Central Asia" connected to the Web.[52]

It is critical not to overstate the affective capacity of the Internet vis-à-vis national identity nor its agency in global politics. Postcolonial writer Ziauddin Sardar rejects the utopian promises of virtual community suggesting that older power structures are so embedded in traditional space that they frequently dominate cyberspace causing the Internet to reinforce, rather than weaken, existing hierarchies.[53] Historian Bruce Lawrence succinctly states, "Cybernauts are doomed to be frustrated 'netizens'; the Information Super Highway will have more dead ends than useful exits, and it will never have a final destination."[54] Dependence on virtual communities also carries the risk of anti-social behavior; as American geographer Joel Kotkin puts it, "By abolishing the need for face-to-face contact, the Internet increases loneliness and social isolation, expanding virtual networks that lack the intimacy of real relationships nurtured by physical proximity. Reliance on electronic communication can lead, research suggests, to too much disengagement from real life."[55] Muslims living outside the *Dar al-Islam* may prove especially susceptible to this phenomenon. As cyberspatial ummah-oriented identification increases, there is the danger that "the virtual [will] become a form of narcosis, providing individuals with 'alternative realities,' which trick their senses through technical manipulation."[56] As David Ardalan points out that, while generally empowering, the Internet allows Muslim women to remain in the home, effectively secluded from Western society, while maintaining virtual contact with Muslims abroad and even engaging in e-Commerce without having to be in the physical presence of non-Muslims.[57] Internet scholar Alexis Kort refers to this as an incipient "computerized *hijab* for women."[58] Ultimately, such disaffection can be a double-edged sword for effective mobilization as cyber-Muslims retreat both from their physical neighbors and mainstream virtual communities of ummahism into idiosyncratic cyberworlds. In such cases, their allegiance either the imagined nation of the ummah and/or the state of residence becomes tenuous. This is perhaps the greatest single impediment to elites seeking to operationalize the current shift towards ummah-centric identity in the Muslim ethnoscape.

Unless one enters cyberspace with an ideological commitment to nation-building, the very structure of the Web tends to subtly but steadily weaken pre-existing nationalist orientations. However, a growing and increasingly influential elite of ummahists have demonstrated such a commitment. Due to a lack of organic solidarity based on geographic proximity, shared culture, commercial exchange, etc., these elites have instead focused on connecting the masses through core values.[59] British activist and researcher Munira Mirza describes this process as a sophisticated attempt at Islamicizing modernity.[60]

This effect is even moving beyond ideological orientations and is impacting physical appearance as Heather Marie Akou points out in her article "Building a New 'World Fashion': Islamic Dress in the Twenty-first Century." She states: "Over the last five years, as the technology and speed of the Internet has improved, websites have begin to play a vital role in spreading fashions between different parts of the Islamic world."[61] Akou argues that a relatively small number of elites have the power to "speak" for the "macroculture" of transnational Muslims; in cyberspace, these elites wield power highly disproportionate to their numbers (she draws an analogy to the U.S. Congress' influence over the American people). Buttressed by what Johan Galtung refers to as *world-encompassing commercialization*,[62] the ability to purchase a common form of Islamic dress from anywhere in the world combined with Web-based discursive pressures to wear such clothing is having a dramatic effect on women's fashion in and outside of the *Dar al-Islam*.

Cyberspace promotes a homogenous, deterritorialized form of Islam, one that has cut its links to many Islamic traditions, which, in turn, enables online ummahists to exert influence displacing traditional authority sources such as the ulema, local leaders, and politicians. Furthermore, Islam makes such an identity building project feasible. More so than Christianity, Buddhism, and other "world religions," the Islamic faith provides robust regulatory capacities for the political, social, and legal lives of its adherents. The nature of cyberspace works against the monopoly of those spokespersons of established institutions and empowers new 'interpreters' of the Islamic ummah.[63] The mere existence of cyber-communities does not guarantee cultural cohesion, political advancement, economic success, or social mobility. Rather, the Web has become an extension for these and other projects. It is the elites who make such dreams into realities.

Über-Ummahists: A New Elite for a Nation in the Making

Islam's first generation of Internet-enabled elites was comprised of students, émigré professionals, political exiles, and labor migrants which socio-cultural anthropologist Jon Anderson describes as "a mobile population, not just of settlers but with ties and the material means to maintain links with homelands in a world shrunken by advances in transportation and communication available to ever more people."[64] This "older" elite is currently being complemented and challenged by elements of the "newer" deterritorialized ummah comprised of second- and third-generation diasporic Muslims who are much more likely to identify with the transnational ummah than their parents.[65] As Gilles Kepel states, "The first generation of university graduates among Muslim immigrants' children in Britain, France, and Germany have already begun to take their place as educated, activist citizens of Europe and the world. They possess the skills and perspective to build bridges to North Africa, the Middle East, or Pakistan."[66] Both of these virtual cliques are reaching out to the traditional Muslim world (particularly the Arab states, Pakistan, Turkey, and Iran) in hopes of building sustainable informational and organizational linkages between the West and *Dar al-Islam*. The extension of influence into Muslim countries is already reaping benefits for the ummahists.

Reflecting the non-ethnic, non-local, non-statist orientations of Muslim digerati, there has been a palpable increase in pan-Muslim solidarity on various questions (though these issues are nearly always global rather than local in nature). As a result, the ummah functions as a nation; however, its membership does not need to fully reject competing national identities (e.g. Persian, Arab, or British) nor does this membership necessarily avert internal divisions (Sunni versus Shi'a, moderate versus fundamentalist, etc.). This tendency to treat membership in the ummah as analogous to membership in some other "nation" appears to be the strongest among de-ethnicized Muslims living outside the Muslim world. In such a milieu, it should be stated that Muslims are not shredding their passports to embrace ummahist identities, but instead are tacking back and forth between the nationalisms of modernity (Iranianism, Jordanianism, etc.) and a new form of postnationalism (ummahism).

Reflecting the diasporic nature of the Internet-enabled ummahists, the language of unity, activism, and intra-Muslim exchange is in flux. "The Muslim 'community of the learned' no longer circulates in a purely Arab-Muslim context, and English is as important as Arabic, if not more so, outside the Arabic-speaking world, which comprises only 20 percent of all Muslims."[67] Ummahist thinkers, activists, and imams are all employing the global lingua franca of English as a tool to speak to their constituencies. "The use of English as the primary language de-emphasizes an Arab/Middle Eastern Arabic speaking monopoly on Islamic discourse, opening up discussion and debate between Muslims worldwide, regardless of their mother tongues."[68] Gary Bunt states, "it is the educated élite, who are literate, use English as a primary language and have access to the web and skills in presenting their message online, who are currently dominating Cyber Islamic Environments."[69] Reflecting the lowered "barriers to entry" for obtaining elite status in the current era of self-publishing and non-governmental activism, these agents of change often lack the academic, political, or cultural bona fides which characterized their predecessors both in Europe during the 1800s and in the developing world in twentieth century.

This effect has only grown more evident in the wake of the 11 September attacks and the consequential backlash against Muslims worldwide.[70]

Any nationally-oriented community is dependent on political and intellectual elites to shape a sense of belonging within the community. Benedict Anderson describes the relationship between the masses and a "strategic strata" of literati in terms of "virtually oriented conduits" which translate ideology from the learned to the illiterate.[71] The ummah has long been riven by the competing interests of religious, economic, and political elites who gained more from dividing than from uniting the world's Muslims. Like Europe's Jews before them, the "gradual elision of national differences" between European Muslims is making it easier and politically profitable for pan-Muslim elites to command spheres of authority in Europe and the greater Muslim world.[72] As Alexis Kort has argued, this decentralization of information and power has also allowed for the voices of Muslim women to be heard loudly around the world.[73]

The emergence of a young, revisionist cadre of intellectuals and activists with few connections to traditional bases of power is analogous to the emergence of national elites in late nineteenth century Austria-Hungary, the interwar Middle East, or sub-Saharan Africa during the Cold War. This novel elite has emerged both as a result of and in reaction to globalization; these actors seek power not for a state, a tribe, or a mosque, but for the entire Muslim ummah (though they recognize that their sphere of influence will never include more than a slice of this polity).

This new elite of Muslim activists should not be underestimated. Their political impact in a world where the current communications infrastructure enables ideas and messages to bridge both time and space is already being felt through controversies such as the Cartoons Affair. In transnational Muslim spheres, Anderson's "strategic strata" is widening as new players take over from the ossified elites. The societal chaos wrought by the diasporic experience has created opportunities for those seeking influence, especially when they leverage the West's dominance of cyberspace for their own benefit. Technological and media savvy further enhance this new cadre's ability to make their voices heard over competing sources of authority (including thoroughly Westernized Muslims in diaspora and traditional elites in the *Dar al-Islam*). By effectively marketing their views as the norm for the imagined ummah, they have created the conditions for an 'information cascade' whereby Muslims—once they have identified themselves as Muslim above all else—tend to believe what others in the group believe.[74] The Copenhagen imam Ahmed Abu Laban's (who administered his sermons alternatively in English and Arabic) decision to conduct a public relations tour of Egypt, Qatar, and Saudi Arabia to publicize the issues surrounding the Muhammad cartoons bring together these threads of media, diaspora, and elite action in a way that demands a reinterpretation of the ummah for the twenty-first century.

The Cartoons Affair and Ummahist National Identity

In early 2006, certain portions of the Muslim world convulsed over the publication of a dozen cartoons of the Prophet Muhammad which contravened Islamic principles against the artistic depiction of the Messenger of God. In what was framed by the world's media as an act of international solidarity against the insult, Muslims around the globe protested—often violently—against Denmark, the West, and America. This event soured diplomatic relations between European states and their Muslim counterparts, resulted in the deaths of more than one hundred protestors, wreaked extensive property damage, cost certain European companies millions in losses from product boycotts, and once again stoked the fires of the "clash of civilizations" within academic and policy circles. The prolonged imbroglio also demonstrated the will, strength, and prominence of transnational, media-savvy ummahists.

The origins of the cartoon controversy lay in the problems Danish writer Kåre Bluitgen had in finding an illustrator for his children's book about Muhammad. After learning that potential artists feared attacks by Islamic extremists, editors at Denmark's leading newspaper *Jyllands-Posten* invited artists to contribute illustrations of the Prophet Muhammad. Twelve of these cartoons were then published on 30 September 2005 in the article "Muhammeds ansigt" ('The Face of Muhammad'), including one with Islam's prophet wearing a bomb-shaped turban. Their publication quickly provoked widespread condemnation among Denmark's Muslim community, but failed to incite controversy beyond the country's borders. In the ensuing months, however, the cartoons were reprinted in other countries, including Egypt, the Netherlands, Germany, and France. After failing to spur action against *Jyllands-Posten* in their home country, several Danish imams began distributing the "Akkari-Laban dossier" (named after its principal authors Ahmad Abu Laban and Ahmed Akkari) abroad in order to "internationalize" the issue so that the Danish government would realize that the "cartoons were not only insulting to Muslims in Denmark but also to Muslims worldwide."[75] The packet included several letters from Muslim organizations explaining their case, the *Jyllands-Posten* cartoons, and other pieces of anti-Islamic material which had purportedly caused "pain and torment" to the authors. In November 2005, a delegation of Danish imams including Abu Laban toured the Middle East distributing the dossier and meeting with representatives of religious, educational, and political institutions. At a December 2005 summit of the Organization of the Islamic Conference (OIC) in Mecca, Egypt's foreign minister Ahmed Abul-Gheit distributed copies of the dossier to the attendees precipitating the OIC's issue of an official communiqué demanding that the United Nations impose international sanctions upon Denmark. The first weeks of the new year saw scattered protests against the cartoons in Muslim states. Word of the controversy then began to "instantly echo in cyberspace" via short message service (SMS), blogs, and email.[76] In February of 2006, rioters in Syria and Lebanon burned Danish embassies beginning a prolonged period of protest and boycotts. Ultimately, the controversy, which Danish Prime Minister Anders Fogh Rasmussen described as the country's worst international crisis since World War II, resulted in scores of deaths, cost Danish companies some €134 million in lost exports to Muslim-majority states, and wreaked untold property damage around the globe.

As Muslims expressed their discontent with Danish flag-burning, threats against Europeans, and assaults on symbols of the West, European policymakers were shocked and horrified. *BBC, FOX News*, and *CNN* were only too ready to cover the story through the optic of 'Muslim rage'; in the words of Palestinian journalist Mohammed Omer, "the Western media have been quick to lump together all Islamic and Arabic protests—whether peaceful or violent, thoughtful or mindless—in places around the world where history and circumstances differ wildly."[77] Moderate Muslims tended to remain (or were portrayed as) silent during the maelstrom, with the notable exception of the Jordanian magazine publisher Jihad Momani, who reprinted the cartoons. He publicly wondered in an accompanying editorial: "Who offends Islam more? A foreigner who endeavors to draw the prophet as described by his followers in the world, or a Muslim with an explosive belt who commits suicide in a wedding party?"[78] He was subsequently fired, arrested, and charged with insulting religion. Such voices—and there were many among Muslims in and outside of the *Dar al-Islam*—were drowned out by self-appointed defenders of the ummah who, in turn, used the event to flex their own muscles calling for boycotts, official apologies, and censorship of Western media outlets. New media played a key role; as one report documented: "There in Cyberspace, instead of noisy street demonstrations, burning flags, and stones hurled through embassy windows, the weapon of choice is the keyboard, the mouse and the economic boycott for 'the Islamic world's' new activists."[79]

The European public and politicians—Danish prime minister Fogh Rasmussen, in particular—seemed baffled by the oddness of it all. To begin with, the cartoons elicited little media attention when originally published. Secondly, Europeans were taken aback by the *apparent solidarity* of Muslims' reaction which differed dramatically from past controversies. When Salman Rushdie published *The Satanic Verses*, the fatwa was issued against him, not against the nation-state that hosted him, i.e., Great Britain. When Dutch filmmaker Theo van Gogh offended Muslims with his provocative comments and films, he as an individual was targeted for assassination, not the Dutch people. Thirdly, the media framing of the issue in religious (and not ethnonational) terms resulted in Europeans seeing the Muslim world's virulent reaction as patently absurd. Unending analogies to *seemingly* similar artistic insults of religious figures in Christian mythology (where there was little or no public outcry) became the mainstay of Western press coverage. Most Europeans agreed that the caricatures were distasteful and publishing them was imprudent, but remained steadfast in their defense of the Continent's hard-won freedom of the press. In response, ummahist elites quickly turned respect for religious figures—the Prophet Muhammad in particular—into a shibboleth for distinguishing the ummah (us) from the non-Muslims (them). In this polarized environment, moderate Muslim voices were even further marginalized. Consequently, the fallout of the controversy has further contributed to the perceptual polarity among Europeans vis-à-vis the 'Islamic other' in their midst. Likewise, the there has been a strengthening the notion that secular European societies fail to afford adequate respect for members of the Islamic ummah living in the West. Thus, the only real 'winners' in the Cartoons Affair have been those individuals and groups mobilizing in the name of the ummah and speaking out against further integration of ethnic Muslims into the fabric of European society.

Through Internet-enabled virtuality and diasporic marginalization, the ummah—more so than any time in the past—is functioning as an ersatz nation. This is the direct result of actions by transnational Muslim elites who are mobilizing their constituencies on multiple levels: ethnic, national, and religious. Technological skill, media savvy, and a keen understanding of the capabilities (as well as the limits) of globalization have endowed this clique with dramatic influence in the Muslim world. Politicized information cascades—like the one associated with the Cartoons

Affair—only add to the power of those acting in defense of the ummah. In constantly seeking to advance the story of "Islam versus the West," Western media have abetted these elites' rapid rise by ignoring competitive actors. As such, it behooves both scholars and policy elites to pay close attention to the actions of the ummahists for they will undoubtedly play a pivotal role in defining relations between the West and the Islamic world in the coming decades. Similarly, the changed environment wrought by global flows of people, ideas, money, entertainment, and information demands the very concept of nation be reworked to accommodate the manifestation of ummahism and similar affinity movements.

Notes

1. "Time to Choose," *The Economist* 368, no. 8331 (5 July 2003): 37
2. James Piscatori, *Islam in a World of Nation-States* (Cambridge: Cambridge University Press, 1986), 86.
3. Ernest Renan, "What is a Nation?" in Vincent Pecora, *Nations and Identities: Classic Readings* (Malden, MA: Blackwell Publishers, 2001 [1882]), 175.
4. Joseph de Maistre, "Study on Sovereignty," in Vincent Pecora, *Nations and Identities: Classic Readings* (Malden, MA: Blackwell Publishers, 2001 [1884]), 109. Earlier thinkers on the topic of nationalism tended to link language, culture, and genetic makeup together into a tightly bound triad of unchanging identity. This approach has been generally discredited; as David W. Anthony points out, "Anyone who *assumes* a simple connection between language and genes, without citing geographic isolation or other special circumstance, is wrong at the outset." See David W. Anthony, *The Horse, the Wheel, and Language: How Bronze-Age Riders from the Eurasian Steppes Shaped the Modern World* (Princeton: Princeton University Press. 2007), 11.
5. Benedict Anderson, *Imagined Communities: Reflections on the Origin and Spread of Nationalism* (London: Verso, 1991), 7.
6. Anthony Smith, *National Identity* (Reno: University of Nevada Press, 1991).
7. Eric J. Hobsbawm, "Introduction: Inventing Traditions," in Eric J. Hobsbawm and Terence Ranger, *The Invention of Tradition* (Cambridge: Cambridge University Press, 1992); Hobsbawm's definition reinforces the previously discussed notion of strategic essentialism for purposes of contemporary nation-building.
8. Miroslav Hroch, *Social Preconditions of National Revival in Europe: A Comparative Analysis of the Social Composition of Patriotic Groups among the Smaller European Nations* (Cambridge: Cambridge University Press, 1985).
9. Max Weber, Hans Heinrich Gerth, and Charles Wright Mills, *From Max Weber: Essays in Sociology* (New York and London: Routledge, 1970), 176.
10. See Piscatori, *Islam in a World of Nation-States*.
11. Piscatori, *Islam in a World of Nation-States*, 31.
12. Ronald Judy, "Sayyid Qutb's *Fiqh al-Waqi'i*, Or New Realist Science," *Boundary* 31, no. 2 (Summer 2004): 113-148.
13. Bassam Tibi, *Islam between Culture and Politics* (Houndsmills, UK: Palgrave, 2001), 128-29.
14. Sayed Khatab, "Arabism and Islamism in Sayyid Qutb's Thought on Nationalism," *The Muslim World* 94, no. 2 (April 2004): 217-244.
15. Fred Halliday, "The Politics of the Umma: States and Community in Islamic Movements," *Mediterranean Politics* 7, no. 3 (Autumn 2002): 20-41.
16. Quoted in Muhittin Ataman, "Islamic Perspective on Ethnicity and Nationalism: Diversity or Uniformity?" *Journal of Muslim Minority Affairs* 23, no. 1 (April 2003): 89-102.
17. Halliday, "The Politics of the Umma," 26.

18. Quoted in Piscatori, *Islam in a World of Nation-States*, 106.
19. Quoted in Piscatori, *Islam in a World of Nation-States*, 103. Despite transnational aspirations, Islamist scholars such as Qutb and Maududi were forced to work within the structure of individual nation-states. However, their 21st century counterparts confront a world where international borders are less salient.
20. See Karl Deutsch, *Nationalism and Social Communication: An Inquiry into the Foundations of Nationality* (Cambridge: The Technology Press of the Massachusetts Institute of Technology, 1953).
21. Ataman, "Islamic Perspective on Ethnicity and Nationalism," 89.
22. Guilain Denoeux, "The Forgotten Swamp: Navigating Political Islam," *Middle East Policy* 9, no. 2 (June 2002): 56-81.
23. Gilles Kepel, *The War for Muslim Minds: Islam and the West* (Cambridge, MA: Harvard University Press, 2004).
24. Quoted in Kepel, *The War for Muslim Minds*, 125-26.
25. John Bowen, "Beyond Migration: Islam as a Transnational Public Space," *Journal of Ethnic and Migration Studies* 30, no. 5 (September 2004): 879-894.
26. Anderson, *Imagined Communities*, 32-36.
27. Anderson, *Imagined Communities*, 39.
28. Peter Mandaville, "Communication and Diasporic Islam," in Karim H. Karim, *The Media of Diaspora* (London: Routledge, 2003), 135.
29. Olivier Roy, "Europe's Response to Radical Islam," *Current History* 104, no. 685 (November 2005): 360-364.
30. See Olivier Roy, *Globalized Islam: The Search for the New Ummah* (New York: Columbia University Press, 2004).
31. Enes Karić, "Is 'Euro-Islam' a Myth, Challenge or a Real Opportunity for Muslims and Europe?" *Journal of Muslim Minority Affairs* 22, no. 2 (October 2002): 435-442.
32. Sander Gilman, "The Parallels of Islam and Judaism in Diaspora," *Palestine - Israel Journal of Politics, Economics & Culture* 12, 2-3 (Summer 2005): 61-66.
33. See Arjun, Appadurai, *Modernity at Large* (Minneapolis: University of Minnesota Press, 1996).
34. Roy, *Globalized Islam*, 103.
35. Ian Johnson and John Carreyrou, "Islam and Europe: A Volatile Mix," *Wall Street Journal*, 11 July 2005.
36. Lawrence Wright, "The Terror Web," *New Yorker*, 2 August 2004.
37. Olivier Roy, "EuroIslam: The Jihad Within?" *National Interest* 71 (Spring 2003): 63-73.
38. Paul Statham, "Resilient Islam: Muslim Controversies in Europe," *Harvard International Review* 26, no. 3 (Fall 2004): 54-61.
39. Johnson and Carreyrou, "Islam and Europe."
40. Ruba Salih, "The Backward and the New: National, Transnational and Post-National Islam in Europe," *Journal of Ethnic and Migration Studies* 30, no. 5 (September 2004): 995–1011.
41. See Gary Bunt, *Virtually Islamic* (Cardiff: University of Wales Press, 2000); Jon Anderson, "The Internet and Islam's New Interpreters," in Dale Eickelman and Jon Anderson, *New Media and the Muslim World: The Emerging Public Sphere*, Second edition (Bloomington: Indiana University Press, 2003); and Peter Mandaville, *Transnational Muslim Politics: Reimagining the Umma* (London and New York: Routledge, 2004).
42. Roy, "EuroIslam," 63. In the UK, "Asian" generally refers to descendents of immigrants from the Indian subcontinent—a large number of whom are Muslims. *Beur* is *verlan* (French youth slang) for a French resident of North African origin regardless of ethnic or national descent.
43. Kepel, *The War for Muslim Minds*, 7-8.

44. Charles Hirschkind, "The Ethics of Listening: Cassette-Sermon Audition in Contemporary Egypt," *American Ethnologist* 28, no. 3 (August 2001): 623-649.

45. Denoeux, "The Forgotten Swamp."

46. Marc Lynch, "Watching al-Jazeera," *Wilson Quarterly* 29, no. 3 (Summer 2005): 36-45.

47. Bunt, *Virtually Islamic*, 103.

48. Quoted in Wright, "The Terror Web."

49. Jon Anderson, "Wiring Up: The Internet Difference for Muslim Networks," in Miriam Cooke and Bruce Lawrence, *Muslim Networks: From Hajj to Hip Hop* (Chapel Hill: University of North Carolina Press, 2005).

50. Peter Mandaville, *Global Political Islam* (London and New York: Routledge, 2007), 324.

51. Mandaville, *Transnational Muslim Politics*, 2.

52. Pablo Escobar, "A Very Peaceful Jihad," *Index on Censorship* 34, no. 1 (Spring 2005): 164-169.

53. Ziauddin Sardar, "alt.civilizations.faq: Cyberspace as the Darker Side of the West," in Ziauddin Sardar and Jerome Ravetz *Cyberfutures: Culture and Politics on the Information Superhighway* (New York: New York University Press, 1998).

54. Bruce B. Lawrence, "Review of New Media in the Muslim World: The Emerging Public Sphere by Dale F. Eickelman; Jon W. Anderson," *International Journal of Middle East Studies* 33, no. 1 (February 2001): 167-169.

55. Joel Kotkin, *The New Geography: How the Digital Revolution Is Shaping the American Landscape* (New York: Random House, 2000), 169.

56. Mihaela Keleman and Warren Smith, "Community and Its 'Virtual' Promises: A Critique of Cyberlibertarian Rhetoric," *Information, Communication & Society* 4, no. 3 (October 2001): 370-387.

57. David Ardalan, "Cyber Fatima—Muslim Women on the Web," National Public Radio, 23 March 2002.

58. Alexis Kort, "Dar al-Cyber Islam: Women, Domestic Violence, and the Islamic Reformation on the World Wide Web," *Journal of Muslim Minority Affairs* 25, no. 3 (December 2005): 363-383.

59. Lenie Brouwer, "Dutch-Muslims on the Internet: A New Discussion Platform," *Journal of Muslim Affairs* 24, no. 1 (April 2004): 47-55.

60. Munira Mirza, Abi Senthilkumaran, and Zein Ja'far, *Living Apart Together: British Muslims and the Paradox of Multiculturalism* (London: Policy Exchange, 2007), 45.

61. Heather Marie Akou, "Building a New 'World Fashion': Islamic Dress in the Twenty-first Century," *Fashion Theory* 11, no 4 (December 2007): 403-422.

62. Johan Galtung, "Cultural Violence, *Journal of Peace Research* 27, no. 3 (August 1990): 291-305.

63. Anderson, "The Internet and Islam's New Interpreters," 48.

64. Jon Anderson, "New Media, New Publics," *Social Research* 70, no. 3 (Summer 2003): 887-906.

65. Mirza, Senthilkumaran, and Ja'far, *Living Apart Together*, 38.

66. Kepel, *The War for Muslim Minds*, 250.

67. Roy, *Globalized Islam*, 109.

68. Kort, "Dar al-Cyber Islam," 364.

69. Bunt, *Virtually Islamic*, 132.

70. See Garbi Schmidt, "The Transnational Umma – Myth or Reality? Examples from the Western Diasporas," *Muslim World* 95, no. 4 (October 2005): 575-586.

71. Anderson, *Imagined Communities*, 15.

72. Gilman, "The Parallels of Islam and Judaism in Diaspora," 63.

73. Kort, "Dar al-Cyber Islam."

74. Mirza, Senthilkumaran, and Ja'far, *Living Apart Together*, 29.

75. Pernille Ammitzbøll and Lorenzo Vidino, "After the Danish Cartoon Controversy," *Middle East Quarterly* 14, no. 1 (Winter 2007): 3-11.

76. Kevin Sullivan, "E-Mail, Blogs, Text Messages Propel Anger over Images," *Washington Post*, 9 February 2006.

77. Mohammed Omer, "Armed with a Mouse, Boycott-Savvy Cyber-Activists Make Their Presence Felt," *Washington Report on Middle East Affairs* 25, no. 3 (April 2006): 30-31.

78. Quoted in Jamal Halaby, "Jordanian Paper Runs Prophet Muhammad Cartoons, Saying They Show 'Danish Offense,'" *Associated Press Worldstream*, 2 February 2006.

79. Omer, "Armed with a Mouse."

Afterword
Toward a Cybernational Future?

In the contemporary world of postnational politics, imagination should not be underestimated as a mechanism for generating new national identities, nor as a potent tool for reviving older ones. Arjun Appadurai has described the democratizing effects of the new technologies on "imagination," arguing that technology has enabled imagination to become a collective, social fact no longer tethered to art, mythology or ritual or dependent on charismatic individuals who would manipulate imagination for their own ends. This is especially salient in relation to the contrived notions of state and national identity. "Even when long-standing identities have been forgotten or buried, the combination of migration and mass mediation assures their reconstruction on a new scale and at larger levels."[1] In this study, I have attempted to demonstrate a number of ways this phenomenon is manifesting.

For diasporic Albanians scattered throughout the Balkans and farther afield, cyberspace has provided an imagined geography where the nation has been redeemed, free from the "artificial" barriers presented by international borders. Among the Russians beached by the ebbing of the Soviet Union's borders, Internet-mediated imagination associated with globalism has proved to be a powerful aid in confronting the challenges of the nationalizing state. Roma elites have similarly gravitated to the Web to build an imaginary landscape that compresses time and space, while simultaneously providing direct connections to a support network and financial opportunities unavailable in their states of residence. Lastly, the Internet has come to function as the forge of the immigrant ummah, enabling a hitherto impossible reification of identity based on membership in the Islamic creed.

Cyberspace represents a remarkably expressive canvas, upon which national identity is being recast on an almost daily basis. There has been a widening and a deepening of the community of authors with the proliferation of the Internet. Furthermore, the entire relationship between producers/authors and consumers/readers has been altered by the advent of the computer-mediated communication.

> [National minorities can now] systematically construct national and cultural identities over time. The other media of communication are constrained by the lack of space and time. A newspaper can contain only so many pages and a radio or television program can run for only so many minutes/hours, whereas material on the Internet, at least in principle, can remain forever. This allows for the slow and careful construction of material, especially that relating to a community's historical and cultural antecedents.[2]

As Menderes Candan and Uwe Hunger parsimoniously states: "The endeavor of nation-building has become easier due to the invention of the Internet." This shift is still in its infancy, but it is clear that the ramifications of the Internet for nations, nationalism, and national identities are substantial.

The Internet has effectively ended Benedict Anderson's statist elite and merchant class monopoly on the national project, although real world elites certain have more tools at their disposal than Internet-based elites. However, the dynamics of computer-mediated interaction undoubtedly allow multiple polities to attempt to define, reinvent, and rediscover nationally-based identity. Cyberspatial national identity projects are a key element of a larger phenomenon based on the withering of the importance of interstate borders, the autonomy of domestic economies, and the assumption of discrete and pristine national cultures.

> Globalization and ethnicity are...closely connected. What is essential to keep in mind, however, is that whereas international migration brings people together from different cultural and historical backgrounds in close proximity, the stratification of these people into various ethnic groups and the nature of ethnic group identities, does not necessarily or automatically reflect preexisting identities, interests or attachments, either on the part of immigrants or established residents...Ethnic identity formation and differentiation emerge from complex processes of interaction, reaction, self-identification, and institutional categorization—all of which play into specific economic, political, and sociocultural contexts.[3]

As explored throughout this text, the Internet is emerging as an important tool for the reification of political, economic, and cultural identities among nationally-defined groups which have hitherto faced marginalization, persecution, or denial of their separateness. As new opportunities emerge, the view of the nation will change to reflect the environment. With the Internet, the options for change increase almost exponentially over time. Some authors contend that minority mobilization via the Internet is resulting in a further weakening of the nation-state. According to Michael Dahan and Gabriel Sheffer, "While...states are weakening, ethnic intrastate and trans-state ethnic groups prosper."[4]

There is little direct evidence to suggest that utilization of the Internet by national minorities has significantly contributed to the weakening of the nation-state. As political scientist Alexander J. Motyl states, "neither the nation—as a self-conscious cultural community—nor the state—as a political organization with a monopoly of violence in some territory—appears to be on the verge of extinction."[5] However, national governments around the world have—sometimes belatedly— begun to recognize that the Internet and cyberspace endow their critics with powerful, postmodern tools of statecraft. Consequently, states are fighting back, attempting to reimpose their influence or prevent minority-based identity projects from producing fruit as cyberspatial identity projects grow in the scope and scale. Authoritarian regimes often choose to limit Internet access based on ethnicity, or some other less overt classification to prevent participation in national identity building in cyberspace. As Rohan Jayasekera states, "[T]he Internet provides very limited security against the depredations of the real world. Web-savvy Turkish security agents can pursue the PKK into the darker corners of cyberspace; Serbs pull the plug on

Montenegrin webservers."[6] Some states are employing sophisticated surveillance techniques that reduce or eliminate the benefit of anonymity that gives cyberspace its relative power as a medium.[7] Other states have used the Web to augment their policies of ethnic and national integration, discursively eradicating or significantly reducing the perception of institutionalized inequality among national minorities. The Internet has also been used by state-building elites to "inculcate" a unifying national culture, effectively becoming a latter day for the daily reproduction of Ernest Renan's plebiscite of the nation.[8] State governments have also counteracted the work of irredentist movements in other states by creating their own Web-based or offline propaganda lauding the contribution, presence and participation of national minorities in society. Such activities were already on display in the 1990s, and were not confined to the developed world. Web-based actors helped shaped the discursive environment of the Ethiopian-Eritrean conflict (1998-2000).

> From the safety of cyberspace, long-distance nationalists encouraged more violence, more suffering in pursuit of Ethiopia's "mission" to demolish "Eritreanism" and replace it with true history, identity and mental purity. Abyssinian fundamentalism rejected the validity of Eritrean identity and insisted Eritreans were "really" Ethiopians, errant family members deceived by postcolonial fantasies and separated from their true nature.[9]

Other strategies have included co-opting the national minority through proactive measures including greater autonomy, special cultural and linguistic programs, etc. Appadurai refers to this as the exercise of "taxonomic control over difference," where small groups are seduced with "the fantasy of self-display on some sort of global or cosmopolitan scale."[10] Lastly, states have even gone as far as to issue military threats regarding nationalist activity originating in neighboring states. Taken together, it is clear that cyberspace is rapidly emerging as important battlefield in the centuries-old struggle between the nations and states.

National identity is and has always been a tool for elites to gather power. The Internet cannot unweave the tapestry of political interactions overnight, nor is it likely to do so in the long term. Cyberspace can, however, provide an outlet for those that feel they deserve more access to the levers of power, and will reward those who are savvy enough to capture some level of local, national, or international influence. For national minorities, challenged ethnic groups, and diasporas, the Web offers a host of new possibilities for identity projects. Concomitantly, states are presented with a plethora of novel challenges to their authority and narratives. The Internet has enabled a world where physical closeness is not required for community building and where anyone with access to the Web can impact national identity. Challenges of distance and politics that might have once prevented physically dispersed nations from communicating across state borders have almost completely evaporated as new virtual relationships develop which are "uninhibited by conventional notions of political territory and national sovereignty."[11] Regardless of state activity intended to counter national identity building in cyberspace, a bell has sounded and it cannot be unrung. Elites among nearly every minority community on the face of the globe are now engaged in some sort of cyberspace-based, mass-mediated national identity project in the name of their kin. The activities are variegated not only in their approach, but also in their aims. Despite their differences, all share a goal of improving the lot of their ethnic brethren.

While virtual ethnic communities might not be poised to replace "real world" bonds of nationality, they allow a range of and depth of ethnic affiliation compatible with a social world in which boundaries have become more permeable and in which the range of possible personal and group identities have expanded. As Jennifer Brinkerhoff states: "The Internet contributes to mobilization by facilitating shared identity, issue framing, and confidence building; acting as an organizing/networking tool; and providing a vehicle for information and referrals."[12] In order to better understand the variegated forms of cybernation-building, it is helpful to apply social identity theory (SIT). The basic principal of SIT is that an individual has more than one "self"; these multiple "selves" are constructed and maintained within a widening circle of group memberships. Social identity theory was developed by John Turner and Henri Tajfel to help understand the psychological basis of intergroup discrimination. As sociologists, they were intrigued by ingroup favoritism which they defined as an "unfair or unjustifiable...tendency to favor the ingroup over the outgroup, in behavior, attitudes, preferences or perception."[13] As the progenitors of SIT, state, "An individual's social identity is those aspects of his [sic] self-concept contributed by the social groups to which he perceives himself to belong."[14] Scholars of nationalism have occasionally employed SIT to explain the existence and absence of nationalist tendencies in group behavior. Group (or collective) identity is based on common belief elements between a set of individuals, which in turn sets that "ingroup" apart from other groups. According to Rogers Brubaker, identity should be "understood as a specifically *collective* phenomenon, [denoting] a fundamental and consequential *sameness* among members of a group or category...this sameness is expected to manifest itself in solidarity, in shared dispositions or consciousness, or in collective action."[15] Since the combinations of orientational traits pulled from members of the group are almost infinite, a lowest common denominator must be established and these traits must be "deep, basic, abiding, and foundational" rather than "superficial, accidental, fleeting, or contingent.[16] Once established, this group identity tends to result in preferential treatment of the ingroup and prejudice against the outgroup. The psychological-social approach offers some clues into the stark differences evidenced in the previous case studies of the Internet-enabled Albanians, near abroad Russians, Roma, and ummahists. In each case, preference for ingroup interactions exist, but with radically different goals for the "nation." By extending these findings to other cybernation-building projects, we can begin to understand the effect of the Web on national identity among minorities.

Among the "electronic irredentists," one finds scores of Web projects aimed redeeming the nation through both violent and peaceful means. Alongside the actions of cyber-Albanians, a wide variety of Internet irredentists have rallied to the Web. Certain aspects of the Albanian case (e.g., international lobbying of foreign government, counter-programming against hostile governments, etc.) have been replicated by other national groups, such as the efficacy of the Internet to broadcast media in an information blackout. As one commentator points out, "Since declaring their independence from the Soviet Union in November 1991, the Chechens have pioneered the use of the website as a weapon to try to break the information blockade that the Russian authorities have attempted to impose over the conflict."[17] Elsewhere, the Web is being used tie to together nations that have been rent asunder by the vagaries of history. As journalist Christopher Farah states, "For the first time in centuries, Kurds have a nation they can call their own—on the Internet."[18] The Albanians, Kurds, and Chechens are not alone in their endeavors. In certain cases, research suggests that these networks of ethnic nationalist Web sites have become so well-developed that they represent "'cyber-states'—nations created in cyber-space because of the lack of a nation in real space."[19] Such progress is proving irresistible for irredentists from Palestine to Pashtunistan.

Regarding the comparatively smaller category of "post-imperial digerati," the Internet principally functions as a personal tool, rather than a platform for concerted political activism or mass cultural change. Mirroring the "beached" Russians of the near abroad, many white South Africans have gravitated to the Internet as a way to promote the new national project of national reconciliation after the soul-crushing decades of apartheid. This is particularly true among Afrikaners, the approximately seven million descendents of French, German, Portuguese, and Dutch settlers who speak Afrikaans, a West Germanic language closely related to Dutch, but indigenous to southern Africa. With the radically-changed political situation in South Africa, the future of Afrikaans has come under threat.[20] But for Afrikaners, the survival of Afrikaans is the keystone in preservation of their unique culture. A new generation of Afrikaners is employing the tools of cyberspace to preserve the existence of their language which faces various threats from globalization, local politicization, and harmonization with modern Dutch. According to South African journalism professor Herman Wasserman, Afrikaners have disproportionately used the Web to promote linguistic and cultural cohesiveness and moderate the drastic loss of political power they have suffered since the late 1990s. Politically, cyberspace also plays a role in the process of reconciliation for the crimes of the "imperial minority's" past through the contemporary promotion of multiculturalism. According to Wasserman, "By serving as a contact zone for different South African languages and literatures, it creates the possibility for transcultural flow, going against the linguistic and literary hierarchy of apartheid which was aimed at preventing social contact between ethnic and racial groups."[21]

Besides South Africa, other Euro-Africans have employed the Internet to help mediate their identity in the wake of decolonization, even when they have been forced to quit the land of their birth. In "Rhodesians in Hyperspace," Tony King's discusses the perpetuation and refining of an anachronistic "Rhodesian" identity through Internet-based communication and commercial contacts across continents:

> [O]n the one hand, many on the Internet are stuck in an idealistic time-warp about the "old days" in the mother country. On the other, the Web is now serving to maintain and develop a sense of Rhodesian identity which has no mother country to look to....These people are not a threat to Zimbabwe. In most cases, they have come to terms with independence, and prefer to keep Rhodesia as memory rather than hope for its resurrection.[22]

In case strikingly similar to that of the Rhodesians, Algeria's *pied-noirs* were denied their homeland as part of the struggle for national liberation.[23] Exiled from the land of their birth, these former colonists preserved their identity through benevolent societies and other cultural organizations in their new states of residence. Over time these "people without a country" have steadily migrated into cyberspace where they are able to continue to share and maintain certain aspects of their unique culture (jokes, argot, traditions, etc.) beyond their small circle of physical propinquity.[24] For such post-imperial digerati, the Internet provides a unique tool for locating and connecting with the ever-shrinking community in which one was born.

For the "cybernetic vanguard," the Basques' use of the Internet for the purpose of preserving a threatened culture is truly paradigmatic. According to Basque experts Andoni Alonso and Iñaki Arzoz, the Web is both a tool for transcending political conflict as well as protecting nation culture. "Cyberspace is the last realm for the consolidation of Basque culture and its normal development."[25] Cyberspace is also proving a godsend for physically-dispersed nations such as the Inuit (Eskimos) who live around the Arctic Circle in multiple countries, an area that is vast, inhospitable, and not linked by modern transportation. According to Oliver Zielke, the chief executive of Web Networks, a non-profit organization based in Canada which provides web services for socially committed groups, "The internet is tailor-made for these groups."[26] Anthropologist Neil Blair Christensen argues that the peripatetic culture of the Inuit (like that of the Roma) makes the migration into cyberspace a natural one, despite institutional and infrastructural hurdles to Internet adoption. "[The nomadic travelling spirit of the Inuit, now being more or less trapped in small communities, could be part of the explanation for why the Inuit and the Internet go so well together. The spirit could still be alive despite decades of more or less forced sedentarisation. Whereas Southerners with their agrarian traditions are at doubt how this nomadic technology will effect (sic) their social integrity, the Arctic case could be profoundly different, as Inuit feel a need to travel."[27] In the long run, the Web could provide absolutely vital for preserving thousands of indigenous languages across the Americas, Australia, and Eurasia.

In regard to my last paragon, the "virtual prophets," the case study demonstrated the power of the Internet to nourish idealized nations which lack a discernible territory, unity in language, and a cogent culture. With its vast numbers and geographic dispersion, the ummah represents perhaps the most hyperbolic manifestation of the "imagined community." Yet in cyberspace, such projects can be sustained indefinitely, assuming the presence of a critical mass of consumers and producers of the "nation." From its very beginnings, the Web has encouraged quixotic national struggles in cyberspace. Internet-only nations such as Melchizedek, Ganjastan, and Freedonia evidence the powerful impact that the growth of cyberspace has had on very concept of geography. Such mass-mediated micronations have used the Web to declare their independence, engage in diplomacy with their neighbors, attract new "citizens," display their flags, play their anthems, and even distribute their currency. Writing about one of these micronations, journalist Andrew Weiner states:

> Most nations start with land and worry about principles later. But having laid claim to a corner of cyberspace, Freedonia—like a handful of other micronations—has begun to assert its sovereignty in other, less virtual realities....This recent surge in do-it-yourself statecraft is entirely due to the establishment of the Internet, a vast and uncharted terra incognita with boundless tolerance for far-fetched ideas.[28]

Generally, these online projects began as libertarian experiments, intended to interrupt or mitigate the exercise of sovereignty by actual nation-states. Cyberspace has also become an important tool for supporting the projects of unrecognized "real world" micronations such as Sealand, located on HM Fort Roughs, a former World

War II sea fort off the coast of Suffolk, England. Sealand's founder, former radio broadcaster and British Army Major Roy Bates, has consistently used the Internet to provide legitimacy to his claims of independence from the United Kingdom. As of late, he has even partnered with well-financed American cyber-libertarians, who operate under the banner of Havenco, to further solidify his status as an independent nation, both on and offline.[29] More closely mirroring the online ummahists, certain Web-based elites have attempted to reinvigorate Yugoslavism through the building of a Cyber-Yugoslavia to replace their lost country. According to researcher Maja Mikula:

> Unlike the numerous online micro-nations, some of which are hardly more than bizarre cyberspace experiments dreamt up by adolescents play-acting an imaginary "adult" world of power and war, Cyber-Yugoslavia is designed as a purposeful media-manipulation project and an astute social commentary....Cyber-Yugoslavia's primary target audience are the like-minded former Yugoslavs, "those who lost their country in 1991 and became citizens of Atlantis," but also those who "feel Yugoslav, regardless of their current nationality and citizenship."[30]

Such projects are especially reflective of original ideation of cyberspace. For William Gibson, cyberspace represented not only a medium, but also a site where human nature undergoes a qualitative change.[31] It is clear that both aspects of the Web are in effect in the twenty-first century. While these curious cybernations may never annex an inch of territory, they have found a new agora that can allow them make their voices heard around the globe. As these minorities raise their voices in cyberspace, the echoes are increasingly resonating in the real world.

Once ARPANET—the U.S. government-funded precursor to today's modern Internet—established the first connections between geographically distant users, the politics of cyberspace began to evolve. With this evolution, there came winners and losers, haves and have-nots, the popular and the pariahs. Power relations in cyberspace are a shadowy reflection of the realities of the offline world. As such, nation-states do possess some inherent advantages in cyberspace, but we should be careful not to overstate their prowess or preeminence.

The globalized world is less defined by nation-states than at any time in the past 300 years. As such, sovereignty—a concept with its roots in the post-Westphalian world—is in need of updating. International relations theorist Barry Buzan defines sovereignty as "the claim to be the ultimate authority, subject to no higher power as regards the making and enforcing of political decisions."[32] The Internet is slowly but steadily creating perforations in the mantle of this "ultimate authority." New congeries of commercial, religious, and social elites are increasingly siphoning off the influence and authority once commanded by the state. This is especially true in the digital landscapes of cyberspace, where wielding political power does not necessitate a seat at the UN General Assembly. Of all these competitors to the nation-state, national minorities and diasporas are proving the most effective at winning authority at the expense of the state.

In this second half of this study, I have explored four cybernations' manipulation of real world political reality through cyberspatial national identity projects.

These varied trajectories merely provide a sampling of the changing nature of politics in the globalized world; however, it is clear that the future of national identity will be less and characterized by physical territory as global communication and media networks expand. When it comes to nation-building, cyberspace is not yet fungible with real space, but it is increasingly proving to be an important—even vital—adjunct.

Notes

1. Arjun Appadurai, *Modernity at Large* (Minneapolis: University of Minnesota Press, 1996), 156.

2. Maya Ranganathan, "Nurturing the Nation on the Net: The Case of Tamil Eelam," *Nationalism and Ethnic Politics* 8, no. 2 (Summer 2002): 51-66.

3. Sheila L. Croucher, *Globalization and Belonging: The Politics of Identity in a Changing World* (Lanham, MD: Rowman & Littlefield Publishers, Inc., 2004), 135-36.

4. Michael Dahan and Gabriel Sheffer, "Ethnic Groups and Distance Shrinking Technologies," *Nationalism & Ethnic Politics* 7, no 1 (Spring 2001): 85-107.

5. Alexander J. Motyl, "The Modernity of Nationalism: Nations, State and Nation-States in the Contemporary World," *Journal of International Affairs* 45, no. 2 (Winter 1992): 311-323.

6. Rohan Jayasekera, "Waiting for the Kingdom: Nations in Cyberspace are No Substitute for the Real Thing," *Index on Censorship* 29, no. 3 (May/June 2000): 140-145.

7. See Shanthi Kalathil and Taylor C. Boas, *Open Networks, Closed Regimes: The Impact of the Internet on Authoritarian Rule* (Washington: Carnegie Endowment for International Peace, 2003) and Shanthi Kalathil, "Dot Com for Dictators," *Foreign Policy* 135 (March/April 2003): 42-49.

8. Maya Ranganathan, "Potential of the Net to Construct and Convey Ethnic and National Identities: Comparison of the Use in the Sri Lankan Tamil and Kashmiri Situations," *Asian Ethnicity* 4, no. 2 (June 2003): 265-279.

9. John Sorenson and Atsuko Matsuoka, "Phantom Wars and Cyberwars: Abyssinian Fundamentalism and Catastrophe in Eritrea," *Dialectical Anthropology* 26, no. 1 (Spring 2001): 37–63.

10. Appadurai, *Modernity at Large*, 39.

11. Bosah Ebo, *Global Relations in the New Electronic Frontier* (Westport, CT: Praeger, 2001), ix.

12. Brinkerhoff, Jennifer M. *Digital Diasporas: Identity and Transnational Engagement* (Cambridge: Cambridge University Press, 2009), 201.

13. John C. Turner, R. J. Brown, and Henri Tajfel, "Social Comparison and Group Interest Ingroup Favouritism," *European Journal of Social Psychology* 9 no. 2 (June 1979): 187-204.

14. Turner, Brown, and Tajfel, "Social Comparison and Group Interest Ingroup Favouritism," 190.

15. Rogers Brubaker and Frederick Cooper, "Beyond 'Identity,'" *Theory and Society* 29, no. 1 (February 2000): 1-47.

16. Brubaker and Cooper, "Beyond 'Identity,'" 7.

17. Paul Goble, "The Web is a Weapon on the Chechnya Front," *Asia Times*, 14 October 1999.

18. Christopher Farah, "Kurdistan Unbound," *Salon.com*, 7 April 2004.

19. Farah, "Kurdistan Unbound."

20. The political legacy of the language's promotion under apartheid combined with its relative lack of utility in today's global information economy discourages many young South

Africans (black and white) from pursuing education in the language, despite its continued recognition as an official language of the country, along with ten others.

21. Herman Wasserman, "Between the Local and Global: South African Languages and the Internet," *African and Asian Studies* 1, no. 4 (December 2002): 303-321.

22. Tony King, "Rhodesians in Hyperspace: The Maintenance of a National and Cultural Identity," in Karim H. Karim, *The Media of Diaspora* (London: Routledge, 2003), 187.

23. After its incorporation into the French empire, a steady trickle of Europeans migrated to Algeria as permanent settlers. These immigrants came from France and various parts of the Mediterranean basin, particularly from Valencia in southern Spain but also Sicily, Malta, and Corsica. Settling in urban areas and the temperate, fertile coastal regions of North Africa, these colonists often intermingled with Jews, Berbers, and Arabs, but observed the tried-and-true Ottoman demographic tradition of residing in socially protected quarters separate from the indigenous population. Over time, the Europeans came to be collectively known as *Pieds-Noirs* ('Black Feet'). By World War II, there were roughly 1 million living in Algeria. Nearly all of these "Europeans" quit Algeria upon independence in 1962.

24. See Antoine Proust, "The Algerian War in French Collective Memory," in J. M. Winter, and Emmanuel Sivan, *War and Remembrance in the Twentieth Century* (Cambridge: Cambridge University Press, 2001).

25. Andoni Alonso and Iñaki Arzoz, *Basque Cyberculture: From Digital Euskadi to CyberEuskalherria* (Reno: Center for Basque Studies, 2006), 17.

26. Quoted in "Inuit Language Finds Home on Net," *BBC News*, 3 November 2004, http://news.bbc.co.uk/2/hi/technology/3975645.stm (3 March 2007).

27. Neil Blair Christensen, *Inuit in Cyberspace: Embedding Offline, Identities Online* (Copenhagen: Museum Tusculanum Press., 2003) 16.

28. Andrew Weiner, "Wanted: Homeland for 300 Webheads," *Metro Santa Cruz*, 22-29 November 2000.

29. John Markoff, "Rebel Outpost on the Fringes of Cyberspace," *New York Times*, 4 June 2000, 14.

30. Maja Mikula, "Virtual Landscapes of Memory," *Information, Communication & Society* 6, no. 2 (June 2003): 169–186.

31. John Johnston, "Mediality in Vineland and Neuromancer," in Joseph Tabbi and Michael Wutz, *Reading Matters: Narratives in the New Media Ecology* (Ithaca: Cornell University Press, 1997), 186.

32. Barry Buzan, "Sovereignty," in Iain McLean, *The Concise Oxford Dictionary of Politics* (Oxford and New York: Oxford University Press, 1996), 464.

Bibliography

Abley, Mark. *Spoken Here: Travels among Threatened Languages.* Boston and New York: Houghton Mifflin, 2003.

Agadjanian, Alexander. "Revising Pandora's Gifts: Religious and National Identity in the Post-Soviet Societal Fabric," *Europe-Asia Studies* 53, no. 3 (May 2001): 473-488.

Akou, Heather Marie. "Building a New 'World Fashion': Islamic Dress in the Twenty-first Century," *Fashion Theory* 11, no 4 (December 2007): 403-422.

Aksoy, Asu and Kevin Robins. "Banal Transnationalism: The Difference the Television Makes," in *The Media of Diaspora*, edited by Karim H. Karim. London: Routledge, 2003, pp. 89-104.

Alonso, Andoni and Iñaki Arzoz. *Basque Cyberculture: From Digital Euskadi to Cyber Euskalherria.* Reno: Center for Basque Studies, 2006

Ammitzbøll, Pernille and Lorenzo Vidino. "After the Danish Cartoon Controversy," *Middle East Quarterly* 14, no. 1 (Winter 2007): 3-11.

Anderson, Benedict. *Imagined Communities: Reflections on the Origin and Spread of Nationalism.* London: Verso, 1991.

Anderson, Jon. "New Media, New Publics," *Social Research* 70, no. 3 (Summer 2003): 887-906.

———. "The Internet and Islam's New Interpreters," in *New Media and the Muslim World: The Emerging Public Sphere*, Second edition, edited by Dale Eickelman and Jon Anderson. Bloomington: Indiana University Press, 2003, pp. 45–60.

———. "Wiring Up: The Internet Difference for Muslim Networks," in Miriam Cooke and Bruce Lawrence, *Muslim Networks: From Hajj to Hip Hop.* Chapel Hill: University of North Carolina Press, 2005, pp. 252-263.

Ang, Ien. "Together-in-Difference: Beyond Diaspora, into Hybridity," *Asian Studies Review* 27, no. 2 (June 2003): 141-154.

Anthony, David W. *The Horse, the Wheel, and Language: How Bronze-Age Riders from the Eurasian Steppes Shaped the Modern World.* Princeton: Princeton University Press, 2007.

Appadurai, Arjun. *Modernity at Large.* Minneapolis: University of Minnesota Press, 1996.

Artisien, Patrick F. R. "A Note on Kosovo and the Future of Yugoslav-Albanian Relations: A Balkan Perspective," *Soviet Studies* 36, no. 2 (April 1984): 267-276.

Ataman, Muhittin. "Islamic Perspective on Ethnicity and Nationalism: Diversity or Uniformity?" *Journal of Muslim Minority Affairs* 23, no. 1 (April 2003): 89-102.

Baark, Erik. *Lightning Wires: The Telegraph and China's Technological Modernization, 1860-1890.* Westport, CT: Greenwood, 1997.

Back, Les. "White Fortresses in Cyberspace," *Unesco Courier* 54, no. 1 (January 2001): 44-46.

———. "Aryans Reading Adorno: Cyber-culture and Twenty-first Century Racism," *Ethnic and Racial Studies* 25, no. 4 (July 2002): 628–651.

Bakker, Peter and Marcia Rooker. "The Political Status of the Romani Language in Europe," Mercator-Working Papers 3, CIEMEN (Escarré International Centre for Ethnic

Minorities and Nations), 2001. PDF available at www.ciemen.org/mercator/pdf/wp3-def-ang.PDF.

Bancroft, Angus. *Roma and Gypsy-Travellers in Europe: Modernity, Race, Space and Exclusion*. Aldershat, UK: Ashgate, 2005.

Baran, Paul. "On Distributed Communications: I. Introduction to Distributed Communications Networks," Memorandum RM-3420-PR, prepared for the United States Air Force Project RAND, 1964. Santa Monica: RAND Corporation, http://www.rand.org/pubs/research_memoranda/2006/RM3420.pdf.

Barany, Zoltan. "The Roma in Macedonia: Ethnic Politics and the Marginal Condition in a Balkan State," *Ethnic and Racial Studies* 18, no. 3 (July 1995): 515-531.

Barber, Benjamin R. "Jihad vs. McWorld," *Atlantic Monthly* 269 (March 1992): 53-65.

———. *Jihad vs. McWorld: How Globalism and Tribalism Are Reshaping the World*. New York: Ballantine Books, 1996.

Benedikt, Michael. "Introduction," in *Cyberspace: First Steps*, edited by Michael Benedikt. Cambridge: The MIT Press, 1992, pp. 1-26.

Bennett, Lance. *News: The Politics of Illusion*, Seventh edition. New York: Longman, 2007.

Bernal, Victoria. "Diaspora, Cyberspace and Political Imagination: The Eritrean Diaspora Online," *Global Networks* 6, no. 2 (April 2006): 161-179.

Berners-Lee, Tim and Mark Fischetti. *Weaving the Web: The Original Design and Ultimate Destiny of the World Wide Web by Its Inventor*. San Francisco: Harper, 1999.

Bhabha, Homi K. "DissemiNation: Time, Narrative, and the Margins of the Modern Nation," in *Nation and Narration*, edited by Homi K. Bhabha. London: Routledge, 1990, pp. 291-232.

———. *The Location of Culture*. London and New York: Routledge, 1994.

———. "Narrating the Nation," in *Nations and Identities: Classic Readings*, edited by Vincent P. Pecor. Malden, MA: Blackwell Publishers, 2001, pp. 359-363.

Bieber, Florian. "Cyberwar or Sideshow? The Internet and the Balkan Wars," *Current History* 99, no. 635 (March 2000): 124-129.

Billig, Michael. *Banal Nationalism*. London: Sage Publications, 1995.

Blevins, Jeffrey Layne. "Counterhegemonic Media: Can Cyberspace Resist Corporate Colonialism?" in *Cyberimperialism? Global Relations in the New Electronic Frontier*, edited by Bosah Ebo. Westport, CT: Praeger, 2001, pp. 139-152.

Blumi, Isa. "Albania," in *Muslim Cultures Today*, edited by Kathryn M. Coughlin. Westport: Greenwood Publishing, 2006.

Borras-Alomar, Susana, Thomas Christiansen and Andres Rodriguez-Pose. "Towards a 'Europe of the Regions?' Visions and Reality from a Critical Perspective," *Regional & Federal Studies* 4, no. 2 (Summer 1994): 1-27.

Boulding, Kenneth E. "National Images and International Systems," *Journal of Conflict Resolution* 3, no. 2 (June 1959): 120-131.

Bowen, John "Beyond Migration: Islam as a Transnational Public Space," *Journal of Ethnic and Migration Studies* 30, no. 5 (September 2004): 879-894.

Bowles, Anna. "RuNet A Cyberian Adventure," *Russian Life* 48, no. 2 (April/May 2005): 41-47.

Boyd, Clark. "Romani Language Report," PRI's *The World*, 7 March 2006.

Brandenberger, David. *National Bolshevism: Stalinist Mass Culture and the Formation of Modern Russian National Identity, 1931-1956*. Cambridge: Harvard University Press, 2002.

Breiner, Laurence A. "Caribbean Voices on the Air: Radio, Poetry, and Nationalism in the Anglophone Caribbean," in *Communities of the Air: Radio Century, Radio Culture*, edited by Susan Merrill Squier. Durham, NC: Duke University Press, 2003, pp. 93-108.

Breuilly, John. *Nationalism and the State*, Second Edition. Chicago: University of Chicago Press, 1994.

Breyfogle, Nicholas B. Abby Schrader, and Willard Sunderland. *Peopling the Russian Periphery: Borderland Colonization in Eurasian History.* Abingdon, UK: Taylor & Francis, 2007.

Brinkerhoff, Jennifer M. *Digital Diasporas: Identity and Transnational Engagement.* Cambridge: Cambridge university Press, 2009.

Brockman, John. *Digerati: Encounters with Cyber-Elite.* San Francisco: HardWired, 1996.

Brouwer, Lenie. "Dutch-Muslims on the Internet: A New Discussion Platform," *Journal of Muslim Affairs* 24, no. 1 (April 2004): 47-55.

Brown, David. "From Peripheral Communities to Ethnic Nations: Separatism in Southeast Asia," *Pacific Affairs* 61, no. 1 (Spring 1998): 51-77.

Brubaker, Rogers. *Nationalism Reframed: Nationhood and the National Question in the New Europe.* Cambridge: Cambridge University Press, 1996.

Brubaker, Rogers and Frederick Cooper. "Beyond 'Identity,'" *Theory and Society* 29, no. 1 (February 2000): 1-47.

Brunn, Stanley D. "Towards an Understanding of the Geopolitics of Cyberspace: Learning, Re-Learning and Unlearning," *Geopolitics* 5, no. 3 (Winter 2000): 144-149.

Brzezinski, Zbigniew. *The Choice: Global Domination or Global Leadership.* New York: Basic Books, 2004.

Bugliarello, George. "Telecommunications, Politics, Economics, and National Sovereignty: A New Game," *Technology in Society* 18, no. 4 (December 1996): 403-418.

Bull, Hedley. *The Anarchical Society: A Study of Order in World Politics.* London: Macmillan Press, 1977.

Bunt, Gary. *Virtually Islamic.* Cardiff: University of Wales Press, 2000.

Bush, Vannevar. "As We May Think," *Atlantic Monthly* 176, no. 1 (July 1945): 101-108.

Buzan, Barry. "Sovereignty," in *The Concise Oxford Dictionary of Politics*, edited by Iain McLean. Oxford and New York: Oxford University Press, 1996, pp. 464-465.

Candan, Menderes and Uwe Hunger. "Nation Building Online: A Case Study of Kurdish Migrants in Germany," *German Policy Studies* 4, no. 4 (2008): 125-153.

Caplan, Richard. "From Collapsing States to Neo-Trusteeship: The Limits to Solving the Problem of 'Precarious Statehood' in the 21st Century," *Third World Quarterly* 28, no. 2 (March 2007): 231-244.

Carey, Nick. "Roma Community Fears Anti-Roma Internet Game," *Radio Prague Enews*, (28 February 2001).

Castells, Manuel. *The Internet Galaxy.* Oxford: Oxford University Press, 2001.

Cerf, Vinton G. and Robert E. Kahn. "A Protocol for Packet Network Intercommunication," *IEEE Transactions on Communications*, Vol. COM-23 (May 1974): 637-648.

Chaturvedi, Sanjay. "Diaspora in India's Geopolitical Visions: Linkages, Categories, and Contestations," *Asian Affairs: An American Review* 32, no. 3 (Fall 2005): 141-168.

Chayko, Mary. *Connecting: How We Form Social Bonds and Communities in the Internet Age.* Albany: SUNY Press, 2002.

Cheshire, Ellen. "Leni Riefenstahl: Documentary Film-Maker or Propagandist?" 2000, http://www.kamera.co.uk/features/leniriefenstahl.html.

Chinn, Jeff and Robert J. Kaiser. *Russians as the New Minority: Ethnicity and Nationalism in Soviet Successor States.* Boulder: Westview Press, Inc., 1996.

Choi, Inbom. "Korean Diaspora in the Making: its Current Status and Impact on the Korean Economy," in *The Korean Diaspora in the World Economy*, edited by C. Fred Bergsten and Inbom Choi. Washington: Peterson Institute, 2003, pp. 9-27.

Christensen, Neil Blair. *Inuit in Cyberspace: Embedding Offline, Identities Online.* Copenhagen: Museum Tusculanum Press, 2003.

Chua, Amy. *World on Fire: How Exporting Free Market Democracy Breeds Ethnic Hatred and Global Instability.* Garden City, NY: Doubleday, 2002.

Cohen, Julie E. "Cyberspace as/and Space," *Columbia Law Review* 107, no. 1 (January 2007): 210-256.

Cooke, Paul. "Surfing for Eastern Difference: *Ostalgie*, Identity, and Cyberspace," *Seminar—A Journal of Germanic Studies 40*, no. 3 (September 2004): 207-220.

Cooks, Leda. "Negotiating National Identity and Social Movements in Cyberspace," in *Cyberimperialism? Global Relations in the New Electronic Frontier*, edited by Bosah Ebo. Westport, CT: Praeger, 2001, pp. 233-252.

Cooper, Jeffrey R. "Diplomacy in the Information Age: Implications for Content and Conduct," *iMP: Information Impacts* (July 2001), http://www.cisp.org/imp/july_2001/07_01cooper.htm.

Corbett, Austin. "Beyond the Ghost in the (Human) Shell," *Journal of Evolution and Technology* 20, no. 1 (March 2009): 43-50.

Croucher, Sheila L. *Globalization and Belonging: The Politics of Identity in a Changing World*. Lanham, MD: Rowman & Littlefield Publishers, Inc., 2004.

Curran, James. "Communications, Power and Social Order," in *Culture, Society and the Media*, edited by Michael Gurevitch, Tony Bennett, James Curran and Janet Woollacott. London and New York: Routledge, 1990, pp. 202-235.

Dahan, Michael and Gabriel Sheffer. "Ethnic Groups and Distance Shrinking Technologies," *Nationalism & Ethnic Politics* 7, no. 1 (Spring 2001): 85-107.

de Maistre, Joseph. "Study on Sovereignty," in *Nations and Identities: Classic Readings*, edited by Vincent Pecora. Malden, MA: Blackwell Publishers, 2001, pp. 107-113.

Deibert, Ronald J. *Parchment, Printing and Hypermedia: Communication in World Order Transformation*. New York: Columbia University Press, 1997.

Delanty, Gerard. "Northern Ireland in a Europe of Regions," *Political Quarterly* 67, no. 2 (April-June 1996): 127-134.

Denning, Dorothy E. "Activism, Hacktivism, and Cyberterrorism: The Internet as a Tool for Influencing Foreign Policy," in *Networks and Netwars: The Future of Terror, Crime, and Militancy*, edited by John Arquilla and David Ronfeldt. Santa Monica, CA: RAND Corporation, 2000, pp. 239-288.

Denoeux, Guilain. "The Forgotten Swamp: Navigating Political Islam," *Middle East Policy* 9, no. 2 (June 2002): 56-81.

Dérens, Jean-Arnault. "Forgotten Peoples of the Balkans," *Le Monde Diplomatique* (4 August 2003).

Deutsch, Karl. *Nationalism and Social Communication: An Inquiry into the Foundations of Nationality*. Cambridge: The Technology Press of the Massachusetts Institute of Technology, 1953.

Drakulic, Mirjana and Ratimir Drakulic. "Balkan Hackers War in Cyberspace," Paper presented at the Fourteenth BILETA Conference: "CYBERSPACE 1999: Crime, Criminal Justice and the Internet," College of Ripon & York St. John, York, England, 29 March 1999.

Draper, Stark. "The Conceptualization of an Albanian Nation," *Ethnic & Racial Studies* 20, no. 1 (January 1997): 123-144.

Drobizheva, L. M. "Etnicheskaya identichnost: Sovetskoye nasledie i sovremennye podkhody" [Ethnic Identity: The Soviet heritage and contemporary approaches], *Demoscope Weekly* (3 March 2003).

Duncan, Peter J. S. "Contemporary Russian Identity between East and West," *Historical Journal* 48, no. 1 (March 2005): 277-294.

Ebo, Bosah. *Global Relations in the New Electronic Frontier*. Westport, CT: Praeger, 2001.

Elison, William. "Netwar: Studying Rebels on the Internet," *Social Studies* 91, no. 3 (May/June 2000): 127-131.

Engel, Christoph. "The Internet and the Nation State," in *Understanding the Impact of Global Networks in Local Social, Political and Cultural Values*, edited by Christoph Engel and Kenneth H. Heller. Baden-Baden: Nomos Verlagsgesellschaft, 2000, pp. 213-272.

Eriksen, Thomas Hylland. "Nationalism and the Internet," *Nations & Nationalism* 13, no. 1 (January 2007): 1-17.

Escobar, Pablo. "A Very Peaceful Jihad," *Index on Censorship* 34, no. 1 (Spring 2005): 164-169.

Evens, Aden. "Concerning the Digital," *Differences: A Journal of Feminist Cultural Studies* 14, no. 2 (Summer 2003): 49-77.

Fair, Benjamin. "Stepping Razor in Orbit: Postmodern Identity and Political Alternatives in William Gibson's *Neuromancer*," *Critique* 46, no. 2 (Winter 2005): 92-103.

Falk, Jim. "The Meaning of the Web," *Information Society* 14, no. 1 (November 1998): 285-293.

Fang, Irving. *A History of Mass Communication: Six Information Revolutions.* Boston: Focal Press, 1997.

Farah, Christopher. "Kurdistan Unbound," *Salon.com* (7 April 2004).

Fawn, Rick. "Czech Attitudes towards the Roma: 'Expecting More of Havel's Country?'" *Europe-Asia Studies* 53, no. 8 (December 2001): 1193-1219.

Feys, Cara. "Towards a New Paradigm of the Nation: The Case of the Roma," *Journal of Public and International Affairs* 8 (1997), http://www.geocities.com/~Patrin/paradigm.htm.

Fishman, Joshua A. "The New Linguistic Order," *Foreign Policy* 113 (Winter 1998-99): 26-40.

Gabrial, Albert. "3,000 Years of History, Yet the Internet is Our Only Home," *Cultural Survival*, 10 June 2001, http://www.atour.com/government/docs/20010610a.html.

Galtung, Johan "Cultural Violence," *Journal of Peace Research* 27, no. 3 (August 1990): 291-305.

Galtung, Johan and Tord Höivik, "Structural and Direct Violence: A Note on Operationalization," *Journal of Peace Research* 8, no. 1 (1971): 73-76.

Ganley, Gladys D. *Unglued Empire: The Soviet Experience with Communications Technologies.* Westport: Ablex Publishing, 1996.

Gawrych, George W. "Tolerant Dimensions of Cultural Pluralism in the Ottoman Empire: The Albanian Community, 1800-1912," *International Journal of Middle East Studies* 15, no. 4 (November 1983): 519-536.

Gellner, Ernest. *Nations and Nationalism.* Ithaca: Cornell University Press, 1983.

Gibson, William. *Neuromancer.* London: Gollancz, 1984.

Gilman, Sander. "The Parallels of Islam and Judaism in Diaspora," *Palestine - Israel Journal of Politics, Economics & Culture* 12, 2-3 (Summer 2005): 61-66.

Glenny, Misha. *The Balkans: Nationalism, War and the Great Powers, 1804-1999.* New York: Viking, 2000.

Goble, Paul. "The Web is a Weapon on the Chechnya Front," *Asia Times* (14 October 1999).

———. "Where 'Putin' is 'Putsin': Russian Nationalist Discontent in Belarus," *Radio Free Europe/Radio Liberty Newsline* (31 August 2004).

Goldberg, Ivan. "Information Warfare," Institute for the Advance Study of Information Warfare (IASIW) Web site, 2001, http://www.psycom.net/iwar.1.html.

Goldberg, Jeffrey. "After Iraq," *Atlantic Monthly* 301, no. 1 (January/February 2008): 68-79.

Goldston, James A. "Roma Rights, Roma Wrongs," *Foreign Affairs* 81, no. 2 (March/April 2002): 146-162.

Graf, Joseph. "Political Influential Online in the 2004 Presidential Campaign," Report published by the Institute for Politics, Democracy & the Internet, The Graduate School of Political Management at George Washington University (Washington, DC), 2004. PDF available at: http://www.ipdi.org/Influentials/Report.pdf.

Gramsci, Antonio. *Selections from the Prison Notebooks.* New York: International Publishers, 1999.

Green, Peter S. "Roma Seeking Sense of Unity to Combat Racial Bias," *New York Times* (10 May 2002).

Grimond, Jessie. "Pristina - War Erupts in Balkan Cyberspace But NATO Is As Quiet As a Mouse," *Independent* (2 May. 2001)

Gros, Jean-Germain. "Towards a Taxonomy of Failed States in the New World Order: Decaying Somalia, Liberia, Rwanda and Haiti," *Third World Quarterly* 17, no. 3 (September 1996): 455-471.

Gudkov, Lev D. *Negativnaya Identichnost* [Negative Identity]. Moscow: Novoe Literaturnoe Obozrenie, 2004.

Guibernau, Montserrat. *Nationalisms: The Nation-State and Nationalism in the Twentieth Century*. Cambridge: Polity Press, 1996.

Habermas, Jürgen. "Citizenship and National Identity: Some Reflections on the Future of Europe," in *Theorizing Citizenship*, edited by Ronald Beiner. Albany: SUNY Press, 1995, pp. 255-282.

———. "The European Nation-State—Its Achievements and Its Limits On the Past and Future of Sovereignty and Citizenship," in *Mapping the Nation*, edited by Gopal Balakrishnan. London: Verso, 1996, pp. 281-294.

———. *The Postnational Constellation: Political Essays*. Cambridge: MIT Press, 2001.

Hafner, Katie and Matthew Lyon. *Where Wizards Stay Up Late: The Origins of the Internet*. New York: Touchstone, 1996.

Hagendoorn, Louk, Hub Linssen, and Sergei Tumanov. *Intergroup Relations in States of the Former Soviet Union: The Perception of Russians*. Hove, UK: Psychology Press Ltd., 2001.

Halaby, Jamal. "Jordanian Paper Runs Prophet Muhammad Cartoons, Saying They Show 'Danish Offense,'" *Associated Press Worldstream* (2 February 2006).

Halavais, Alexander. "National Borders on the World Wide Web," *New Media & Society* 2, no. 1 (March 2000): 7-28.

Halliday, Fred. "The Politics of the Umma: States and Community in Islamic Movements," *Mediterranean Politics* 7, no. 3 (Autumn 2002): 20-41.

Hancock, Ian. "The Struggle for the Control of Identity," *Transitions* 4, no. 4 (September 1997): 34-44.

Harrison, Martin. "Government and Press in France during the Algerian War," *American Political Science Review* 58, no. 2 (June 1964): 273-285.

Harvey, P. D. A. *Maps in Tudor England*. Chicago: University Of Chicago Press, 1994.

Hauben, Michael and Ronda Hauben. *Netizens: On the History and Impact of Usenet and the Internet*. Hoboken: Wiley—IEEE Computer Society Press, 1997.

Heleniak, Tim. "Ethnic Unmixing and Forced Migration in the Transition States," *Beyond Transition* 10, No. 4 (August 1999), http://www.worldbank.org/html/prddr/trans/julaug99/contents.htm.

Henderson, David R. "Information Technology as a Universal Solvent for Removing State Stains," *Independent Review* 4, no. 4 (Spring 2000): 517-523.

Hirschkind, Charles. "The Ethics of Listening: Cassette-Sermon Audition in Contemporary Egypt," *American Ethnologist* 28, no. 3 (August 2001): 623-649.

Hobsbawm, Eric J. "Introduction: Inventing Traditions," in *The Invention of Tradition*, edited by Eric J. Hobsbawm and Terence Ranger. Cambridge: Cambridge University Press, 1992, pp. 1-14.

Holland, Tom. "Nothing Will Ever Be the Same Again. Or Will It?" *New Statesman* 128, no. 4463 (November 1999): 33-35.

Hroch, Miroslav. *Social Preconditions of National Revival in Europe: A Comparative Analysis of the Social Composition of Patriotic Groups among the Smaller European Nations*. Cambridge: Cambridge University Press, 1985.

———. "From National Movement to the Fully-Formed Nation: The Nation-Building Process in Europe. in *Mapping the Nation*, edited by Gopal Balakrishnan. New York and London: Verso, 1996, pp. 78–97.

Hugill, Peter J. *Global Communications since 1844: Geopolitics and Technology*. Baltimore: Johns Hopkins Press, 1999.

Humphreys, Peter J. *Mass Media and Media Policy in Western Europe*. Manchester: Manchester University Press, 1996.

Hunt, Lynn. *Politics, Culture and Class in the French Revolution.* Berkeley: University of California Press, 1984.

Huntington, Samuel P. "Clash of Civilizations," *Foreign Affairs* 72, no. 3 (Summer 1993): 22-49.

———. *The Clash of Civilizations and the Remaking of World Order.* New York: Simon and Schuster, 1997.

Hutchinson, John and Anthony Smith. *Nationalism.* Oxford: Oxford University Press, 1994.

Ibraimi, Fatmir Fanda. "Albanian Cyberspace," Lajmet.com Web site (22 January 2006).

Innis, Harold A. *Empire and Communications.* Toronto: University of Toronto Press, 1972.

Ioviţă, Radu P. and Theodore G. Schurr. "Reconstructing the Origins and Migrations of Diasporic Populations: The Case of the European Gypsies," *American Anthropologist* 106, no. 2 (June 2004): 267-281.

Iseke-Barnes, Judy M. "Aboriginal and Indigenous People's Resistance, the Internet, and Education," *Race, Ethnicity and Education* 5, no. 2 (Summer 2002): 171-198.

Jackson, Patrick. "News Fuels Russian Internet Boom," *BBC News Online* (10 April 2006).

Jayasekera, Rohan. "Waiting for the Kingdom: Nations in Cyberspace are No Substitute for the Real Thing," *Index on Censorship* 29, no. 3 (May/June 2000): 140-145.

Jelavich, Barbara. *History of the Balkans: Twentieth Century (Volume Two).* Cambridge: Cambridge University Press, 1991.

Johnson, Barnabas D. "The Cybernetics of Society: The Governance of Self and Civilization," Jurlandia web site, 2004, http://www.jurlandia.org/cybsoc.htm.

Johnson, Ian and John Carreyrou. "Islam and Europe: A Volatile Mix," *Wall Street Journal* (11 July 2005).

Johnston, John. "Mediality in Vineland and Neuromancer," in *Reading Matters: Narratives in the New Media Ecology,* edited by Joseph Tabbi and Michael Wutz. Ithaca: Cornell University Press, 1997, pp. 173-192.

Jones, Calvert. "Online Impression Management: Case Studies of Activist Web Sites and Their Credibility Enhancing Tactics During the Kosovo War," Paper prepared for presentation at the conference "Safety and Security in a Networked World," Oxford Internet Institute (OII), Oxford University, UK, 8-10 September 2005.

Jordan, Michael J. "New Refugee Aid Worker: Cell Phone," *Christian Science Monitor* 91, no. 104 (26 April 1999): 7-7.

Judy, Ronald. "Sayyid Qutb's *Fiqh al-Waqi'i*, Or New Realist Science," *Boundary* 31, no. 2 (Summer 2004): 113-148.

Kagan, Robert. *Paradise and Power: America and Europe in the New World Order.* Conshohocken, PA: Atlantic Books, 2004.

Kalathil, Shanthi. "Dot Com for Dictators," *Foreign Policy* 135 (March/April 2003): 42-49.

Kalathil, Shanthi and Taylor C. Boas. *Open Networks, Closed Regimes: The Impact of the Internet on Authoritarian Rule.* Washington: Carnegie Endowment for International Peace, 2003.

Kaldor-Robinson, Joshua. "The Virtual and the Imaginary: The Role of Diasphoric New Media in the Construction of a National Identity during the Break-up of Yugoslavia," *Oxford Development Studies* 30, no. 2 (June 2002): 177-187.

Kanat, Kilic. "Ethnic Media and Politics: The Case of the Use of the Internet by the Uyghur Diaspora," *First Monday* 10, no. 7 (July 2005): 1-6.

Kaplan, Robert D. "The Coming Anarchy," *Atlantic Monthly* 273, no. 2 (February 1994): 44-77.

Karić, Enes. "Is 'Euro-Islam' a Myth, Challenge or a Real Opportunity for Muslims and Europe?" *Journal of Muslim Minority Affairs* 22, no. 2 (October 2002): 435-442.

Karim, Karim H. *The Media of Diaspora.* London: Routledge, 2003.

Karny, Yo'av. *Highlanders: A Journey to Caucasus in Quest of Memory.* New York: Farrar Straus Giroux, 2000.

Kauppila, Laura E. "The Baltic Puzzle: Russia's Policy towards Estonia and Latvia, 1992-
    1997," Pro Gradu Thesis in Political History, Department of Social Science History,
    University of Helsinki, 1999.
Keenan, Thomas. "Looking like Flames and Falling Like Stars: Kosovo, 'The First Internet
    War,'" *Social Identities* 7, no. 4 (December 2001): 539-550.
Keleman, Mihaela and Warren Smith. "Community and Its 'Virtual' Promises: A Critique of
    Cyberlibertarian Rhetoric," *Information, Communication & Society* 4, no. 3 (October
    2001): 370-387.
Kepel, Gilles. *The Revenge of God: The Resurgence of Islam, Christianity, and Judaism in the
    Modern World*. University Park: Penn State University Press, 1994.
———. *The War for Muslim Minds: Islam and the West*. Cambridge, MA: Harvard
    University Press, 2004.
Kerényi, György. "Roma in the Hungarian Media," *Media Studies Journal* 13, no. 3 (Fall
    1999): 140-147.
Khatab, Sayed. "Arabism and Islamism in Sayyid Qutb's Thought on Nationalism," *The
    Muslim World* 94, no. 2 (April 2004): 217-244.
King, Tony. "Rhodesians in Hyperspace: The Maintenance of a National and Cultural
    Identity," in *The Media of Diaspora*, edited by Karim H. Karim. London: Routledge,
    2003, pp. 177-188.
Kita, Chigusa Ishikawa. "J.C.R. Licklider's Vision for the IPTO," *IEEE Annals of the History
    of Computing* 25, no. 3 (July-September 2003): 62-77.
Kitchin, Robert M. *Cyberspace: The World in Wires*. Chichester, UK: John Wiley and Sons,
    1998.
———. "Towards Geographies of Cyberspace," *Progress in Human Geography* 22, no. 3
    (September 1998): 385-406.
Kligman, Gail. "On the Social Construction of 'Otherness': Identifying 'the Roma' in Post-
    Socialist Communities," *Review of Sociology* 7, no. 2 (November 2001): 61-78.
Klímová-Alexander, Ilona. *The Romani Voice in World Politics: The United Nations and
    Non-State Actors*. Aldershat, UK: Ashgate, 2005.
Kluver, Randy. "Globalization, Informatization, and Intercultural Communication," *American
    Communication Journal* 3, no. 3 (June 2000), http://acjournal.org/.
Kolendic, Dubravko. "Serb-Albanian War Rages over the Internet Too," *Deutsche Presse-
    Agentur* (1 August 1998).
Kolstø, Pål. "The New Russian Diaspora—An Identity of Its Own?" *Ethnic and Racial
    Studies* 19, no. 3 (July 1996): 609-39.
———. "Territorialising Diasporas: The Case of the Russians in the Former Soviet
    Republics," *Millennium: Journal of International Studies* 28, no. 3 (December 1999):
    607-631.
Kort, Alexis. "Dar al-Cyber Islam: Women, Domestic Violence, and the Islamic Reformation
    on the World Wide Web," *Journal of Muslim Minority Affairs* 25, no. 3 (December
    2005): 363-383.
Koslowski, Rey. *International Migration and the Globalization of Domestic Politics*. London
    and New York: Routledge, 2005.
Kosta, Barjaba. "Albania: Looking Beyond Borders," Migration Policy Institute Web site
    (August 2004), http://www.migrationinformation.org/Profiles/display.cfm?id=239.
Kotkin, Joel. *The New Geography: How the Digital Revolution Is Shaping the American
    Landscape*. New York: Random House, 2000.
Kowal, Donna M. "Digitizing and Globalizing Indigenous Voices: The Zapatista Movement,"
    in *Critical Perspective in the Internet*, edited by Greg Elmer. Lanham: Roman &
    Littlefield Publishers, Inc., 2002, pp. 105-126.
Kuo, Franklin F. "ALOHA Packet Broadcasting System," in Fritz E. Froehlich and Allen
    Kent, *The Froehlich/Kent Encyclopedia of Telecommunications*. Boca Raton: CRC
    Press, 1991.

Kurlantzick, Joshua. "The Unsettled West," *Foreign Affairs* 83, no. 4 (July/August 2004): 136-143.

Kutolowski, John F. "Mid-Victorian Public Opinion, Polish Propaganda, and the Uprising of 1863," *Journal of British Studies* 8, no. 2 (May 1969): 86-110.

Kuzio, Taras. "Russian National Identity and Foreign Policy Toward the 'Near Abroad,'" *Prism* 8, no. 4 (30 April 2002).

Laitin, David. *Identity in Formation: Russian-Speaking Populations in the Near Abroad.* Ithaca: Cornell University Press, 1998.

Langhorne, Richard. *The Coming of Globalization: Its Evolution and Contemporary Consequences.* Houndmills: Palgrave, 2001.

———. *The Essentials of Global Politics.* London: Hodder Arnold, 2006.

Lawrence, Bruce B. "Review of New Media in the Muslim World: The Emerging Public Sphere by Dale F. Eickelman; Jon W. Anderson," *International Journal of Middle East Studies* 33, no. 1 (February 2001): 167-169.

Lee, Rachel C. and Sau-ling Cynthia Wong. *AsianAmerica.Net: Ethnicity, Nationalism, and Cyberspace.* New York: Routledge, 2003.

Lefebvre, Henri. *The Production of Space.* Cambridge: Blackwell, 1991.

Lengel, Laura B. and Patrick D. Murphy, "Cultural Identity and Cyberimperialism: Computer-Mediated Exploration of Ethnicity, Nation and Censorship," in *Cyberimperialism? Global Relations in the New Electronic Frontier,* edited by Bosah Ebo. Westport, CT: Praeger, 2001, pp. 187-203.

Leung, Linda. *Virtual Ethnicity: Race, Resistance and the World Wide Web.* Farnham, UK: Ashgate, 2005.

Licklider, J.C.R. "Man-Computer Symbiosis," *IRE Transactions on Human Factors in Electronics,* HFE-1 (March 1960): 4-11.

Louw, Eric P. *The Media and Political Process.* London: Sage, 2005.

Lynch, Marc. "Watching al-Jazeera," *Wilson Quarterly* 29, no. 3 (Summer 2005): 36-45.

MacKenzie, Donald. "Perestroika and Parallelism: Advanced Information Technology and the Soviet Union," *Technology Analysis & Strategic Management* 1, no. 2 (June 1989): 145-156.

Mai, Nicola. "The Albanian Diaspora-in-the-Making: Media, Migration and Social Exclusion," *Journal of Ethnic and Migration Studies* 31, no. 3 (May 2005): 543-561.

Maksymiuk, Jan. "Dynko: Soviet Nationalism as Lukashenka's Strategy of Survival," *Radio Free Europe/Radio Liberty Newsline* (10 December 2003).

Mandaville, Peter. "Communication and Diasporic Islam," in *The Media of Diaspora,* edited by Karim H. Karim. London: Routledge, 2003, pp. 135-147.

———. *Transnational Muslim Politics: Reimagining the Umma.* London and New York: Routledge, 2004.

———. *Global Political Islam.* London and New York: Routledge, 2007.

Marien, Michael. "New Communications Technology: A Survey of Impacts and Issues," *Telecommunications Policy* 20, no. 5 (June 1996): 375-387.

Markoff, John. "Rebel Outpost on the Fringes of Cyberspace," *New York Times* (4 June 2000).

Martin, Terry. *The Affirmative Action Empire: Nations and Nationalism in the Soviet Union, 1923-1939.* Ithaca and London: Cornell University Press, 2001.

Matjunin, Sergei. "Bonded by the Past, Culture and Language," *A Minority Different from Others,* EuroDialog Web site, 1998, http://www.znak.com.pl/eurodialog/ed/aktualny/index.html.en.

Matthews, Jessica T. "Power Shift," *Foreign Affairs* 76, no. 1 (January/February 1997): 50-66.

Mayall, David. *Gypsy Identities 1500-2000: From Egipcyans and Moon-men to the Ethnic Romany.* London and New York: Routledge, 2004.

McLuhan, Marshall. "Effects of the Improvements of Communication Media," *Journal of Economic History* 20, no. 4. (December 1960): 566-575.

————. *The Gutenberg Galaxy: The Making of Typographic Man.* Toronto: University of Toronto Press, 1962.

McLuhan, Marshall and Quentin Fiore. *The Media Is the Massage: An Inventory of Effects.* London: Penguin Books, 1967.

Mickiewicz, Ellen. *Media and the Russian Public.* New York: Praeger, 1981.

Mikula, Maja. "Virtual Landscapes of Memory," *Information, Communication & Society* 6, no. 2 (June 2003): 169–186.

Miller, Daniel and Don Slater. *The Internet: An Ethnographic Approach.* Oxford: Berg, 2000.

Mills, Kurt. "Cybernations: Identity, Self-determination, Democracy and the 'Internet Effect' in the Emerging Information Order," *Global Society* 16, no. 1 (January 2002): 69-87.

Mindich, David T. Z. "The Young and the Restless," *Wilson Quarterly* 29, no. 2 (Spring 2005): 48-53.

Minority Rights Group. *World Directory of Minorities.* Harlow, Essex: Longman Group UK Ltd., 1991.

Mirza, Munira, Abi Senthilkumaran, and Zein Ja'far. *Living Apart Together: British Muslims and the Paradox of Multiculturalism.* London: Policy Exchange, 2007.

Morozov, Evgeny. "A Melting Pot It's Not," *Foreign Policy* 171 (March/April 2009): 26.

Mosco, Vincent. "Communication and Information Technology for War and Peace," in *Communication and Culture in War and Peace*, edited by Colleen Roach. Newbury Park: Sage, 1993.

Mott, William H. *Globalization: People, Perspectives, and Progress.* Westport: Greenwood, 2004.

Motyl, Alexander J. "The Modernity of Nationalism: Nations, State and Nation-States in the Contemporary World," *Journal of International Affairs* 45, no. 2 (Winter 1992): 311-323.

Muller, Jerry Z. "Us and Them," *Foreign Affairs* 87, no. 2 (March/April 2008): 18-35.

Murray, Laura. "Examining Irredentism: Irredentism and International Politics (Review)," *Journal of International Affairs* 45, no. 2 (Winter 1992): 648-652.

Myers, Tony. "The Postmodern Imaginary in William Gibson's *Neuromancer*," *Modern Fiction Studies* 47, no. 4 (Winter 2001): 887-909.

Naegele, Jolyon. "A People Scattered," *New Presence: The Prague Journal of Central European Affairs* 7, no. 3 (Autumn 2005): 32-33.

Naím, Moisés. "The YouTube Effect," *Foreign Policy* 158 (January/February 2007): 103-104.

Nakamura, Lisa. *Cybertypes: Race, Ethnicity and Identity on the Internet.* London: Routledge: 2002.

Nelson, Diane E. "Maya Hackers and the Cyberspatialized Nation-State: Modernity, Ethnostalgia, and a Lizard Queen in Guatemala," *Cultural Anthropology* 11, no. 3 (August 1996): 287-308.

Nicolae, Valeriu. 2006. "Anti-Gypsyism – A Definition," European Roma Information Office website, 2006, http://www.erionet.org/Antigypsyism.html.

Nune, Alfred. "Internet and Albania: a Paradoxical Ambivalence?" in *New Media in Southeast Europe*, edited by Orlin Spassov and Christo Todorov. Sofia: Southeast European Media Centre, 2003.

Omer, Mohammed. "Armed with a Mouse, Boycott-Savvy Cyber-Activists Make Their Presence Felt," *Washington Report on Middle East Affairs* 25, no. 3 (April 2006): 30-31.

Ong, Aihwa. *Flexible Citizenship: The Cultural Logistics of Transnationality.* Durham: Duke University Press, 1999.

Oushakine, Serguei A. "The Terrifying Mimicry of Samizdat," *Public Culture* 13, no. 2 (Spring 2001): 191-214.

Paert, Irina *Old Believers: Religious Dissent and Gender in Russia, 1760-1850.* Manchester: Manchester University Press, 2003.

Panayi, Panikos. *An Ethnic History of Europe since 1945: Nations, States and Minorities.* Harlow: Longman, 2001.

Pavlowitch, Stevan K. *The Improbable Survivor: Yugoslavia and its Problems, 1918-1988.* Columbus: Ohio State University Press, 1988.

Payin, Emil. "The Disintegration of the Empire and the Fate of the 'Imperial Minority,'" in *The New Russian Diaspora: Russian Minorities in the Former Soviet Republics*, edited by Vladimir Shlapentokh, Munir Sendich, and Emil Payin. Armonk, NY: M. E. Sharpe, 1994, pp. 21-36.

Pervez, Kiran. "Narrating the 'Nation': A Relational Methodology Exploring the India-Pakistan Conflict," Paper presented at the annual meeting of the International Studies Association, Montreal, Quebec, Canada, 20 March 2004.

Pieterse, Jan Nederveen. *Globalization & Culture: A Global Mélange.* Lanham, MD: Rowman & Littlefield, 2003.

Piscatori, James. *Islam in a World of Nation-States.* Cambridge: Cambridge University Press, 1986.

Plomin, Joe. "Linguists Track Romani Dialects across Europe," *Guardian Unlimited* (25 May 2001).

Pogany, Istvan. "Accommodating an Emergent National Identity: The Roma of Central and Eastern Europe," *International Journal on Minority and Group Rights* 6, nos. 1-2 (Spring 1999): 149-167.

Polyuha, Mikula. "Ukrainian Internet Identity," *Western Journal of Graduate Research* 12, no. 1 (Fall 2005): 82-91.

Poster, Mark. "National Identities and Communications Technologies," *Information Society* 15, no. 4 (October-December 1999): 235-240.

Price, Monroe Edwin. *Television, the Public Sphere, and National Identity.* Oxford: Oxford University Press, 1995.

Proust, Antoine. "The Algerian War in French Collective Memory," in *War and Remembrance in the Twentieth Century*, edited by J. M. Winter and Emmanuel Sivan. Cambridge: Cambridge University Press, 2000, pp. 161-174.

Raack, R. C. "Nazi Film Propaganda and the Horrors of War," *Historical Journal of Film, Radio and Television* 6, no. 2 (January 1986): 189-195.

Ramusovic, Aida. "Playing With Ethnic Regionalism," *Transitions* (22 January 2004).

Ranganathan, Maya. "Nurturing the Nation on the Net: The Case of Tamil Eelam," *Nationalism and Ethnic Politics* 8, no. 2 (Summer 2002): 51-66.

———. "Potential of the Net to Construct and Convey Ethnic and National Identities: Comparison of the Use in the Sri Lankan Tamil and Kashmiri Situations," *Asian Ethnicity* 4, no. 2 (June 2003): 265-279.

Rantanen, Terhi. "The Old and the New: Communications Technology and Globalization in Russia," *New Media & Society* 3, no. 1 (March 2001): 85-105.

———. *The Global and the National: Media and Communications in Post-Communist Russia.* Lanham: Rowman & Littlefield, 2002.

Renan, Ernest. "What is a Nation?" in *Nations and Identities: Classic Readings*, edited by Vincent Pecora. Malden, MA: Blackwell Publishers, 2001, pp. 162–76.

Reynolds, David. *One World Divisible: A Global History since 1945.* New York: W.W. Norton & Co., 2000.

Ricoeur, Paul. *Memory, History, Forgetting*, trans. Kathleen Blamey and David Pellauer. Chicago: University of Chicago Press, 2004.

Riegel, Oscar W. "Nationalism in Press, Radio and Cinema," *American Sociological Review* 3, no. 4. (August 1938): 510-515.

Rosecrance, Ricard. "The Rise of the Virtual State," *Foreign Affairs* 74, no. 4 (July/August 1996): 45-61.

Rosenzweig, Roy. "Wizards, Bureaucrats, Warriors, and Hackers: Writing the History of the Internet," *American Historical Review* 103, no. 5 (December 1998): 1530-1552.

Roth, Lorna *Something in the Air: The Story of First Peoples Television Broadcasting Canada.* Montreal: McGill-Queen's University Press, 2005.

Roy, Olivier. "EuroIslam: The Jihad Within?" *National Interest* 71 (Spring 2003): 63-73.

————. *Globalized Islam: The Search for the New Ummah*. New York: Columbia University Press, 2004.

————. "Europe's Response to Radical Islam," *Current History* 104, no. 685 (November 2005): 360-364.

Rusciano, Frank Louis. "The Three Faces of Cyberimperialism," in *Cyberimperialism? Global Relations in the New Electronic Frontier*, edited by Bosah Ebo. Westport, CT: Praeger, 2001, pp. 9-26.

Rushkoff, Douglas. "The People's Net," *Yahoo! Internet Life* 7 (July 2001): 78-84.

Said, Edward. *Orientalism*. New York: Vintage Books, 1979.

Salih, Ruba. "The Backward and the New: National, Transnational and Post-National Islam in Europe," *Journal of Ethnic and Migration Studies* 30, no. 5 (September 2004): 995–1011.

San Juan, Jr., E. "Ethnic Identity and Popular Sovereignty," *Ethnicities* 6, no.3 (September 2006): 391-422.

Sanders, Rickie. "The Triumph of Geography," *Progress in Human Geography* 32, no. 2 (April 2008): 179–182.

Santianni, Michael. "The Movement for a Free Tibet: Cyberspace and the Ambivalence of Cultural Translation," in *The Media of Diaspora*, edited by Karim H. Karim. London: Routledge, 2003, pp. 189-202.

Sardar, Ziauddin. "alt.civilizations.faq: Cyberspace as the Darker Side of the West," in *Cyberfutures: Culture and Politics on the Information Superhighway*, edited by Ziauddin Sardar and Jerome Ravetz. New York: New York University Press, 1998, pp. 14-41.

Sardar, Ziauddin and Jerome R. Ravetz. "Introduction: Reaping the Technological Whirlwind," in *Cyberfutures: Culture and Politics on the Information Superhighway*, edited by Ziauddin Sardar and Jerome Ravetz. New York: New York University Press, 1998, pp. 1-13.

Sassen, Saskia. "The Impact of the Internet on Sovereignty: Unfounded and Real Worries," in *Understanding the Impact of Global Networks in Local Social, Political and Cultural Values*, edited by Christoph Engel and Kenneth H. Heller. Baden-Baden: Nomos Verlagsgesellschaft, 2000, pp. 195-209.

————. "Globalization or Denationalization?" *Review of International Political Economy* 10, no. 1 (February 2003): 1-22.

Satchell, Michael. "Captain Dragan's Serbian Cybercorps," *U.S. News & World Report* 126, no. 18 (10 May 1999): 42.

Saunders, Robert A. "Building New National Identities in Cyberspace: The Digital Pan-Turkic Movement, Cyber-Russians in the Near Abroad and Some Reflections on State Sovereignty in the Age of the Internet," Unpublished paper presented at the Central Eurasian Studies Society Fourth Annual Conference, Harvard University, 4 October 2003.

————. "Happy Slapping: Transatlantic Contagion or Home-Grown, Mass-Mediated Nihilism?" *Static* 1 (Autumn 2005), http://static.londonconsortium.com/issue01/saunders_happyslapping.html.

————. "Denationalized Digerati in the Virtual Near Abroad: The Paradoxical Impact of the Internet on National Identity among Minority Russians," *Global Media and Communication* 2, no. 1 (April 2006): 43-69.

————. "A Conjurer's Game: Vladimir Putin and the Politics of Presidential Prestidigitation," in *Playing Politics with Terrorism: A User's Guide*, edited by George Kassimeris. London: Hurst & Company, 2007, pp. 220-249.

————. "Buying into Brand Borat: Kazakhstan's Cautious Embrace of Its Unwanted 'Son,'" *Slavic Review* 67, no. 1 (Spring 2008): 63-80.

Schlesinger, Philip. "Mass Media and Cultural Identity," in *International Encyclopedia of the Social & Behavioral Sciences*, edited by Neil J. Smelser and Paul B. Baltes. Oxford: Elsevier Science Ltd., 2001, pp. 9341-9346.

Schmidt, Garbi. "The Transnational Umma – Myth or Reality? Examples from the Western Diasporas," *Muslim World* 95, no. 4 (October 2005): 575-586.

Schmidt, Henrike and Katy Teubener. "'Our RuNet'?: Cultural Identity and Media Usage," in *Control + Shift: Public and Private Uses of the Russian Internet,* edited by Henrike Schmidt, Katy Teubener, and Natalja Konradov. Norderstedt: Books on Demand, 2006, pp. 14-21.

Schmidt, Henrike, Katy Teubener, and Nils Zurawski. 2006. "Virtual (Re)Unification?: Diasporic Cultures on the Russian Internet," in *Control + Shift: Public and Private Uses of the Russian Internet,* edited by Henrike Schmidt, Katy Teubener, and Natalja Konradov. Norderstedt: Books on Demand, 2006, pp. 120-131.

Ščuka, Emil. "Declaration of a Roma Nation," International Romani Union, 1 January 2001, http://www.hartford-hwp.com/archives/60/132.html.

Selnow, Gary. "The Internet: The Soul of Democracy," *Vital Speeches of the Day* 67, no. 2 (November 2000): 58-60.

Sher, Julian. "Ethnic Albanians Use Web in Fight Against Serb Control," *Globe and Mail* (12 October 2000).

———. "Using the Web to Reconnect and Rebuild in Kosovo," CNN Interactive, 24 August 2000, http://www.journalismnet.com/articles/kosovo.htm.

Sherrell, Kathy and Jennifer Hyndman, "Global Minds, Local Bodies: Kosovar Transnational Connections beyond British Columbia," *Refuge* 23, no. 1 (2006): 16-26.

Shlapentokh, Vladimir, Munir Sendich, and Emil Payin. *The New Russian Diaspora: Russian Minorities in the Former Soviet Republics.* Armonk, NY: M. E. Sharpe. 1994.

Siebert, Fredrick S., Theodore Peterson, and Wilbur Schramm. *Four Theories of the Press: The Authoritarian, Libertarian, Social Responsibility, and Soviet Communist Concepts of What the Press Should Be and Do.* Chicago: University of Illinois Press, 1963.

Smith, Anthony. *National Identity.* Reno: University of Nevada Press, 1991.

———. "When is a Nation?" *Geopolitics* 7, no. 2 (Autumn 2002): 5-32.

Socor, Vladimir. "East of the Oder: Introducing the Baltic 'Interfront' Candidates," *Wall Street Journal Europe* (11 June 2004)

Sorenson, John and Atsuko Matsuoka. "Phantom Wars and Cyberwars: Abyssinian Fundamentalism and Catastrophe in Eritrea," *Dialectical Anthropology* 26, no. 1 (Spring 2001): 37–63.

Spivak, Gayatri C. "Can the Subaltern Speak?" in *The Post-Colonial Studies Reader,* edited by Bill Ashcroft, Gareth Griffiths, and Helen Tiffin. London and New York: Routledge, 1995, pp. 28-37.

Spoonley, Paul, Richard Bedford, and Cluny Macpherson. "Divided Loyalties and Fractured Sovereignty: Transnationalism and the Nation-State in Aotearoa/New Zealand," *Journal of Ethnic & Migration Studies* 29, no. 1 (January 2003): 27-46.

Starr, Paul. *The Creation of the Media: The Political Origins of Modern Communications.* New York: Basic Books, 2004.

Statham, Paul. "Resilient Islam: Muslim Controversies in Europe," *Harvard International Review* 26, no. 3 (Fall 2004): 54-61.

Stiglitz, Joseph E. *Globalization and Its Discontents.* New York: W.W. Norton & Co., 2002.

Straubhaar, Joseph D. *World Television: From Global to Local.* Los Angeles. Sage Publications Inc., 2007.

Sullivan, Kevin. "E-Mail, Blogs, Text Messages Propel Anger over Images," *Washington Post* (9 February 2006).

Suny, Ronald Grigor. *The Revenge of the Past: Nationalism, Revolution, and the Collapse of the Soviet Union.* Stanford: Stanford University Press, 1993.

Szerszynski, Bronislaw and John Urry. "Visuality, Mobility and the Cosmopolitan: Inhabiting the World from Afar," *British Journal of Sociology* 57, no. 1 (March 2006): 113-131.

Szurmiński, Łukasz. "The Kosovo Conflict in the Internet," Asociacioni Kosovar i Studentëve të Shkencave Politike Web site, 2003, http://www.asshp.org/downloads/Publications%20Eng/The%20Kosovo%20conflict%20in%20the%20Internet.pdf.

Tai, Zixue. *The Internet in China: Cyberspace and Civil Society.* New York; London: Routledge, 2006.

Tibi, Bassam. *Islam between Culture and Politics.* Houndsmills, UK: Palgrave, 2001.

Tishkov, Valery A. "Forget the Nation: Post-Nationalist Understanding of Nationalism," *Ethnic and Racial Studies* 23, no. 4 (November/December 2000): 625-650.

Todorova, Maria. *Imagining the Balkans.* Oxford: Oxford University Press, 1997.

Tolz, Vera. "Forging the Nation: National Identity and Nation Building in Post-Communist Russia," *Europe-Asia Studies* 50, no. 6 (September 1998): 993-1022.

Tönnies, Ferdinand. *Community and Society*, English edition. Mineola, NY: Dover Publications Inc., 2002.

Torpey, John. *The Invention of the Passport: Surveillance, Citizenship and the State.* Cambridge: Cambridge University Press, 2000.

Trigo, Abril. "Cybernation (Or, *La Patria Cibernetica*)," *Journal of Latin American Cultural Studies* 12, no. 1 (March 2003): 95-117.

Tsekos, Mary Ellen. "Minority Rights: The Failure of International Law to Protect the Roma," *Human Rights Brief* 9, no. 3 (Spring 2002): 26-29.

Tuminez, Astrid S. *Russian Nationalism since 1956: Ideology and the Making of Foreign Policy.* Lanham: Rowman & Littlefield, 2000.

Turner, John C., R. J. Brown, and Henri Tajfel. "Social Comparison and Group Interest Ingroup Favouritism," *European Journal of Social Psychology* 9 no. 2 (June 1979): 187-204.

Tyner, James and Olaf Kuhlke. "Pan-National Identities: Representations of the Philippine Diaspora on the World Wide Web," *Asia Pacific Viewpoint* 41, no. 3 (December 2000): 231–252

Vande Winkel, Roel. "Nazi Newsreels in Europe, 1939–1945: The Many Faces of UFA's Foreign Weekly Newsreel (*Auslandstonwoche*) Versus German's Weekly Newsreel (*Deutsche Wochenschau*)," *Historical Journal of Film, Radio and Television* 24, no. 1 (Fall 2004): 5-34.

Varfolomeyev, Oleg. "Notes from Kiev: Where Have All the Russians Gone?" *Transitions* (10 February 2003).

Vermeersch, Peter. "Ethnic Minority Identity and Movement Politics: The Case of the Roma in the Czech Republic and Slovakia," *Ethnic and Racial Studies* 26, no. 5 (September 2003): 879-901.

Voskanian, Vardan. "The Iranian Loan-words in Lomavren, the Secret Language of the Armenian Gypsies," *Iran and the Caucasus* 6, nos. 1-2 (Summer 2002): 169-180.

Wæver, Ole. "Europe since 1945: Crisis to Renewal," in *What is Europe? The History of the Idea of Europe*, edited by Kevin Wilson and W. J. van der Dussen. New York: Routledge, 1995, pp. 151-210.

Waringo, Karin. "Europe: Bark Louder, Please," *Transitions* (28 February 2005).

Wasserman, Herman. "Between the Local and Global: South African Languages and the Internet," *African and Asian Studies* 1, no. 4 (December 2002): 303-321.

Watson, Iarfhlaith. "The Irish Language and Television: National Identity, Preservation, Restoration and Minority Rights," *British Journal of Sociology* 47, no. 2 (June 1996): 255-274.

Weber, Eugen. *Peasants into Frenchmen: The Modernization of Rural France, 1870-1914.* Stanford: Stanford University Press, 1976.

Weber, Max, Hans Heinrich Gerth, and Charles Wright Mills. *From Max Weber: Essays in Sociology.* New York and London: Routledge, 1970.

Wegren, Stephen K. and Andrew Konitzer. "Prospects for Managed Democracy in Russia," *Europe-Asia Studies* 59, no. 6 (September 2007): 1025-1047.

Weiner, Andrew. "Wanted: Homeland for 300 Webheads," *Metro Santa Cruz* (22-29 November 2000).

Wellman, Barry, Janet Salaff, Dimitrina Dimitrova, Laura Garton, Milena Gulia and Caroline Haythornthwaite. "Computer Networks as Social Networks: Collaborative Work,

Telework, and Virtual Community," *Annual Review of Sociology* 22, no. 1 (1996): 213-238.

Wentz, Larry K. *Lessons from Kosovo: KFOR Experience (CCRP Publication Series).* Washington, DC: Department of Defense, 2002.

Wolff, Stefan and Marc Weller. "Self-Determination and Autonomy: A Conceptual Introduction," in *Autonomy, Self-governance and Conflict Resolution*, edited by Marc Weller and Stefan Wolff. London: Routledge, 2005, pp. 1-25.

Woo-Young, Chang and Lee Won-Tae. "Cyberactivism and Political Empowerment in Civil Society: A Comparative Analysis of Korean Cases," *Korea Journal* 46, no. 4 (Winter 2006): 136-167.

Wright, Lawrence. "The Terror Web," *New Yorker* (2 August 2004).

Yinger, J. Milton *Ethnicity: Source of Strength? Source of Conflict?* Albany: State University of New York Press, 1994.

Zeman, Z. A. B. *Nazi Propaganda*, Second edition. Oxford: Oxford University Press, 1973.

Index

About the Author

Robert A. Saunders is assistant professor in the Department of History, Economics, and Politics at the Farmingdale State College, a campus of the State University of New York, where he teaches courses on new media, globalization, and Russia and the former Soviet Union. He received his PhD from the Division of Global Affairs at Rutgers University in 2005.

Dr. Saunders is the author of *The Many Faces of Sacha Baron Cohen: Politics, Parody, and the Battle over Borat* (Lexington Books, 2008) and the co-author of the *Historical Dictionary of the Russian Federation* (Scarecrow Press, 2010). His research has appeared in *Nations and Nationalism, Identities: Global Studies in Power and Culture, Nationalism & Ethnic Politics, Journal of Conflict Studies, Russia in Global Affairs, Global Media and Communication,* and *Slavic Review.* He is a founding editor of *Digital Icons: Studies in Russian, Eurasian and Central European New Media* (formerly known as *The Russian Cyberspace Journal*) and an assistant editor of the *Globality Studies Journal.*

Prior to completing his doctorate, he held the position of Director at The Eastern Management Group, an international consultancy specializing in information and communications technology. Dr. Saunders received his MA in Russian History from the State University of New York at Stony Brook and his BA in History from the University of Florida.